BOLDLY

into the

WILDERNESS

Travelers in Upstate New York
1010-1646

Betty Ahearn Buckell

buckle press ~ queensbury, ny
1999

other books by buckle press ...

by betty ahearn buckell
No Dull Days At Huletts
Old Lake George Hotels
Lake George Boats
Stuff

reprints
Battle Of Lake George, Society Of Colonial Wars
Isaac Jogues, TJ Campbell, SJ

editors ~ Bev Lewis, Ann Buckell
design & art work ~ Betty Buckell
computer consultant ~ Ann Buckell

prints ~ primarily from the Buckell collection, also: Caldwell-Lake George Library; Crandall Library; and SALS and MVLA systems.

ISBN ~ 0-9616809-6-2
copyright [of new material and original art] ~ 1999

The second seal of Albany shows how important the beaver was to the economy.

RAMBLINGS

One day, while searching through the Warren County Historian's files, I found a paper that had been presented by Agnes Gilligan, of Bolton, before the Washington County Historical Society on 28 April 1956.

Contained in this paper were names of men she believed had traveled through Lake George before Isaac Jogues -- who is credited with discovering the lake in 1646. I decided that it would be very satisfying, a lot of fun and might create a new perspective of the area's history, if I wrote a book on the subject.

I determined that my geographic boundaries would be: south, Albany; north, the Canadian border; east, Vermont; and west, the eastern shore of Lake Ontario. In other words, the area covered would be larger than the territory located behind the current blue line of the Adirondacks.

Agnes Gilligan listed: David Ingram, 1568; Samuel Champlain, 1609; two Dutchmen, 1614; Jean Nicolet, 1618; William Poulain, 1621; Pierre Magnan, 1627; Thomas Godefroy and Francois Marguerie, 1639; and Henry, 1643. She also thought that Etienne Brule had traveled to the Mohawk Valley with the Iroquois.

I added: Henry Hudson; Champlain again in 1615; Kleynties; Dutch and French fur traders; fishermen from Bristol, Brittany, Spain and Portugal; Francis Bressani; Ardent Van Curler; Thorfinn Karlsefni; Johannes Megapolensis; Prince Madoc; The Greenland Company, Daniel van Krieckenbeeck; Castle Island; a journal; and even a pet rock, the Pompey Stone. I changed: Nicolet's date from 1618 to 1633; also Godefroy and Marguerie's to 1641.

I tried to flesh them all out: I found much material for some, but unfortunately very little for others. I found almost nothing on Henry, was he Henry Stontrats, who escaped from Bressani's ambush, 1644? If so, Stontrats never was in New York. Or was he the Henry who had traveled with Jogues? Father Poulain, a Recollect, worked among the Canadian tribes, and as far as I could determine, never was in upstate New York. Therefore, I did not include Henry or Poulain.

I have redrawn or retraced some of the maps because most ancient ones do not reproduce clearly. In some cases I drew only what is necessary to make a point.

I felt that editing was needed to correct never ending sentences and paragraphs, too many capitals, especially when quoting from, *The Jesuit Relations* and Megapolensis' "Letter." Champlain's reports of his battles needed a great deal of work, just to understand them.

There were different and creative ways to spell names and locations, so I included as many variations as possible. Regarding brackets that appear -- ( ) denotes information included in the original text; [ ] shows that I added clarification. The term, "Native American" had not been coined, before 1646, therefore I used what was considered correct for the period, "Indian."

As you continue reading to find out what I discovered and concluded -- forget what you learned in school -- then draw your own conclusions.

Of course America had often been discovered before, but it had always been hushed up.
Oscar Wilde

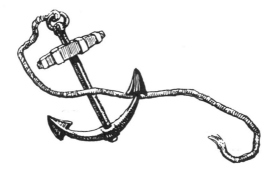

TABLE OF CONTENTS

Strangers have been coming to the eastern shores of North America long before Christopher Columbus: Phoenicians, Portuguese, Basques, Bretons, Irish, Welch, Africans and Vikings to name a few.

St Brendan and his fellow monks celebrating Mass on an island in the Atlantic -- finally they realized the island was a whale!

1010 to 1646 NAVIGATION

A feel for the sea is even more important than technical navigation.
Admiral Samuel Morison

After the Phoenicians, there was a void in the ancient sailing world. Rumors have drifted down through the ages of wondrous voyages in the Atlantic: St Brendan, the Navigator and his fellow monks searched for the Isles of Brasylle; the Archbishop of Oporto sailed to Antilia in 734; and the Basques fished for whales out in the Atlantic in the 700s. It remained for the Vikings to take over the high seas. Even though their ships were small, they were fearless enough to sail into the west during the sailing season of April to October.

How did they do it without radar, GPS, a compass, a clock, correct charts and most important of all exact knowledge of latitude and longitude? Longitude would not be available for some centuries but early sailors did have the ability to determine how many miles the trip would be and how many days it would take under favorable conditions.

Vikings were able to hold a course on fixed latitude. After mastering coastal navigation, they determined how to sail into the unknown. They learned that if they sailed to a particular landmark on the Norwegian coast, turned westward, and kept on that route, they would reach the Shetlands, then the Faeroes, eventually Iceland and finally Greenland. Of course, there was a considerable amount of tacking that had to be done. They simply reversed the procedure to return home, which was much easier because they were helped by the North Atlantic current. This was latitude sailing.

It was not all pure luck, or guesswork, for Irish monks had already found Iceland and this knowledge certainly was well known in the ports of northern Europe.

In northern waters, the sun helped them to navigate more than the North or Guiding Star. While sailing due east or west, a sailor would eyeball the sun's height above the horizon -- measured by an arm, a stick of wood, whatever. The ship had to be on an even keel, so a reading during rough seas was impossible. The ideal time to take this reading is when the sun is highest, at mid day, a difficult feat without a water clock. How many Vikings knew what one was, or could afford one? This technique is known as relative latitude. If there was no sun, there was a problem, but experienced sailors then relied on the wind.

A mariner could also sail north-south by applying the simple rules he had learned from latitude sailing. If a sailor knew the height of the noon day sun for Cuba, at that particular time of the year, he could sail south from Newfoundland and expect to reach the southern island. That is if he could manage to keep his ship on course. When the ship's noon sun matched the known position of the noon sun at Cuba, the mariner simply turned west until Cuba came into view.

Until recently, it was thought that the only instrument the Vikings had was the sounding lead, which only helped in harbors, along coasts, or over sand bars.

Early in the 11th century, Oddi Helgason created a table of the sun's azimuth figured in a half wheel, based on half of the sun's diameter. His calculations were accurate to within three degrees. However, few early sailors had the ability to use his table, or any other table.

Sailors of today use up to date charts to plot their course. Vikings did not chart: all calculations were made in their head. Currently, mariners use as their bible, *The American Practical Navigator* by Bowditch, 2,346 pages of convoluted thinking. Vikings somehow managed to get around quite nicely without Bowditch. Quite a feat.

By the end of the 15th century, ships were able to stay on a set line for latitude sailing, instead of veering off course. Ships were sturdy enough to withstand the rigors of long sea voyages: maps and charts were getting more accurate. The time was ripe for discovery and exploration of new lands.

These Sensory Clues Were Used To Guide The Mariner Towards Land ...

- Birds are first seen about 150 miles from land
- Islands sighted
- The swell surrounding small isolated islands
- Glaciers off Iceland and Greenland
- The feel of the colder Greenland polar current
- The color of the water near Greenland
- Iceland's volcanoes were the first lighthouses
- Mountains are sighted far away
- Whales mean an island could be near, even if socked in by fog
- Schools of fish
- Driftwood ... floating seaweed
- Angle of waves in relation to the ship were used when the weather was overcast
- Change of wind causes wavelets over larger waves
- The locations of prevailing fog banks
- At night, they sailed by the moon and the stars
- Ravens were kept aboard: one would be released and was easily tracked against a pale sky. The bird then circled looking for land, if none were seen it would return to the ship. If the bird kept on flying, the ship followed it -- for land was only a couple of days away.

A mirage in the Bering Strait. Arctic mirage/fata morgana/refraction/ice blink/Vailian canopy is a phenomenon that is rather hard to believe, but with the right conditions of water and air temperatures, ice crystals are suspended in the sky. This occurs when normal light waves are bent to the curvature of the earth, then crystals form a huge viewing screen that shows the land ahead for approximately 250 miles. Sometimes the mirage appears upside down.

It is beginning to be accepted that this arctic mirage occurred frequently centuries ago and helped early sailors to actually see the land that lay ahead.

glossary

ECIDS, RCDS, ECS, ARCS, S57 ... these initials stand for the latest in electronic charting systems that make navigation easier, more efficient, and cost effective. It is felt that paper charts will soon be obsolete.

GPS ... Global Positioning System. The latest help in determining where a ship is and her relation to other vessels and to land, plainly shown on a screen. This up to the minute information is sent to the ship by satellite and is not affected by weather.

LONGITUDE ... finally in 1759, John Harrison devised a way of figuring longitude, that was correct. He constructed the first practical marine chronometer that was in reality a large clock with a bimetal strip that compensated for temperature variation. Harrison was awarded 20,000 pounds for his invention, but had to wait until 1773 until he was completely paid. The British government was a tad slow.

RUTTER/Routier ... a book of sailing directions, possibly with charts and maps, compiled by cartographers, giving explicit directions how to sail from point A to point B. It usually told where water, stores and refitting could be found.

Somewhere, an ancient mariner figured out a way to take a reading of the sun or stars by bending his arm to form an angle with the celestial bodies, or with the horizon. Or, he simply cut a notch on the mast.

Slowly these crude aides evolved into the following devices ...

CROSS STAFF ... [A] a device that could be used quickly for a solar angle. A navigator took one crosspiece and placed it on the staff so that the crosspiece lined up with the sun at the top crossing, while the bottom crossing was lined up with the horizon. The distance of this device from the eye, gave the sun's altitude. It was very hard on the eyes, because the person had to look directly into the sun.

QUADRANT/Backstaff ... [B] an extremely long device that allowed a mariner to find the altitude of the sun above the horizon to fix a ship's latitude. The degrees were placed on a quarter circle. This newer staff did not harm the eyes because the mariner did not have to look directly into the sun. It was the forerunner of the sextant.

BEARING DIAL ... [C] a wooden dial with a hole in the center that had 32 notches placed equally around the edge. A shaft was in the center, plus a gnomon [an upright pin that was a shadow caster], and a horizontal pointer. This early device was used to take the bearings of the sun, or of a landmark. When it was noon, the navigator held the dial, then looked at the shadow cast by the pin to determine where north was. This crude compass would only work for voyages along one degree latitude. A different pattern on the dial was needed for the same voyage taken at another time of the year

This could be the husa snotra/husanotra, a wooden device, made and used by Thorfinn Karlsefni to locate Vinland.

... Or it was a flat piece of wood shaped into a quarter circle and marked into degrees on the arc. By holding the instrument so that its flat base touches the horizon and the north star touches the edge of the arc, the sailor can read off his degree of latitude. This is accurate to within 1/4 of a degree of latitude. This could also be the husa snotra.

HOUR GLASS ... [D] was used by early sailors to determine time. The problem was to remember to turn the glass over at the correct moment

KNOTS ... [E] a ship's speed was calculated by throwing out a small piece of wood to which was tied a rope with equal distant knots. By keeping count of the knots, that slipped through the hands, during a timed period, speed can be determined -- in knots.

MAGNETIC COMPASS ... [F] was first mentioned by Alexander Neckam, in 1180, who wrote that it was a needle, "Placed upon a dart." The compass was precise enough c1300 to allow ships to sail the Mediterranean even if visibility was poor: it was the best instrument that early sailors had and was accurate to within a few degrees.

SUNSTONE/Solarstein ... certain stones can produce polarized light, reflecting the sun even though it is mostly obscured by a cloud cover. Adventurine feldspar is also known as sunstone.

ASTROLABE ... see back cover.

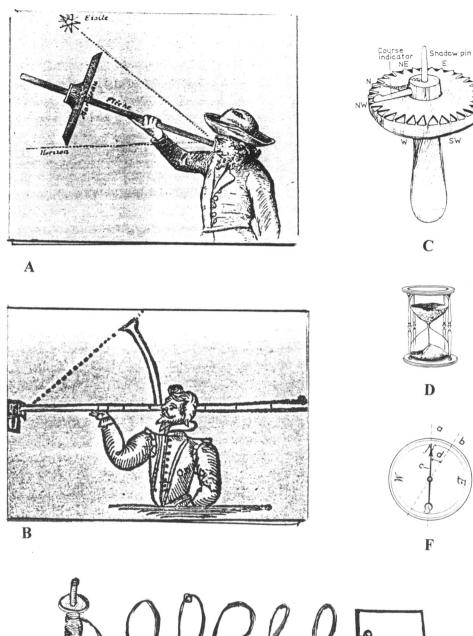

A

B

C

D

F

E

11

Thorfinn's ship was a knorr/knarr. A knorr was a double ended, clinker built, small boat that was swift and could plane after it reached a certain speed. Oars were used in emergency and when going up narrow waterways. It was decked at the fore and aft ends and connected by a gangway along the gunwale. The open space between the decks could carry 15 to 20 tons of cargo, or cattle, that was protected by skins stretched as tarpaulins.

There were only five heavy timbers -- the mast, the mast block, the stempost, the keel, and the sternpost. Most hulls were made of oak. The pine mast was about 35' tall, which enabled a lookout to scan the horizon up to seven and a half miles away. This mast was removable and supported a squarish sail that was larger at the bottom than at the top. A rudder was lashed on the outside starboard quarter. The anchor could have been of iron, for iron was worked in Iceland and Greenland.

A large boat was frequently towed behind the knorr and could carry up to 20 persons. In addition, a smaller craft was often carried upon the ship.

THORFINN KARLSEFNI, c1010

The lower Hudson is ... the world's lowest latitude fjord.
Dean Snow

Thorfinn Karlsefni was born in Iceland about 980. There are three sources that tell of his ventures, *The Fatley Book, The Karlsefni Saga* [in *Hawk's Book*] and *The Saga Of Eric The Red* -- who discovered Vinland. Because there are three sources and a bit of discrepancy among them, a scholar has some picking and choosing and weeding to do.

One Theory That Is Most Interesting And Fits Upstate New York Is ...

The Viking settlers of Iceland and Greenland believed their elders, who related that there was no frost at Leif's Shelters, in Vinland, and that cattle could graze all winter in the tall lush grasses that barely withered. So around 1004-1010, Thorfinn a successful merchant, gathered approximately 160 men and women, equipment, supplies and cattle, loaded them onto three ships and sailed from Iceland to Vinland.

The ships sailed south and southwest along the coast for a long time. Finally they came upon a cape -- Cape Cod. They tacked keeping the cape on their starboard and saw long strands and sands that they called Wonderstrands because it took them so long to sail past. They decided to row to shore, and on the cape, they found the keel of a ship that they thought was Eric's, so they called the cape, Keelness.

They sailed beyond Wonderstrands and the coast became indented with bays. They steered their ships into a bay. Leif Ericson had been given two Gaels, Haki and Hekja, when he had been at the court of King Olaf Trgvasonto. Leif lent them to the expedition because they could run faster than a deer. The pair went ashore and Karlsefni told them to run southwards to see what the country had to offer, but to return in three day's [daegr] time. After three days, the Gaels returned to the waiting ships. Haki bore grapes in his hand, while the woman, Hekja, held wild wheat. Karlsefni declared that they had discovered a country rich in resources. If they had sailed past Cape Cod along the New England coast, Long Island would be to their south and would be the only place where the pair could run southward.

They continued, most likely southwest, until they reached a place where the shoreline was broken by a fjord so they steered their ships into it and called it Streamfjord. Frederick Pohl believes that Streamfjord is the Hudson River because there are only two fjords located along the Atlantic coast, Somes Sound in Mt Desert Island, Maine and the Hudson. It was the custom of the Norsemen to sail as far as possible up a fjord, or a river, because experience had taught them that the farther the location was from the ocean, the better the weather would be. Therefore if Thorfinn sailed into the Hudson, eventually he would have gone up to the head of navigation, or the Albany-Troy area.

At the mouth of the fjord there was an island round which there were, according to most translations, strong currents -- but Tornoe argues that instead of currents there were sounds around it.

Somewhere on the shore of the fjord, around Manhattan, or as far up as the Albany area, they set up a camp. They had brought along all kinds of livestock and unloaded them so they could graze in the tall grass. There were mountains thereabouts and the country was beautiful. The men spent all their time exploring but unfortunately did not gather any provisions, assuming that the land would support them year round. During the summer, the fishing began to fail. They stayed through the winter, which was very severe, and food became short. So, they went out to the island in the hope that something would turn up, either in the way of fishing or flotsam. There was not much food on the island, even though their cattle were getting along fine: they prayed to God to send them some food, but nothing appeared.

After a while, a whale was beached and the men cut it up, but they did not know what kind of whale it was: even Karlsefni, who was an expert on whales, did not know. When it was cooked, they ate it, and all became sick. They threw the whale into the sea and then uplifted their voices to ask for the mercy of God. Spring came and the weather got better so they could row out to fish and from then on, they had no lack of provisions, for they could hunt game on the land and catch fish in the sea. They went out to the island to gather eggs and there were so many eider ducks that it was almost impossible to step between their eggs.

The first autumn Thorfinn and his wife Gudrid had a son, Snorri, the first white child presumed to have been born in North America.

The next year they left their Hudson winter headquarters and sailed a long way south to Hop. If they had sailed from any point in New England, they would have sailed west. Below New York Harbor, the New Jersey sea coast bends south and a bit westward.

Finally, because of clashes with the natives, they returned home to Iceland: Snorri was three years old.

conclusion
They found mountains and it was beautiful.

Considering that there are only two fjords found along the eastern coast, and that there is only one west or southwest of Cape Cod, then the Hudson River becomes Thorfinn's fjord. The Vikings always sailed as far into a fjord as possible, and because their boats required only five or six feet of water, they were then able to ascend the Hudson as far as Waterford. And perhaps further: it would depend on the time of the year when they arrived and how much water was in the river. The after boats, or smaller craft, could have enabled them to go above the Riffs. They spent much time exploring the surrounding country and would have covered quite a distance in all directions from their camp.

Pohl decided that they wintered, not in the Manhattan area, but somewhere around Albany. Close to the Menands Bridge, that connects Menands to South Troy, there used to be a highly desirable farm that was originally called de Vlackte, but later known as The Flatts. This was where Van Curler lived when he was agent for the Patroon. This site would certainly fit for Thorfinn's winter home: and there is an island opposite, Breaker Island.

14

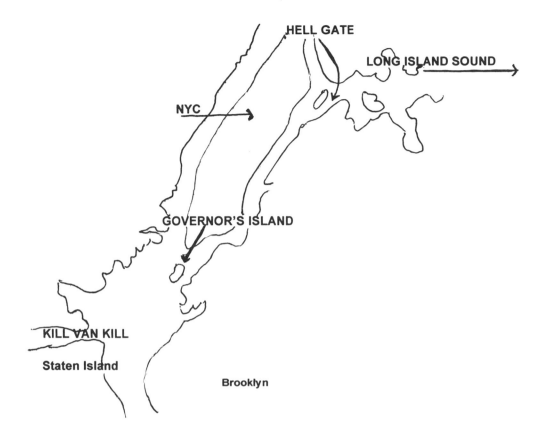

HELL GATE

LONG ISLAND SOUND

NYC

GOVERNOR'S ISLAND

KILL VAN KILL

Staten Island

Brooklyn

Captain Bill Huus said that, "The Harlem River is really a sound -- which is a body of water connecting two bodies of water. A river has a source but a sound does not. There is slack water around Manhattan for about 20 minutes, which means that you can dock a boat within that time without a tug because there is no tide. Then, the rivers are like a lake.

But, at Hell Gate there are only four to eight minutes. There much rock was blasted before WW I or WW II. Today there is a very deep channel, about 150', this is kept fairly clean of silt because of the swift water."

STREAM FJORD ... according to *The National Geographic,* March 1962, "In this 150 mile stretch the Hudson really is not a river at all but an inlet of the sea," and an inlet of the sea is a fjord.

STREAM ISLAND/Straumey ... in the fjord there lay an island, around which flowed very strong currents, and is believed by Pohl, et al, to be Governor's Island. According to Bill Huus, "When the tide runs, the tide is very strong around Governor's Island."

The Viking word Straumr means -- stream, current, race of the sea, tide, or river. But Tornoe in, *Early American History,* states that Straumey means sound. If so, there is Long Island Sound, the Harlem River, the Kill Van Kull, and the Staten Island Sound in the area.

15

whales

TRAIN OIL ... oil produced by boiling the blubber of whales.
WHALES ... "A whale was driven up there," *The Flatley Book*. Note the use of the word, "Up."

Two whales ascended the Hudson according to Anthony DeHooge's, "Memorandum Book". On 29 March 1647, he noted that a white whale was in the river before Fort Orange; and, on 19 April 1647, another whale, this time a brown one, was before Fort Orange.

One wag even wrote a longish poem about it, here is a portion of it ...

THE TALE OF THE WHALE
Benj. Hall

As the spring floods subsided, the yeomanry came
To see the great monster without any name;
Among them a skipper, renowned on the sea
With a knowledge of fishes like Barnum, PT
This skipper climbed up on the animal's back,
Then wandered about on a varying tack,
Pulled away at his flippers, examined his tail,
And said to the Dutchmen, "This here is a whale."
As when in years later, obedient to fate,
The rocks flowed with oil in a neighboring state,
And hundreds forsook their homes, firesides, and friends
For the spot where the stream of petroleum wends,
So now from the hillsides, the plains, and the town
The people all came where the animal brown
Lay dead on the quicksand, with hatchets and saws,
And axes and cleavers, and meat-hooks and claws,
Determined to turn to their own private use
What before they had thought was a public abuse,
Prepared in great kettles his blubber to broil,
And try the great whale into barrels of oil.

16

On the 1767 map "Of The Settlements In The Manor Of Rensselaerwyck" drawn by Jno Bleeker there is an island in the second sprout that does not appear in later maps. Could this be Whale Island?

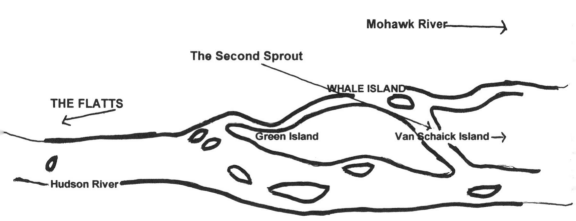

The location of The Flatts and Whale Island.

Whale Island was in the second Sprout of the Mohawk River. Silt carried by the Mohawk was deposited where it joins the Hudson that formed large and small islands. Four channels or, sprouts, now are the exit for the Mohawk. Whale Island was submerged after the state dam was built between Green Island and Troy in 1823, to permit sloops to ascend as far as Lansingburg.

The effect of the tide from the Atlantic is felt to the current State Dam opposite Troy, about 175 miles from the ocean.

17

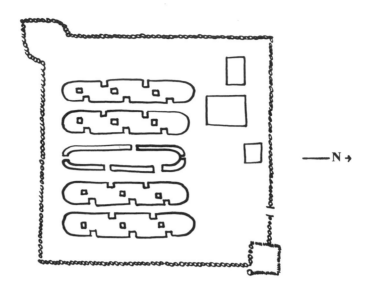

The Indian fort at The Flatts.   Courtesy of the Colonie Town Historian.

However, the beached whale seems impossible for this location. But is it really? There was an island at the meeting of the Mohawk and Hudson Rivers that the Dutch named Walvisch Island, or Whale Island. Van der Donck wrote how this island got its name ...

In March [of 1647] a great freshet occurred, by which, the water of the river became nearly fresh to the bay [New York Harbor] ... At this season two whales of common size swam up the river 40 miles [Dutch miles], from which place one of them returned and stranded about 12 miles from the sea, near which four others stranded the same year. The other ran further up the river and grounded near the great Cahoes Falls, about 43 miles from the sea. This fish was tolerably fat, for, although the citizens of Rensselaerwyck broiled out a great quantity of train oil, still the whole river, (the current being still rapid) was oily for three weeks and covered with grease. As the fish lay rotting, the air was infected with its stench to such a degree that the smell was offensive and perceptible for two miles leeward.

The spring of 1996, a harbor seal swam all the way from the coast of Maine to the Corning Preserve and stayed for a few days, much to the delight of Albanians. Recently, there have been sightings of a whale and a dolphin in a New Jersey river and a manatee was cruising the waters of the North Atlantic. If these creatures are swimming in foreign waters now, consider how far out of today's range they must have gone a few hundred years ago, when there was no pollution or motor boat traffic.

Whether the Vikings spent the winter in the Albany area is not that important, what is important is that they sailed up the Hudson to the head of navigation. All things considered there is a 50% chance that they did, which becomes 100% if Cape Cod is proved to be where Lief's Shelter was located.

L'Anse aux Meadows, Newfoundland
A World Heritage Site, which was excavated by Helge Ingstad and his wife, Anne.

Helge and Anne Ingstad sought a Viking settlement along the North Atlantic shores for years. Perhaps they used the theory of; WA Munn, V Tanner, AH Mallery and Jorgen Meldgaard, that there were ruins of one at Epaves Bay. At last, George Decker, a resident of the area, told Helge about outlines of ancient buildings at L'Anse aux Meadows. Anne, an archeologist, started excavating. The pair soon announced to the world that they had found a Viking settlement that they believed to be Vinland.

The whorl found at the site.

Surprisingly, only a few artifacts were found, among them a spindle whorl and needles. The Ingstads claim that these finds mean women had been there and because Thorfinn brought women on his journey, this proves that the site was Vinland.

The Newfoundland newspaper clippings about Helge leave the reader with a single adjective -- stubborn. The talk regarding Anne is that she made -- things fit.

Helge and Anne, to make this site fit Vinland, rewrote a part of the sagas. They claim that through the years, the ink oxidized on the ancient manuscript. Hence the Viking word for "Meadows" became the word for "Vin." Therefore, in the Ingstads' minds the name L'Anse aux Meadows backed up their theory that the site's name matched the Saga that stated that where Thorfinn wintered, there were vast meadows. However, the term L'Anse aux Meadows does not mean "meadows" as stated by the Ingstads. The original name was L'Anse au Meduse, which means "Jellyfish Bay," and was bastardized, by the English, into L'Anse aux Meadows.

That Anne made things fit is evident in her and her husband's stating that the spindle whorl and needles found, meant that women were there because spinning is woman's work. Not necessarily, men have been shown using whorls on TV [and I saw men using a whorl when I traveled around the Mediterranean in 1958].

Anne also had the village recreated in her idea of what an early Viking settlement should look like. The walls discovered were about three feet wide, whereas the new ones are nine. There is no indication that the roofs would have been made of sod; rather it is now felt that the Vikings simply would have lifted their boats over the sod walls to serve as the roof.

19

L'Anse aux Meadows. The top photo shows the reconstructed site, with a later fence. The bottom photo shows the very narrow Black Duck Brook. [Buckell photos]

Mowat believes that this site was only a Viking stopover: later used by whalers. He wonders if the, "great building" is Norse. He feels that it does not resemble ...

Anything known from either Greenland or Iceland of this period [and that] between it and the sea there is a large pit filled with burned and fire-cracked stones and pebbles, which has no parallel in Greenland c1000 AD. However, this pit closely resembles the tryworks fire pits used at early Basque, French, Dutch and English shore-whaling stations in northern regions. One large "wing" of the structure is fitted with a complex floor drainage system and does not show convincing evidence that it was ever a walled room at all. It could have been a blubber-cutting platform.

Inasmuch as Red Bay, Labrador is almost across the bay, Mowat's theory makes much sense. Red Bay is considered to be the first factory in Canada and was used by Basque whalers in the early 1400s, possibly before.

If L'Anse aux Meadows was used by the Vikings, it most likely was used as a half way station between Greenland and Vinland, to the south. It is highly unlikely that it was Thorfinn's winter home for the simple reason that so little of the site fits Eric's Saga.

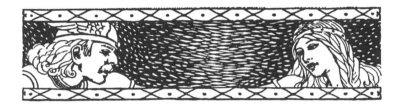

In Eric's Saga		*L'Anse aux Meadows*	*Hudson River*
There is a difference in reading about a site and actually visiting it.			
grapes	no	too cold and too acidic	yes
self sown wheat	"	not enough dry land	"
large timber	"	only a bit of scrubby growth	"
meadows	"	wet boggy land, with an alpine growth	"
mountains	"	foothills	"
beautiful	"	dreary and bleak	"
fjord	"	small brook	"
cattle could graze	"	would sink in bogs	"
harsh winters	yes		"
strong currents	"		"
sounds	no		"
island nearby	yes		"

glossary

DAEGR/Doegr ... is a measure of time. One daegr equals either a 12 or a 24 hour day. Usually it meant how many nights were spent traveling. It is thought that the Vikings could sail 144 nautical miles in one daegr.

EAR OF CULTIVATED WHEAT ... has to be Indian corn. Corn, of this period, was a great deal smaller than the corn we know today. Would the Vikings have confused it with wheat, which was known to them?

However, some feel that it was wild rice that grows along the margins of marshes, ponds, streams and lakes of eastern North America. Rice is a member of the grass family and was an important food for various Indian tribes.

EIDER DUCK ... there are two eider types, the common eider and the king eider. Today, the common's winter range is as far south as Long Island and the summer range reaches to Maine. In warmer areas they may remain near the breeding grounds all year. The king winters as far south as New Jersey but summers in Greenland and Hudson Bay.

The temperature was warmer during Thorfinn's time. How would it have affected the eider's range? Currently in New Jersey, Canadian geese are wintering over probably due to a year round supply of food, and have increased so rapidly that they have become a nuisance and a traffic hazard. So ranges do change depending upon food availability and weather.

The eider was greatly prized for its down, which was gathered from abandoned nests and used to fill pillows, mattresses, coverlets and as an interlining of clothing.

Pohl feels that the many eggs on Current Island were not found the fall of Thorfinn's arrival, but rather during the following spring. This is logical because the Vikings went to the island, in the spring, to gather eggs.

GAELS ... were Celts, either Irish or Highland Scots.

GRAPES ... according to a letter sent back to Holland, 1624 by the *Mackarel* [*Mackerel*], "We were greatly surprised when we arrived in this country. Here we found ... wild grapes [in the Hudson Valley.]"

True wild grapes were found all along the eastern seaboard from Maine to Mexico, but not at L'Anse aux Meadows. Those who argue for this location state that cranberries, or wineberries are what the Vikings found there. If so, there is a vast difference between grapes and cranberries. The Vikings certainly knew what wineberries/cranberries were -- even if they had never seen grape vines. The Sagas mention, not once but quite a few times, about grapes and grape vines that were to be found in Vinland.

grapes	wineberries	cranberries
purple	red, it is the red currant	red, or red and white, or pink and white
vines	bush	shrubs, low or high
true wine	currant wine	juice

North America is the world's most prolific center of wild grapes. Today cultivated grapes are grown from 34 to 50 degrees latitude.

SAGAS ... there are different types of these medieval epics, dealing with myths, legends, history, romances, or family histories. They were orally passed down from one generation to the other until finally some scribe started to write them. They, for the most part have the ring of truth and are finally being accepted instead of being considered myths.

It is estimated that about 80% of the Sagas have been lost. An early Bishop of Iceland went around the countryside gathering what many considered to be worthless scraps, even pulling vellum out of windows, where it had been inserted to keep out the elements. It is felt that if we had all the Sagas available, there would be a complete record of these intrepid people and their incredible journeys.

geography

DUTCH MILE ... one Dutch mile equals three English miles.
FJORD ... is a narrow, deep coastal arm of the sea formed by glacial movement.
FREEZING OF THE HUDSON ... the winter of 1995-1996 saw temperatures drop to 30 degrees below zero, the coldest winter in the memory of most locals. The US Coast Guard has maintained an ice cutter in the upper Hudson for decades.
RIFFS/Rifts ... a natural barrier of rock/stones, in the Hudson, above Waterford that caused deep drafted ships to stop. Of course during high tide, excessive high tides or freshets, it would be easier to cross this barrier.

Thorfinn and Gudrid in Vinland.

23

Forts at Oswego.

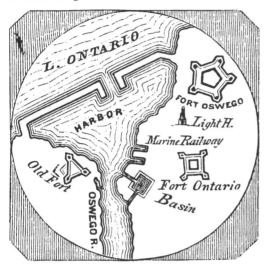

Francis Lewis.

24

PRINCE MADOC, 1170

Were there Welch Indians in New York State before 1646?

The story of an early Prince of Wales' voyage to America in 1170, has often been repeated to explain blue eyed, fair haired Indians who spoke Welsh. Madoc's tale became popular during the period of the great explorations of the Americas when England was striving to lay claim to all, or almost all, of North America.

Tradition claims that the colonists Prince Madoc brought to North America became known as a Welch speaking tribe that moved westward from the Atlantic shore until they became the Mandans of the west.

The first published work in Tudor times to relate the discovery of America by Madoc was a pamphlet entitled, *A Time Reporte* written by Sir George Peckham and dedicated to Sir Francis Walsingham. This pamphlet was written, "To prove Queen Elizabeth's lawful title to the New World, based on not only upon Sir Humphrey Gilbert's discoveries, but also those of Madoc's." It referred to David Ingram, as one source and to, "An ancient Welch chronicle" as another. Ingram claimed that he had heard Welch words spoken in America, as did other travelers, some of whom published vocabularies.

The pamphlet was followed the next year by a much more detailed account ...

Madoc ... left the land in contention betwixt his brethren and prepared certain shipps with men and munition, and sought adventures by seas, sailing west, leaving the coast of Ireland so farre north, that he came to a land unknown where he saw manie strange things. This land must needs be some part of that countrie of which the Spaniards affirme themselves to be the first founders since Haunoe's time; for, by reason and order of cosmogrophie, this land to which Madoc came, must needs be some part of Nova Hispaniola, or Florida. Whereupon it is manifest that that country was long before by Brytaines discovered, afore either Columbus or Americus Vesputius led any Spaniarde thither.
The Historie Of Cambria
1584
Dr Powell

There are two points that need explanation. First, mostly all North America was called Florida, therefore it does not mean Madoc landed in what is now known as Florida. Second, the phrase, "Leaving the coast of Ireland so farre north," means that Madoc gave Ireland a wide berth to the north.

Why Madoc Is Being Considered ...

There are a few writers who spin a tale about Francis Lewis, a son of a Welch clergyman, who emigrated to America in 1738 at the age of 21. He became a merchant and a leading citizen of New York City.

So far all sources agree: but apparently beginning with Roger Butterfield's article, the reader is told some additional curious facts ...

Francis Lewis, a rich, weather-beaten New York City merchant in his 60s, had seen quite a bit of the world. He was ... shipwrecked a couple of times and once was captured by the Lake Ontario Indians during the Colonial Wars with France. According to his story, he escaped being tied to a stake and burned alive because he began talking to the Indians in Welch -- and they understood him!
"They Signed Their Lives For You"
1947

Then Richard Deacon wrote that Lewis ...

Fought in the French-Indian War and was captured by Montcalm in 1757, when he was taken to Canada with other prisoners. After his release he was elected a delegate to the General Congress in 1757 ... After the fall of Oswego, he was captured by the Indians near Albany. According to his story of that incident, he escaped from being tied to a stake and burned alive because he began talking to the Indians in Welch; they understood him and he was released.
Madoc And The Discovery Of America
1966

Next Ellen Pugh stated that ...

He took part in the French and Indian War, was captured by Montcalm in 1757 and taken along with other prisoners -- to Canada. Later he was released; but after the fall of Oswego, in New York, he was taken by Indians near Albany. At that time ... [he] was tied to a stake to be burned alive, when he began speaking to his captives in his native Welch tongue. They understood him and promptly released him.
Brave His Soul
1970

Reading these three sources, it is apparent that Pugh copied Deacon almost word for word and Deacon relied on Butterfield: but where did Butterfield learn that Lewis was weather-beaten, ship wrecked, tied to a stake, spoke Welch and that the Indians understood him?

From these sources it would appear that there were Indians who lived near Albany who spoke or understood Welch: were they the descendants of Prince Madoc's colonists? Had Madoc settled near Albany?

Before any conclusion can be drawn, it would be wise to check on Julia Delafield's 1887 biography of her ancestor, the same Francis Lewis who ...

Obtained a contract for clothing the British Army, and was in Oswego attending to the business when Montcalm advanced upon the place with a body of French, Canadians and Indians. Lewis who had long been intimate with Mercer, the commander of the fort, agreed to remain with him and act as his aide. Montcalm opened a battery and Mercer was killed, Lewis standing by his side. In a few hours the fort was untenable. To avoid an assault, the garrison, consisting of 1,600 men surrendered.

Montcalm allowed his Indian allies to select 30 prisoners as their share of the booty, and Lewis was one of the number. The Indians retreated northward. Toward the close of each day, when they found by the side of a mountain stream, or in a sheltered valley, a pleasant spot that invited them to rest or to feast, they lit their fires and celebrated victory by the sacrifice of a captive.

The bloody rite was repeated so often that Lewis was certain of the fate that awaited him. He was not a man under any circumstances to lose his presence of mind, or to despair. He seemed to submit, watched and waited. Two warriors were selected for his guard. As the prisoner showed no disposition to escape, they were satisfied with binding his arms, allowing him to walk otherwise unshackled, whilst they beguiled the time talking together. Presently words familiar to his childhood struck his ear. Acquainted with both the Gaelic and Cymraeg [Welsh] dialects, it was easy for him to join in their conversation. It may be that Lewis was gifted with the power of controlling men -- it may be that his calm and dignified bearing already had an influence upon the savages. When they found that there was the tie of a common language between them, he was no longer a prisoner -- he was treated as a friend and a brother. They conducted him to Montreal, recommended him to the protection of the Governor, and requested that he might be permitted to return at once to his home. This permission, however, was not granted. He was sent to France in a cartel and exchanged.

Lewis made every effort to discover from the Indians themselves, and from such of the whites as had any knowledge of the aborigines what was the home and origin of the red-faced brethren who understood an obscure European dialect. All that he could learn was that they were from the far west; that they were few in number, and that it was seldom that any of them were seen near the Atlantic coast.

I received it from my Father

        Mother -- Mrs Maturin Livingston ... they had it from Lewis himself.

Julia also noted that ...

It is not true, as has been asserted, that Lewis represented the Indians who understood Cymraeg as being Mingos [Manduns] - nor is it true that he spoke of the party as generally understanding Cymraeg: what he said was, that he was able to communicate in Cymraeg with the warriors who had him in custody.

Lewis returned immediately to America after he was exchanged and the colonial government presented him with 5,000 acres as an acknowledgment of his military service. He was elected a delegate to the General Congress in 1757, by the convention of deputies in New York State and was a signer of The Declaration Of Independence.

conclusion

There is no doubt that Lewis was captured during the French and Indian War and that he was brought through upstate New York. These warriors were in New York State, to support their Indian allies, during the French and Indian War.

Julia Delafield wrote that Lewis never said they were Mandans. All he could learn from them is that they were from the far west and that they were seldom near the Atlantic coast. She did not state that they had ever lived, or traveled to or into New York State before 1646. Nor has any reputable writer even suggested that the Mandans were ever in the state for that early date.

Therefore, it should be discounted that Madoc, and his colonists, had settled in upper New York State.

Deceiving Wolf and his family drawn by George Catlin. Catlin wrote that the Mandan males pulled their hair back from the forehead in flattened bunches and painted it red, which made it impossible to determine what color it was. Women let their hair grow as long as possible, oiled it frequently, and painted the part with red paint. The women's hair was all colors, except red, and many had hair without color. These unusual colors helped perpetuate the idea that the Mandans were Welch.

glossary

ALBINISM/Partial Albinism ... according to the, *Encyclopaedia Britannica*, the word albinism refers to the absence of yellow, red, brown or black pigments in the eyes, skin or hair. This condition is inherited. Albinism in the human is caused by the absence of melanin, the dark brown pigment normally present in the skin, hair and eyes. There are three different degrees depending on the degree of lack of melanin: 1) total albinism, involving the skin, hair and eyes; 2) ocular albinism, in which only the eyes are affected; 3) localized albinism, in which small areas of the body lack pigment [white locks, spottings]. All three forms are hereditary. Other types of pigment deficiencies, such as the graying of hair during aging, are not examples of albinism. This condition should be considered to explain the fairness of the Mandans.

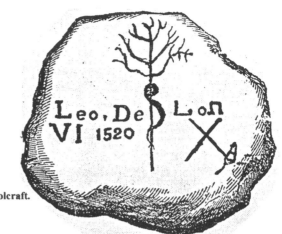

The Pompey stone as sketched by Schoolcraft.

The Pompey stone after 1894.

the Papal tiara.

30

THE POMPEY STONE, 1520
A comedy of errors.

1820

Farmer Philo Cleveland [Cleaveland] was clearing a field on Watervale Road, just north of Pompey Center and pulled yet another rock out of the dirt. He noticed some marks on the stone, but as he was about to quit, he simply moved it to a nearby pile of debris. A few days later he decided to check it: by then, the rain had washed away surface dirt so that a, "Rude engraving was much more distinctly to be seen." Puzzled by what he saw, he asked his neighbors to see what they thought it meant. It was decided to place the stone in a blacksmith's shop in Watervale, where the locals gawked at it for some six months.

1821-1864

About a year later the curiosity was moved to the village of Manlius, where it was examined by ...

Several gentlemen of science, most of who were disposed to admit that it was genuine. It remained in this village nearly a year and was finally deposited in the museum of The Albany Institute [Of History And Art] now under the care of Dr T Romeyn Beck. The nature and objects of the inscription will best appear by a minute examination of the engraving. The stone is about 14", by 12" and 8" in thickness. It is a hard, oval shaped boulder, of a gneisoid character, and bears the evidence of attrition common to all the erratic block groupe. By the figure of a serpent climbing a tree, a well-known passage in the Pentateuch is clearly referred to. By the date, the sixth year of the reign of the Roman Pontiff Leo X, has been thought to be denoted. This appears to be probable, less clearly from the inscriptive phrase, Leo de Lon VI, than from the plain date, 1520, being six years after this Pontiff took the Papal Chair.

It has been stated in newspaper notices, that Mexico had been fully explored and settled previous to 1521. In the appendix to Stone's Brant, this is narrowed down to the declaration that Mexico was settled at that date. Neither is strictly true. Cortez first attacked the city in 1519, whence he was expelled under the short but energetic reign of Guatamozin, but he finally prevailed, after taking the troops of Narvaez and carried the city and razed it to the ground, as he entered it, in 1521. His army entered it finally on the 13th August. No exploration of the territory, far less settlement was made, or attempted until after this date. We cannot look to Mexico, as having originated any measure which led to a visit, however isolated, of the Iroquois country, a region possessed then, as afterwards, by brave muscular warriors, very different, in these respects, from the mild and luxurious Aztecs.

Gaspar Cotereal, a Portuguese, had explored nearly the whole coast of North America in 1501. The fishing grounds of Newfoundland were well known and were occupied by the French as early as 1505. The Italian navigator, Verrizano [sic], examined the shores of the United States in 1525 [should be 1524]. Jacques Cartier reached Hochelaga, the present site of Montreal, in 1535.

It has been said that the inscription is due to persons connected with the celebrated expedition of De Soto. This explorer, who set out with the spirit of a Cortez, and who had the bril-

liant success of the latter to stimulate him to the deeds of heroism, examined both banks of the Mississippi, for some leagues and penetrated as far north as latitude 36 degrees. It has been related by some that he with his party rambled over a considerable part of Florida, which then embraced nearly all the country now known as the southern states. During their travels, it is said, they fell in with a party of northern Indians, having with them a Spaniard taken from the party of Narvaez, who had proceeded over much of Florida 10 years before; and that by their guidance, the captive Spaniard was led to this spot.

It is further suggested by Sanford in his Aborigines, in which he was followed by Stone, in his Life of Brant, that DeSoto had probably gone as far north as the Susquehanna, from the analogies to this name found in the word "Saquechama" which is employed by the historian of the expedition. But it is quite overlooked, that De Soto did not set out on his expedition till 1538, 18 years after the date of the Onondaga inscription.

Florida had, however, then been known to the Spaniards for many years, having been discovered by De Leon in 1512 [should be 1513], the very year that Leo X assumed the Papal Chair. Its coasts and bays were known, as far west, at least, as the mouth of the Mississippi, which was evidently discovered by the Spaniards from Cuba in 1527. It was De Leon, however, whom first visited the interior and his visionary search for the spring endowed with the property of restoring perpetual youth, would hardly be credited, did it not rest on the best historical testimony.

It is far more likely that some straggling party had reached the Iroquois, from this Quixotic era of exploration, from the mouth of the St Lawrence, whence the Cotereals were in 1501. And with this idea in view, it may be thought that the name De Leon is intended, by the words De Lon. The date, VI, would tally exactly with the sixth year after his landing in, and the discovery of Florida, in 1512; the Onondaga country being there, as much a part of Florida as any other part of the Atlantic and interior coasts. If by the prefix of Leo, or lion, a compliment to a brave and hardy explorer was designed to have been expressed, it would have well corresponded with the chivalric character of that age. As a mere historical question, a claim to the discovery of the interior of New York, by the Spanish crown, might, in this view, find something to base itself on.

History Of The Iroquois
1846
Henry Schoolcraft

1865

The New York World sent a reporter to view the stone, which was still in The Albany Institute Of History And Art. He brought Dr O'Callaghan, NYS Historian; NYS Senator Henry Murphy; James Hall, who would soon be in charge of the stone when it was removed to the NYS Cabinet; and a few days later, Frederic De Peyster, President of the New York Historical Society, who expressed a desire for his association to own it. The article stated, "It was found very carefully put away in a glass case and covered with a dust that indicated that for some years, at least, its quiet had not been disturbed."

The reporter went on to say that, "It must be remembered that this stone was found when there was no pecuniary inducement for the forging of such relics." All the authorities, who accompanied the writer, believed it was authentic.

This article made a noteworthy observation that, "The stone was merely lent to the late Dr Beck for examination and ought long since to have returned."

1870

The Albany Institute Of History And Art decided to divest itself of anything that did not pertain to art and donated the stone to The NYS Cabinet, as the State Museum was then called. Sadly they did not keep any records regarding the stone, so that today The Albany Institute has no memory of ever displaying it.

The NYS Cabinet published in, *The Twenty-fourth Report On The State Museum*, that it had received the Pompey Stone, dated 1520, and quoted Schoolcraft [see above]. They wrote ...

In accordance with a resolution of the Albany Institute, adopted at a regular meeting held on the 18th day of January 1870, the undersigned in behalf of the trustees and officers of the New York State Cabinet of Natural History, hereby acknowledge the receipt, on deposit, of a boulder found many years since in the county of Onondaga, in this state, and bearing an ancient inscription, subject to the further order of the Albany Institute.

1879

Dr Henry Holmes, NYS Librarian, read a paper on the stone before the Oneida Historical Society during November, which was later published. In his speech he stated that, "The genuineness of the inscriptions upon it have never been questioned by any of those who have written, down to Mr Haven of the American Antiquarian Society, who very lately has declared them to be well authenticated."

He closed with this statement, "I think we are authorized to regard the Pompey inscribed stone with its genuineness and authenticity, as the earliest monument either in the State of New York or the United States ... "

Holmes also stated, "This stone is the property of the Albany Institute, though for the present deposited in the State Museum."

Holmes gave the date of the Pompey Stone as 1520.

1894

Syracuse planned to celebrate its centennial during the year, and decided to bring back the Pompey Stone.

Imagine everyone's surprise when Reverend Beauchamp, after viewing it at the Centennial exhibit, proclaimed to the world that the stone was a HOAX! This is his scathing letter printed in a Syracuse paper ...

Dr HA Holmes' paper on the Pompey Stone could not be found when I returned home ... I can, however, give you its substance. He referred to the many instances of wandering white men in the 16th century, held as captives or adopted by the Indians and so far his argument was good. Then he supposed this stone, which he thought a true relic, the monument of such a captive in Pompey, raised by a surviving companion. To this I answered that there were no Indian villages in Pompey at that date and the moist ground in which it was found was not suitable for burial. Accepting as genuine I hazarded the conjecture that some exploring party had placed it, as the French buried or placed lead plates, as an act and sign of possession. We neither of us questioned the truth of the date, as I think well might, for his knowledge of old books would have shown him features of doubt.

I owe it to your kindness that I could make a close examination of the stone this afternoon and certainly with unexpected results. The inscription was not cut with a knife, but with several and somewhat differing tools, and with blows from a hammer and mallet. Two of these tools were cold chisels of good quality, one having a straight and very sharp edge, nearly three-eighths of an inch wide, and another a little narrower and rounder and dulled by use. These were used in certain parts of the work and the lines at the tops of the letters were made with a single stroke of the hammer. At the ornament in the right hand lower corner and elsewhere, a smith's punch was used, one with a dull but not broad point. What other tools were employed it is not necessary to say. A hammer, two cold chisels and a good punch would make a pretty good kit of tools for a wandering Spaniard and he may have found these enough. If anyone thinks he carried them so far, he may believe in the Pompey Stone.

There is another feature which has received no notice. The characters are purely modern. The letter L is that of this century, not of the 16th. It is the fashion now to use old fashioned type and if any one will look at the letter in question the distinction will be seen. I have gone through a number of my books of that century, as well as some of the next, and in all the terminal point of the capital L slopes forward instead of being upright as on the stone. I think this was invariable from 1500 to 1600 and general for a century later, but an expert would determine this and the next point at once.

The next point is that the numericals are modern characters, of uniform height and not reaching distinctly above or below the line. I find no figures like these until a long time after the date carved on the stone. Anyone can see this also, by taking a book of 150 or 200 years old. Especially it may be noted that he will find no figure 5 like that on the stone. If no such book is accessible he may turn to books printed in the fashionable old types of today. These forms were in general use up to the beginning of this century.

Mr Clark accounted for the fresh appearance of the work by the fact that as it stood in a blacksmith's shop for some weeks, people would, "Take a horse nail or an old file and scrape all the cracks, seams and carvings, giving it somewhat the appearance of new work." This does not account for the clear, sharp cuts made by the cold chisel. I may add that I have investigated several frauds in every way more antique in character than this inscription.

You may ask my opinion, and I simply give the facts, submitting the question to you in turn. According to the statement of the find the spot was unsuitable for either dwelling, camp or grove. At the date given there were no Indians living in Pompey and few in the county. The work was done by a man of skill and fair knowledge of modern, not of early books. He had a good supply of smith's or stonecutter's tools. The characters are those of the nineteenth, not of the sixteenth century ...

Thanks to your consideration, I have now a close copy of the inscription, something not before obtained. It differs much from Clark's figures and all others which I have seen. No intelligent judgment can be rendered without this exactness. I wish a "squeeze" might be made, but am too busy to do it. The full notes I made will also be of future use and for the present will find a safe place in the sixth volume of my "Onondaga Antiquities."

The Journal, 9 June 1894

W Beauchamp

Local people noted that the stone had mysteriously changed from the one that they remembered. It was apparent that: the date had changed from 1520 to 1589; most of the carving had been reworked; the "L'N" was missing; and two horizontal lines on the bottom appeared.

Most amazing.

A couple of days later, a letter from a John Sweet appeared in *The Syracuse Daily Journal*, 11 June edition. He wrote that his Uncle Cyrus Avery told him, the last time he saw him in 1867, "That he and his nephew, William Willard of this city, cut the figures on the Pompey Stone, and just to see what would come of it. When it came out in Clark's history so much had come of it, they thought it best to keep still altogether. I have no doubt the tools used were those mentioned by Mr Beauchamp, as such tools were exactly the ones most likely to be at hand in Grandfather Avery's blacksmith shop at Oran."

1909

Martin Luther

Arthur Parker, NYS Archeologist, wrote a letter to Dr John Clarke at the NYS Cabinet. He claimed that Cyrus Avery was religious, of Pilgrim stock, and was taught that Luther broke with Pope Leo X in 1520. When Cyrus was a boy, the Mohawk Valley was the path for the Protestant "Great Awakening," that swept the center of New York State like a tidal wave. Parker also wrote that Beauchamp, "Made a miscroscopic examination and inspection." However, Beauchamp did a lot on the day he penned his letter to the editor. According to his diary, he went to Syracuse, went to the exhibit, returned home and then composed a lengthy letter -- hardly the stuff of, "Consuming miscroscopic examinations".

Somehow this letter escaped the 1911 fire.

1911

The NYS Capitol fire destroyed museum records.

1937

NYS Archaeologist Noah Clark wrote to the Onondaga Historical Association that, "There is a decided difference in the inscription which now appears from the one," in the original sketches. "I am at a loss to give a reason for this unless in the years since its discovery someone has made an attempt to restore the faint lines by scratching them deeper and in doing so lost a part or erred in the date."

1976

Pompey was planning a Bicentennial celebration and contacted the state about the loan of the town's treasured rock.

The NYS Museum wondered if the stone is, "A hoax of a hoax" ... Charles Gillette, NYS Senior Scientist, wrote to the committee that the stone's inscription does not match, "certain particulars" for instance the date was changed from 1520 to 1589. He also thought that one of his predecessors believed that the stone was lost in the Capitol fire and that a duplicate had been created. But his best statement was, "The original inscription was inaccurate for the record it propounded to be and was so changed to establish harmony by a person or persons unknown." [What exactly does he mean?]

So, Johanne Alexander, of Pompey, made a rubbing of the stone that showed the 1520 date under the 1589 one.

1998

The stone sadly sits in The Pompey Historical Museum, huddled close to the door, so close that it could be missed.

conclusion

Is the stone ... a hoax? A hoax of a hoax? Genuine?

If Leo was an explorer who suddenly died, his companions would bury him where he drew his last breath regardless of damp soil. Weather conditions change, so, was the area wet in 1520? Currently El Nino is creating a dust bowl out of fertile lands in Texas. Also, if the area was so wet during 1820, why did Cleveland bother to clear it?

When the stone was brought to the blacksmith shop quite a few of the locals, who gathered around to view and discuss it, traced the engravings with whatever was at hand. Sometimes it was only a finger, or a piece of straw, but consider where they were -- in a blacksmith's shop. There had to be metal scraps that could point, trace, and scratch. Scratching and tracing would naturally affect the pristine quality of the original engraving.

After the stone arrived in Albany, it was kept in a glass case, at least until 1865, which means that it was protected from curious fingers and sharp instruments.

Henry Schoolcraft, eminent historian and writer of early American history and Indian culture, and others, went to the Institute to gaze at the stone and all proclaimed it authentic. There was not one nay amongst them, it is hard to imagine that these men, especially Schoolcraft, could be so easily duped.

Holmes, the NYS Historian in 1879, wrote that it was a headstone of a Spaniard named Leo who had died. This is the best supposition of all.

Then, at the 1894 Syracuse Centennial exhibition, a "strange" stone was displayed, one that had decidedly been reworked and even the date had been changed, from 1520 to 1589! Dr Beauchamp saw it and sputtered that it was a hoax.

Beauchamp insisted that the letters on the stone are modern. But, the photo reproduced copy of Ingram's *Relations* prove otherwise ... the "L" shown is straight and resembles type used today. Margaret Coffin, an authority on old tombstones, said that carving stone is different from setting type. Also, the person who carved this stone, in such a primitive location, certainly would not be aware of what the accepted style should be, he just did the best he could. Under these conditions, Margaret said that a straight line can be accepted for the "L".

A day or so later, a letter appeared in the paper from John Sweet, who wrote that two of his relatives created a hoax. Did Avery and Willard really create the stone? If they did, why did Avery wait so long to tell anyone? One person can keep a secret, but it is quite difficult for two to keep one: because of the temptation to gloat.

Sweet's letter leaves us with these unanswered questions ...
- Where was the stone created?
- Why did the boys carve what they did?
- What was it suppose to mean?
- How did they transport the 128 pound stone?
- Why did they select Cleveland's farm to bury the stone?
- Should Sweet be believed? Perhaps he was the one who wanted to be noticed.

Consider the crop circles of England and the pair who recently claimed that they had made them. They even gave demonstrations of how they created the circles. But, they were quickly declared to be frauds. The point is, there are people who are willing to claim that, "They did it," from murders to crop circles.

It was suggested that the stone was destroyed in the 1911 blaze, which is hard to believe. But maybe not, because the people of the Pompey area, stated that the shape of the stone had changed.

The best calculated guess of what happened is that the stone was dirty when the request came, in 1894, to send it to the Syracuse exhibition. Old James Hall, must have given the word to the only person working under him to, "Clean it." During that period, no underling would attempt to do anything, on his own, unless it was authorized by his superior. Another scenario would have Hall, himself cleaning it. Apparently the cleaner, Hall or the assistant, did not see the "L'N" marking, for that was not enhanced. Were the horizontal lines at the bottom added then? They are not shown in the old drawings. Unfortunately, there is no paper trail for what happened.

Another curious fact is what, *The New York World* wrote in 1865, that the stone had only been, "loaned to Dr Beck," of The Albany Institute Of History And Art, and that it should be returned. There is no document, legal or otherwise, that is in the possession of the Albany Institute, The NYS Museum, or The Pompey Historical Museum, stating that the stone had ever been given to the Institute. In the, *Twenty-fourth Report On The State Museum* it is printed on page 20 that, "In order to afford to the public better facilities for the inspection of this interesting relic, it was deemed proper by the members of the Albany Institute to deposit it in the State Cabinet."

Even though The Albany Institute, "deemed it proper," it had no title to the stone. Therefore the Institute made an illegal transfer of the Pompey Stone to a second party -- The State Cabinet.

Johanne Alexander of Pompey, who had experience in gravestone rubbings, decided to make a rubbing of the stone in 1976. She discovered that 1520 was under the 1589 date and rediscovered the "L' N" marking. Her work appears to have been the only scientific work done on the stone and proves that the stone is not a hoax of a hoax.

Sadly, it is too late to prove if the stone is authentic when one considers all the reworking that was done.

It has to be ...

1) The first fake produced in New York State ... it predates the Cardiff Giant, made in 1868 but discovered in 1869 at Cardiff, south of Syracuse.

2) Possibly the oldest fake produced in the country ... it predates the: Grave Creek tablet found in Moundsville, West Virginia, 1838; the Holy Stones of Ohio found between 1860 and 1867; and the Kensington Stone found in 1898. There has been much controversy regarding these objects: they have only been mentioned to compare a time frame.

or:

3) The oldest authentic European made object produced in New York State.

38

Men Who Played A Part ...

AVERY, Cyrus ... was born 1807 in Pompey. Avery told his nephew, Professor Sweet in 1867, that he and another nephew, William Willard, created the stone when he was 13 years old. Sweet also added that Avery was given to practical jokes..

BEAUCHAMP, William ... 1830-1925. Beauchamp was: an Episcopal Minister, Rector of Grace Church In Baldwinsville 1865-1900; an amateur archaeologist; writer of several historical books, many articles on history for Syracuse newspapers; and an historian. He pronounced his name BEECHAM

CLARK, Joshua ... even though he is credited with being an authority on Onondaga County, it is surprising how much of his material on the stone was lifted, almost word by word, from Schoolcraft.

CLARKE, John ... 1857-1925. Clarke became Hall's assistant in 1886. He was made director of the NYS Cabinet in 1904. It can be assumed from these dates that Clarke must have been involved in the cleaning of the stone, c 1894.

During 1907, as head of the NYS Cabinet, he received a letter from Arthur Parker, NYS Archeologist about the stone -- from that letter it can be assumed there had been a dialogue about this puzzle. If so, why didn't Clarke write about what he had either done or must have seen done to the stone?

HALL, James ... 1811-1898. Hall graduated from RPI as a geologist. He was curator of the NYS Cabinet of Natural History, 1866-1893, NYS Geologist, 1893 until his death in 1895. He was 83 years old when the stone was shipped to Syracuse and it is felt that he had only one assistant, who would have been John Clarke.

George Kunz wrote in *Natural History*, Jan 1923 issue, that Dr Hall was, "At times over-zealous," and that he used, "dictatorial methods." So, it is hard to believe that anyone other than Hall was responsible for the cleaning of the stone.

Hall also stated that the Cardiff Giant, a proven hoax, was, "The most remarkable object yet brought to light in this country." Remarkable?

SCHOOLCRAFT, Henry ... 1793-1864. He attended Union and Middlebury Colleges. He was a geologist on an exploration trip to the Lake Superior copper area and upper Mississippi during 1820. He was the Indian Agent for the tribes around Lake Superior, 1822; commanded the 1832 expedition that discovered the sources of the Mississippi; and negotiated treaties with various tribes enabling the United States Government to acquisition 16,000,000 acres of land. Schoolcraft was a likable man who wrote a number of books about his explorations and on the ethnology of the Indians, which are still of great value to the historian.

Somehow, he also found the time to work at his father's glassworks in Guilderland, Albany County, just off Route 20.

WILLARD, William ... 1808-1876. When he was 12, he assisted his uncle, Cyrus Avery, in carving the Pompey Stone. He was a resident of Syracuse at the time.

Sir Francis Drake.

John Hawkins.

The Jesus.

40

DAVID INGRAM, 1568
Was he a pitch man for an early land deal, did he embellish, or did he tell the truth?

John Hawkins, that old sea dog, set sail during 1567, on his third slaving venture with seven ships. Hawkins commanded the *Jesus*, 700 tons. He was accompanied by the *Minion*, 300 tons; the *William*, 150 tons; the *John*, 150 tons; the *Swallow*, 100 tons; the *Judith*, 50 tons; and the *Angel*, 33 tons. A young Francis Drake, a relative of Hawkins, sailed with the fleet. Everything was successful until September 1568, in the harbor of San Juan de Ulua, when the Spanish Plate Fleet scuttled all but two of the English ships. It was this disaster that would ultimately lead to the war with Spain in 1585.

The remaining ships were too tiny to accommodate the sailors, most of the survivors of the *Jesus* had to follow the *Minion* in a small boat. There was not enough food to go around, so some 100 sailors begged to be set ashore. According to Ingram it was 100 men, but Hortop/Hartop claimed that it was 96, while Philips/Phillips said 114.

Hawkins promised to return in a year. He sailed back to England aboard the *Minion* with 200 crammed aboard. They had so little food they ate: the ship's cats; the ever present rats; and stewed ox hides from the cargo. Finally they ate the parrots which would have fetched high prices in Europe. Hawkins did not relate how Drake managed to be aboard the *Judith*: the silence about her return voyage is puzzling.

The sailors, who had been put ashore were attacked by the natives at least once a day: quickly all their clothing, and the bits of trade goods that Hawkins had been able to spare, were taken. A few men died in the attacks. Perhaps 70 decided to try to reach Mexico City -- they would not be heard of again for 20 years.

The remainder, some 23 according to Miles Philips, decided to trek northward to see if they could contact a ship near the Great Banks. They had to hurry to reach the north before the winter of 1569 set in -- or they would freeze to death from the cold. Somehow, their number dwindled down to three. David Ingram, Richard Browne and Richard Twide made it to about 50 or 60 leagues from Cape Breton and returned to England, where they were rewarded by a joyous Hawkins. Miles Philips thought that the other 20 sailors probably had been tempted to stay with Indian women met along the way.

England, during the period of the 1570s, was experiencing extreme problems of unrest. "Lustie youthes" were roving the country and rioting was feared because of lack of work. Food prices were rising but wages, if any were paid, were far too low. A novel solution was seized upon by the court -- send the trouble makers to North America. Sir Humprey Gilbert was given a grant, valid for six years, with title for all the lands that he could discover and occupy in the New World.

By 1582, the scheme had not started and the charter's time limit was almost ended. Therefore, a group of men led by Sir Francis Walsingham decided to question Ingram about the eastern seaboard through which he had traveled. Sir George Peckham, a sponsor and friend of Sir Humphrey Gilbert, was present at the inquiry, and Gilbert himself may have been there too. Gilbert was preparing a fleet to sail during the following summer.

Therefore, all the questions asked were relative to this one purpose -- the future colonists needed to know what reception they might expect from the Indians, how nature might aid them in establishing the first English settlement, and whether gold or precious stones would reward their enterprise.

The accuracy of what he said about his travels could not, at that time, be checked: Browne had been killed on board the *Elizabeth* five years before, and Twide had died ashore in 1579. Ingram alone possessed the facts and did not fear contradiction. One must remember that Ingram had traveled extensively and apparently kept no diary, hence his recollections, at times, are a bit fuzzy. Regardless, Walsingham must have checked Ingram for accuracy.

Miles Philips returned in 1582 from Mexico and Job Hortop in 1590. They eventually gave their accounts of what had happened which were printed by Hakluyt. Unfortunately they were not on hand for Walsingham's gathering of information.

The name Florida first appeared on the Cantino map of 1502. Then Florida reached far north and it depends on which map is viewed as to where its northern borders were. Mostly its boundaries met Norumbega. This 1582 map locates the River of Norumbega at about the correct latitude, running north to Hochelaga, and the island of Claudia to its east. The River of May is north of present day Florida.

The Relation of David Ingram of Barking, in the County of Essex Sailor, of sundry things which he with others did see, in traveling by land from the most northerly parts of the Baie of Mexico (where he with many others were set on shore by Master Hawkins) through a great part of America, until he came within fifty leagues or there abouts of Cape Britton

Translation of the old English, including the exact punctuation, or lack of it, by B Buckell.

About the beginning of October, Anno 1568 David Ingram with the rest of his company being 100. persons in all, were set on land by M. John Hawkins, about six Leagues to the West of the river La mina, or Rio de Minas, which standeth about 140 leagues west by North from the cape of Florida, who traveling toward cape Britton, spent about 12 months in the whole, And about seven months thereof in those Countries, which lie towards the North of the river of May, in which time, (as the said Ingram thinketh) he traveled by land 2,000 miles at the least, and never continued in anyone place above three or four days, saving only at the City of Balma, where he stayed six or seven days.

The River of May is now known as the Altamaha, in Georgia and noted for the Indian ford at Macon. Some historians claim that this river is the St John in Florida; if so, that meant that Ingram turned south, instead of keeping on a northerly course.

Kings
There are in those parts (saith he) very many kings, commonly within 100 or 120 miles one from another, who are at continual wars together: The first King that they came before dwelt in a country called Giricka, who caused them to be stripped naked, and wondering greatly at the whiteness of their skins, let them depart without further harm.

Large precious stones
The Kings in those countries are clothed with painted or colored garments, and thereby you may know them, and they wear great precious stones, which commonly are Rubies, being 4 inches long and two inches broad. And if the same be taken from them, either by force or sleight, they are presently deprived of their kingdoms.

The Kings in their majesty
When they mean to speak with any person publicly they are always carried by men in a sumptuous chair of Silver or Crystal garnished with divers sorts of precious stones.

The manner of saluting their kings
And if you will speak with the king at your first approaching near to him, you must kneel down on both your knees, and then arise again and come somewhat nearer him, within your length, then kneel down again as you did before. Then take of the earth or grass between both your hands, kissing the backside of each of them, and put the earth or grass on the crown of your head, & to come, & kiss the kings feet. Which circumstances being performed, you may then arise and stand up, and talk with him.

How to know the noble men
The Noble men and such as be in special favor with the King, do commonly wear feathers in the hair of their heads for the most part, of a Bird as big as a goose of color. And this is the best mark that this Ingram can give to know him by.

The turkey is a possibility for, "A bird as big as a goose of russet color."

Litters were used by the Indians of North America. The Queen of Cafitachequi received De Soto on a sumptuous litter. The Great Sun, of the Natchez, was always carried in one.

The men and the maidens, in the print, are nearly naked and one man is blowing a trumpet while another is carrying his.

The Indians of the south adorned themselves with great ropes of pearls and buried them with their dead. A mound near Hamilton, Ohio had more than 60,000 pearls in it. No doubt they were traded as far as Peru, or given as gifts to great rulers.

The Spanish came, saw and coveted them. De Soto found about 350 pounds of pearls in mounds by the Savannah River. In a few short years, it is estimated that the Conquistadors shipped nearly 1,000 pounds to Spain. [A string of 57, 8mm pearls with a light clasp, weighs about 1 ounce.] Vespucci, during his 1499 voyage, was given 150 pearls and some gold at one place; at another he was gifted with an oyster that had 130 pearls in it.

Contemporary pictures of Queen Elizabeth show her usually dripping with pearls; pearls roped and roped around her neck, pearls hanging from her ears, pearls in her hair, pearls in a crown, pearls sewn onto her dress and no doubt even sewn on her shoes. Probably the only place she did not sport these treasures was on her undergarments. Pearls, on the Queen, were an advertisement to show the world that England was rich. Naturally, the nobles and wealthy followed Elizabeth's style.

The demand for pearls was great.

Pearl

There is in some of those Countries great abundance of pearl, for in every cottage, he found pearl, in some houses a quart, in some a pottle, in some a peck, more or less, where he did see some as great as a bean. And Richard Browne, one of his companions, found one of these great pearls in one of their Canoes or boats, which pearl he gave to Monsieur Campain [Champaigne], who took them aboard their ship, and brought them to Newhaven in France.

Bracelets of Gold

All the people generally do wear Manilios or Bracelets, as big as a man's finger, upon each of their arms, and the like on the small of each of their legs, whereof commonly one is gold and two silver.

Curets of Gold

And many of the women also do wear plates of gold, covering their bodies in manner of a pair of curets, and many bracelets and chains of great pearl.

The favour and shape of the people

The people commonly are of good favor, feature & shape of body, of growth about five foot high, somewhat thick, with their faces and skins of color like an olive, and toward the North somewhat tawny, but some of them are painted with divers colors, they are very swift of foot, the hair of their heads is shaven in sundry spots and the rest of their head is traced.

Naked people

In the South parts of these countries they go all naked, saving that the Noble mens privates are covered with the neck of a gourd, and the womens privates with the hair or leaf of the palm tree. But in the North parts they are clothed with beasts skins, the hairy side being next to their bodies in winter.

Brutish behavior

They are so brutish & beastly, that they will not forbear the use of their wives in open presence.

People courteous

They are naturally very courteous, if you do not abuse them, either in their persons or goods, but use them courteously. The killing or taking of their beasts, birds, fishes, or fruits, cannot offend them, except it being of their cattle which they keep about their houses, as Kine, Guinea hens, or such like.

A sure token of friendship

If any of them do hold up both their hands at length together, and kiss the backs of them on both sides, then you may undoubtedly trust them, for it is the greatest token of friendship that may be.

Messengers from the king

If any of them shall come unto you with a horsetail in his hand, then you may assure your self that he is a Messenger from the King, and to him you may safely commit your person, or go to the king, or anywhere else, or by him send any thing or message to the king. For these men are always either Ensign bearers in the wars, or the kings messengers, who will never betray you.

To allure the people to approach

If you will have any of the people come aboard your ship, hang out some white cloth upon a staff, for that is a sign of amity.

The manner of trafique and dealing with them

If you will bargain for ware with them, leave the thing that you will sell upon the ground, and go from it a pretty way off: then will they come and take it, and set down such wares as they will give for it in the place: And if you think it not sufficient, leave the wares with signs that you like it not, and they will bring more, until either they or you be satisfied, or will give no more. Otherwise you may hang your wares upon a long poles end, and so put more or less on it, until you have agreed on the bargain

How they march in battle

When they go to the wars, they march in battle array two or three in a rank.

Their weapons and instruments for war

Their Trumpets they do make of certain beasts teeth, they have a kind of Drum which they make of beasts skins, they make shields and Targets of the skins of beasts, compassed with willow twigs, and being dried, they are strong and defensible.

Their weapons are darts, headed with iron, the heads are two fingers broad, and half a foot long, which are fastened within a socket.

They have also short bows, strung with the bark of trees, being half an inch broad, and the arrows are of bone, a yard long, notched and headed with silver and bone, and their arrows are of small force within a stones cast of them, and you may put them by with a staff a pretty way off.

They have short broad swords of black iron of the length of a yard, or very near an ell, bearing edges thicker than backs of knives, somewhat like the foils in our fence schools.

They have crooked knives of iron somewhat like a woodknife, or hanger, wherewith they will carve excellently both in wood and bone.

Their Ensign is a horsetail, with glass or Crystal in some of them being dyed in sundry colors, as red, yellow, green, etc.

Cannibals

The people in those Countries are professed enemies to the Cannibals or men eaters: The Cannibals do most inhabit between Norumbega & Bariniah, they have teeth like dogs teeth, and thereby you may know them. In the wars they do pitch their camp as near as they may unto some wood of Palm tree, which yields them meat, drink, and present remedy against poisoned arrows.

This woodcut, printed c1497, is believed to be, "The first representation of the people of the New World" and shows that the people of America ate "each other."

If Norumbega was on the lower Hudson River and Bariniah was near the Saguenay River, then the cannibals would be the Mohawks/Iroquois. Beauchamp in his, *Notes On Cusick's Six Nations* wrote ...

The name Seneca appears on the Dutch Map of 1616 [Figurative Map of 1616] and has been thought an Algonquin term for eaters of flesh, or cannibals. The eastern Indians gave the Mohawks a name with the same meaning, and that none of the Five Nations were adverse to human flesh ... In 1643, Roger Williams said that, "The Mauguauoga, or man eaters, that live 300-400 miles west of us, make a delicious monstrous dish of the heads and brains of their enemies." The Dutch knew the Five Nations only as Mohawks and Senecas. Williams further wrote ... "They say Etoniochtochguari, *which is human flesh tastes like bear's meat, that the hands are not good eating: they are* yongarat *bitter."*

The *Jesuit Relations* state that ...

"He was baptized toward 8 o'clock in the evening; and half an hour after, his soul, purified in the Blood of the Lamb, took its flight to Heaven" ... Such is the report, both written and verbal, of those whose eyes had witnessed the felicity of a Hiroquois [Iroquois], who had perhaps, eaten his share of more than 50 men.

De Lamverville noted that 600 captives were eaten in one expedition against the Illinois. The Ottawas dug up dead Senecas and ate them, during Denonville's attack.

WIGWAM
Eastern North
American Indian.

Their houses and buildings
Their buildings are weak and of small force, their houses are made round like Dove houses, and they do dwell together in Towns and Villages. And some of them have banqueting houses in the top of them made like the louver of a hall, builded with pillars of massive silver, and crystal, framed square: whereof many of them are as big as boys leg of fifteen years of age, and some less.

Towns and Villages
This Ingram did also see divers Towns and Villages, as
GUNDA ... a Town a flight shot in length.
OCHALA ... a great Town a mile long.
BALMA ... a rich City, a mile and a half long.
BEGA ... a Country, and Town of that name, three quarters of a mile long, where are good store of ox hides.
SAGUANAH ... a Town almost a mile in length.
BARINIAH ... a City a mile and a quarter long: Also there is a River and a Town of that name, but less than the first above named.
GUINDA ... a small Town and a River, both of that name. And this is the most Northerly part, that this Ingram was at.
There are besides those Towns aforenamed, many other great Towns which this Ingram passed by, commonly distant six or eight miles one from the other, which have divers small Villages within eight or ten miles from them.

Kettles of massive silver, for common uses
They have in every house scoops, buckets, and divers other vessels of massive silver, wherewith they do throw out water and dust, and otherwise do employ them to their necessary uses in their houses. All which this Ingram did see common and usual in some of the countries, especially where he found the great Pearls.

Gold in the heads of Rivers
There are also great rivers, at the heads whereof, this Ingram and his companions did find sundry pieces of gold, some as big as a mans fist, the earth being washed away with the water.

50

There was much gold, silver and copper found in the rivers that flowed from the Appalachian Mountains. This early print shows that the Indians dug trenches near river banks to catch sand brought down by the water. When water filled up the trenches, they pushed the sand away with reeds and put the minerals in canoes and brought it down the great river, or the River of May.

   Pieces of gold that weighed 300 pounds were found, in the New World, and even one that was 3,000 pounds.

51

Rocks of crystal

And in other places, they did see great rocks of Crystal which grew at the heads of great and many Rivers, being in quantity to load ships.

Crystal during this period was a highly desirable commodity. This stone was carved into chalices, bowls, plates and coffers. Sometimes, bronze, gold or enameling was entwined around the item and further embellished with precious gems. Crystal could be carved into impressive gems and set into jewelry and decorative objects.

The Patroon considered mining crystal. In 1649, he instructed that samples be sent back to Holland to determine if the cost was feasible. Jasper Danckaerts wrote that, "mountain crystal" was located on the Robert Saunders farm, between Albany and Cohoes.

King Arthur is believed to be buried in a crystal cave -- was Ingram familiar with this legend?

Ingram started walking northward during October and almost reached Cape Breton 11 months later. He traveled during the winter months and could have seen large chunks of ice at the mouths of rivers.

However, the best assumption is that he saw icebergs, which flow down the Belle Isle Straight during the early summer months -- and possibly later. Tim Severin recreated St Brendan's journey and wrote in his book, *The Brendan Voyage*, that the icebergs the crew saw were like Brendan's, "Great Pillar of Crystal." He added that, "It is difficult for the scholar to understand the illusion unless he too has seen the northern icebergs."

Fine furs

There are also in those parts, plenty of fine Furs, unknown to this Ingram, dressed after the manner of the Country.

Sweet turf to burn

The people there do burn a kind of white Turf or earth, which they dig out of the marshes a fathom deep in the ground. It burneth very clear, and smelleth as sweet as musk, and that earth is as wholesome, sweet, and comfortable, to smell unto, as any Pomander. They do make their fire of this earth for the sweetness thereof, having great abundance of wood.

Their manner of kindling fire

When they want fire they take briars, and rub them very hard together between their fists, and so with hard and often rubbing they kindle and make fire.

Iron and mineral salt

They have great plenty of Iron, and there is also great plenty of mineral salt, in the marsh ground which looketh reddish, a thing necessary for the great fishings near the sea shore, which are there abundant, and the fish very large and huge.

The fertility of the soil. Plains. Great woods. Palms. Closes and Pastures

The ground and Country is most excellent, fertile and pleasant, & especially towards the River of May, For the grass of the rest is not so green, as it is in these parts, for the other is burnt away with the heat of the Sun. And as all the Country is good and most delicate, having great plains, as large & as fair in many places as may be seen, being as plain as a board: And then great & huge woods of sundry kind of trees, as cedar, Lingum vitae, Bombasse (silk cotton tree), plants and bushes, bark that biteth like Pepper, (of which kind, young M. Winter brought home part from the Straight of Magelane), with the fruitful Palm tree, & great plenty of other sweet trees to this Ingram unknown. And after that plains again, and in other places great closes of pasture, environed with most delicate trees in stead of hedges: they being as it were set by the hands of men: Yet the best grass for the most part is in the high Countries, somewhat far from the Sea side, and great Rivers, by reason that the low grounds there be so rank, that the grass groweth faster than it can be eaten, whereby the old grass lieth withered thick, and the new grass growing through it. Whereas in the upper parts, the grass and ground is most excellent and green. The ground not being overcharged with any old withered grass as is afore specified.

The Palm tree

The Palm tree aforesaid carrieth hairs on the leaves thereof, which reach to the ground, Whereof the Indians do make ropes and cords for their Cotten beds, and do use the same to many other purposes.

Wine of the Palm

The which Tree if you prick it with your knife, about two foot from the root, it will yield a Wine in color like whey, but in taste strong and somewhat like Bastard, which is most excel-

lent drink. But it will distemper both your head and body, if you drink too much thereof, as our strong Wines will do in these parts.

Meat of the Palm
The branches of the top of the tree, are most excellent meat raw, after you have pared away the bark.

Oil against poisoned arrows
 Also there is a red oil that cometh out of the root of this tree, which is most excellent against poisoned arrows & weapons: for by it they do recover themselves of their poisoned wounds.

The Plantine with its fruits
There is a tree called a Plantine, with fruit growing on it like a pudding (sausage), which is most excellent meat raw.

   They have also a red berry like a pescod, called Guyathos, two or three inches long, which groweth on short bushes full of pricks like the Sloe or Thorn tree, and the fruit eateth like a green Raisin, but sharper somewhat: They stamp this berry and make Wine thereof, which they keep in vessels made of wood.

Vines with great grapes
They have also in many places, Vines which bear Grapes as big as a man's thumb.

Herbs and flowers
There is also great plenty of herbs, and of all kinds of flowers, as Roses and Gillyflowers, like ours in England, and many others which he knew not.

Grain
Also, they have a kind of Grain, the ear whereof is as big as the wrist of a mans arm: the Grain is like a flat pease; it maketh very good bread and white.

Bread of a Cassava
They do also make bread of the root called Cassava, which they do dry, and beat it as small as they can, and temper it with water and so bake it in cakes on a stone.

Kinds of beasts. Deer. Sheep
There is also a great plently of Buffs, Bears, Horses, Kine, Wolves, Foxes, Deer, Goats, Sheep, Hares, and Conies. Also other cattle like ours, to this Examinate unknown, the most part being wild. The Hides and skins of them are good Merchandise. There is very great store of those Buffs, which are beasts as big as two Oxen, in length almost twenty foot, having long ears like a Bloodhound with long hairs about their ears, their horns be crooked like Rams horns, their eyes black, their hairs long, black, rough, and shagged as a Goat. The Hides of these beasts are sold very dear, this Beast doth keep company only by couples, male and female, and doth always fight with others of the same kind when they do meet. There is also great plenty of Deer, both red, white and speckled. This last sort this Examinate knoweth not.

An early rendition of a buff. Ingram was the first Englishman to describe the buffalo.

There is also great plenty of another kind of Sheep which carry a kind of course wool. This Sheep is very good meat, although the flesh be very red. They are exceeding fat, and of nature loath to rise when they are laid, which is always from five a clock at night until five a clock in the morning: between which time you easily kill them, but after they be on foot they are very wild, and rest not in one place, but live together in herds, in some 500 as it happeneth, more or less: And these red Sheep are most about the Bay of Saint Marie, as this Examinate guesseth.

There are Bears both black and white. There are Wolves. The Foxes have their skins more grizzled than ours in England. There are Conies both black and red, and grey in every place great plently.

White bears are polar bears. Currently, during summer, these animals come down as far as the southern end of Hudson Bay; a portion of eastern Quebec, that boarders on the sea; the eastern coast of Labrador; and the northern tip of Newfoundland.

The earliest date of exporting polar bears from Iceland was about 880. Two cubs were given to King Harold the Fairhaired of Norway. He was so delighted that the gave Imgimundr, the giver, an ocean going ship loaded with lumber.

It was discovered that if the bears were captured when they were young, they could be easily tamed. They became a fashionable pet for nobles, kings and the wealthy -- it was the ultimate gift.

A strange Beast

This Examinate did also see in those Countries a Monstrous beast twice as big as a Horse, and in proportion like to a Horse, both in mane, hoof, hair, and neighing, saving it was small towards the hinder parts like a Greyhound. These Beasts hath two teeth or horns of a foot long growing straight forth by their nostrils: they are natural enemies to the Horses.

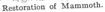
Restoration of Mammoth.

MUSK OX

ELK

MONSTROUS BEAST	*buffalo*	*walrus*	*musk ox*
2x size of horse	yes	yes	yes
proportion of horse	yes	yes	yes
small hindquarters, like greyhound	yes	yes	yes
mane	shaggy one	no	yes
hoofs	yes	no	yes
hair	yes	yes	yes
neighs	?	barks	?
2 teeth, or horns, a foot long, from front of ears on side of face, growing straight forth by nostrils	2 horns top of head	yes	yes

Canadian Indians told of the Big Elk. This huge beast was very dangerous, could navigate through eight feet of snow, had skin so tough that their weapons could hardly penetrate it, and wonder of wonders, "Had some sort of an arm which comes out of his shoulder and which he uses as we do."

The Delaware Indians knew of a herd of shaggy animals that were so powerful they drove off all the animals in their vicinity. Finally the God of the Indians became so incensed that he killed off most of the creatures and after a tremendous struggle managed to wound the leader of the herd .... the herd then fled.

Thomas Jefferson wrote that local Indians told him that they had seen mammoths and he believed, "That this animal still exists in the southern and western parts of America."

Elephants and Ounces. A strange Beast

He did also see in that Country both Elephants and Ounces. He did also see one other strange Beast bigger than a Bear, he had neither head nor neck: his eyes and mouth were in his breast. This beast is very ugly to behold, and cowardly of kind. It beareth a very fine skin like a Rat, full of silver hairs.

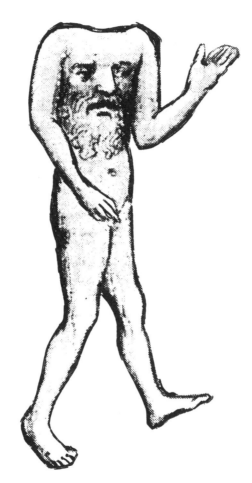

Europe had a myth of men with their heads on their chests. One such creature is drawn on the Piri Re'is chart of 1513. Fifteenth century editions of Marco Polo's adventures show headless men.

Shakespeare wrote in *The Tempest*, "Who would believe ... that there were such men whose heads stood in their breast." *Act III Scene III.* As Shakespeare was born in 1564, the play was written after Ingram's trip, and shows that the European mind still accepted this belief.

The National Geographical Society wrote, February 1997, that, "Ignorance of East Asia led Europeans into wild imaginings of monstrous creatures."

58

Russet Parrots. Birds like ours. Guinea Hens. Red Birds. Penguins

There are in those Countries abundance of Russet Parrots, but very few green. There are also Birds of all sorts as we have, and many strange Birds to this Examinate unknown. There are great plenty of Guinea hens which are tame Birds and proper to the inhabitants, as big as Geese, very black of color, having feathers like Down. There is also a bird called a Flamingo whose feathers are very red, and is bigger than a Goose, billed like a Shovel, and is very good meat. There is also another kind of Fowl in that Country which hunteth the Rivers near unto the Islands: They are of shape and bigness of a goose but their wings are covered with small yellow feathers, and cannot fly. You may drive them before you like sheep: They are exceeding fat and very delicate meat, they have white heads and therefore the Country men call them Penguins (which seemeth to be a Welch name). And they have also in use divers other Welsh words, a matter worth noting.

The great auk, now extinct, was a black and white flightless bird that lived along northern coastal areas. From Cartier's time sailors would salt casks of the birds to either, eat on their return voyages, or bring back to Europe to sell as food. It was an oily bird, so oil was produced. It has been reported that some ships made 10 to 12 puncheons of it. A puncheon, a liquid cask, can hold 72 to 120 gallons [12x100 gallons = 1,200 gallons.]

Richard Strong, master of the *Marigold* wrote in 1593, "We beat about a very long time ... and fell in with Cape Briton ... Heere divers of our men went on land upon the very cape, where, at their arrivall they found ... penguins."

The russet parrot is a puzzle. It has been suggested that it was a passenger pigeon, but that extinct bird was grey, very much like the mourning dove.

There is also a very strange Bird, thrice as big as an Eagle, very beautiful to behold, his feathers are more orient than a Peacocks feathers, his eyes are glittering as a Hawks eyes, but as great as a mans eyes, his head and thigh as big as a mans head and thigh. It hath a crest and tuff of feathers of sundry colors on the top of the head like a Lapwing, hanging backwards: His beak and talons in proportion like Eagles but very huge and large.

In Arabian legend there is an enormous bird of prey called the roc. This bird was so large that it carried elephants in its claws to feed its young.

Tempests
Touching Tempests and other strange monstrous things in these parts, this Examina
that he hath seen it Lighten and Thunder in summer season by the space of four ̄ ̄ ̄ ̄ ̄
hours together: the cause whereof he judgeth to be the heat of the Climate.

Hurricanes, Tornadoes
He further saith that there is a Cloud sometime of the year seen in the air, which commonly
turneth to great Tempests. And that sometimes of the year there are great winds in manner of
Whirlwinds.

Their manner of Religion
Touching their Religion, he saith that they honor for their God a Devil, which they call Col-
luchio, who speaketh unto them sometimes in the likeness of a black Dog and sometimes in
the likeness of a black Calf.
And some do honor the Sun, the Moon, and the Stars.

Adultery punished with death
He saith to the people in those Countries are allowed many Wives, some five, some ten, & a
king sometimes an hundred: And that Adultery is very severely punished in manner follow-
ing, that is to say: the woman taken in adultery, must with her own hands cut the throat of the
Adulterer, and the next of his kindred doth likewise cut the throat of the Adulteress. And be-
ing asked in what manner they take their executions, he saith That they are brought to execu-
tion by certain Magistrates, who do deliver unto the woman the knife, wherewith she cutteth
the throat of the Adulterer.
Then appeareth their Colluchio or Devil, in the likeness aforesaid, and speaketh unto them,
and to that Devil the parties brought to execution do great reverence, and with many prayers
to it do take their death.

Their manner of Burials
He saith that such persons as are put to death in such sort, have not any of their friends bur-
ied with them: but such as die naturally, have always buried quick with them one of their
dearest friends to keep them company, and to provide necessaries and victual for them, who
do willingly consent thereto, being thereto persuaded by their Collunchio or Devil, who they
do worship.

The Devil fled away at the name of the holy Trinity
He saith further, that he & his two fellows, namely Richard Browne, and Richard Twide, went
into a poor mans house, & there they did see the said Colluchio or Devil, with very great eyes
like a black Calf: Upon the sight whereof Browne said, There is the Devil, and thereupon he
blessed himself: In the name of Father, and of the Son, and of the Holy Ghost. And Twice
said very vehemently, I defy thee and all thy works. And presently the Colluchio shrank away
in a stealing manner forth of the doors, and was seen no more unto them.

Great Rivers

Also they passed over many great Rivers in those Countries, in Canoes or Boats: some four, some six, some eight, some ten miles over; whereof one was so large, that they could scarce cross the same in four and twenty hours.

Musical instruments

Also he saith, that in the same Country the people have instruments of Music made of a piece of a cane, almost a foot long, being open at both ends: which sitting down, they smite upon their thighs and one of their hands, making a pleasant kind of sound.

And they do use another kind of instrument like a Taber, covered with a white skin somewhat like Parchment.

This Examinate can very well describe their gestures, dancing, and songs.

After long travail, the aforesaid David Ingram with his two companions Browne and Twide, came to the head of a river called Garinda, which is 60 Leagues West from Cape Britton: where they understood by the people of that Country of the arrival of a Christian. Whereupon they made their repair to the Seaside, and there found a French Captain named Monsieur Champaigne, who took them into his Ship and brought them unto Newhaven, & from thence they were transported into England, Anno Dom. 1569.

Silver in exchange of trifles

This Monsieur Champaigne with divers of his company was brought into the Village of Bariniah, about 20 miles up into the Country by the same Examinate and his two Companions, by whose means he had a trade with the people of divers sorts of fine furs, & of great red leaves of trees almost a yard long, & about a foot broad, which he thinketh are good for dying.

Also the said Monsieur Champaigne, had there for exchange of trifling wares, a good quantity of rude, and wrought silver.

He saith further, that divers of the said Frenchmen which were in the said Ship called the Gargarine, *are yet living in Homfleure upon the coast of France, as he thinketh, for he did speak with some of them within these three years.*

About a fortnight after their coming from Newhaven into England, this said Examinate and his two companions came to master John Hawkins, who had set them on shore upon the Bay of Mexico, and unto each of them he gave a reward.

Richard Browne, his companion, was slain about five years past in the Elizabeth of master Cockins of London: And Richard Twide, his other companion, died at Ratcliffe in John Sherewoods house there, about three years past.

The language of some of the Countries

GWANDO ... Is a word of Salutation, as among us; Good morrow, Good even, God save you, or such like.
CARICONA ... A King.
CARRACCONA ... A Lord.
FONA ... Bread.
CARMUGNAR ... The Privates.
KERUCCA ... The Sun.

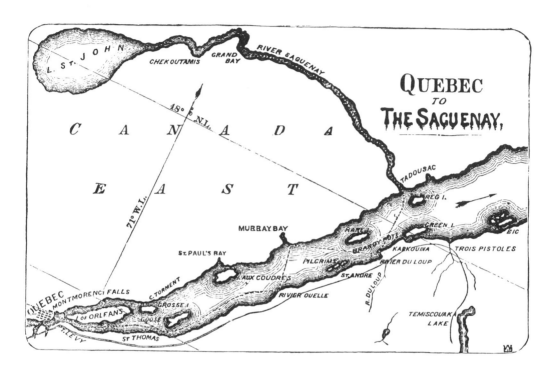

The location of Tadoussac and the Saguenay River.

Ingram stated that the head of the River of Garinda was about 60 leagues west of Cape Britton, which could be the St Lawrence -- then the city of Garinda, a mile and a half long, would be Tadoussac. Champlain would later complain about the Basques who had been fur trading there for years before his arrival. Because of their toehold, he therefore decided to sail further upstream to start his new settlement, of Quebec.

Bariniah was, "About 20 miles up into the country," after the trio met Captain Champaigne. It could have been an Indian village on the Saguenay River.

The Saguenay is also spelled Sague/Saguenai/Sagnay/Sagne/Saghung/Sadilege. "On the 15th of January 1540-1 Letters patent from Francis I to Roberval that appointed him to lead an expedition against the Kingdom of Saguenay"... the territory surrounding the river was known as the Kingdom of the Saguenay.

The main Sea on the Northpart of America

Also the said David Ingram traveling towards the North, found the main sea upon the North-side of America, and traveling in the sight thereof the space of two whole days, where the people signified unto him, that they had seen ships on that coast, and did draw upon the ground the shape and figure of ships, and of their sails and flags. Which thing especially proveth the passage of the Northwest, and is agreeable to the experience of Yasques de Coronado, which found the ship of China of Cataia upon the Northwest of America.

Corrasau Island

Also the examinate saith, that there is an Island called Corrasau, and that there are in it five or six thousand Indians at the least, and all those are governed by one only Negro, who is but a slave to a Spaniard. And moreover the Spaniards will send but one of their slaves with a 100 or 200 of the Indians, when they go to gather gold in the Rivers descending from the mountains. And when they shall be absent by the space of 20 or 30 days at the least, every one of the Indians will nevertheless obey all the Slaves commandments with as great reverence, as if he were their natural King, although there be never a Christian near them by the space of 100 or 200 miles: which argueth the great obedience of those people, and how easily they may be governed when they be once conquered.

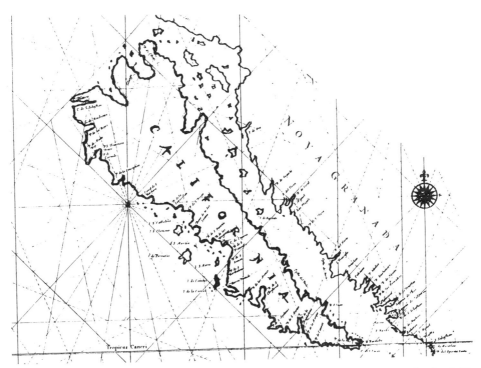

The island of Corrasau certainly seems that it should be Curacao. Some historians have dismissed this possibility because they feel Ingram's description does not fit. It could be any island in the Atlantic.

However, since he referred to Chinese ships, California is a remote possibility because early maps show it as an island.

64

conclusion

Ingram's *Relation* was not meant to be a heroic travel adventure but rather was planned as an inducement, for people of Great Britain, to settle lands held by Walsingham and his cronies. Ingram was probably interviewed days or weeks before the formal questioning, which would have given the Walsingham group time to carefully craft the questions Ingram would be asked. The questioners did not care about the exact route, what they cared about was: water; grazing; cattle and fowl for food; and that there were precious gems, metals and other treasures for the taking. Just about all of Ingram's answers would be considered a drawing card for colonization.

It is a known fact that 96 to 114 men were put ashore near Tampico, Mexico and that the group split into two, one went towards Mexico City while the other trudged northwards. About 20 years later, Job Hortop and Miles Philips, two of the group who had headed toward Mexico City, returned to England and their stories did back up Ingram's.

Hawkins was still alive and it would be plausible to think that Walsingham's group had checked with him about the veracity of Ingram's account. Captain Champaigne was living, according to Ingram, and could have been contacted. Then too the ship's landing at Homfleure, France and later at England could have been verified with the harbor masters.

Hakluyt was the foremost English geographer of his time. However, he ignored the writings of many Europeans who were writing about recent travels and discoveries: he even ignored the *Jesuit Relations*. Why did he ignore these important writings? It could be that he considered himself above the European mentality. Did he feel that only he was capable of determining what was true and worthy to print? Does this quirky thinking have anything to do with why he did not reprint Ingram's *Relation*?

The question has been asked whether Ingram and his two companions could have trekked as far as they did in such a short time because they must have traveled at least 2,700 miles -- if they did not do any backtracking.

WHAT WAS IIIS ROUTE?

If they were traveling today, they would fly, go by train, bus, or sail. Naturally all these options were unavailable then. In other words, since a ship was not available they had to walk.

It is known that the sailors were set ashore near Tampico. Ingram and his two companions were picked up near Cape Breton, which could have been Tadoussac/ Tadousac. When Samuel de Champlain arrived in New France, he found this established trading center at the juncture of the Saguenay and St Lawrence Rivers.

The first leg of the long walk would be between Tampico and the northeastern part of Texas. It is the vast territory between Texas and the eastern shore of Canada that has presented a puzzle to historians.

If they had paddled up the Mississippi-Ohio River system, they would have reached the southern tier of New York State, Ingram certainly would have written that they paddled for days on end and against the flow. Since there is no mention of

TRIP LOG ... one, or possibly all three, of the group had a tremendous sense of direction, especially when compared to deVaca's mindless wandering about the southern part of the United States.

Divide the total mileage, about 2,700 miles, by 335 days [11 months], and the trio would have averaged 8 miles each day. However, since Ingram stated that they stayed a few days at some sites, it is more probable that they must have averaged 15 miles per day, which is certainly possible.

NIAGARA FALLS

MISSISSIPPI-OHIO RIVERS

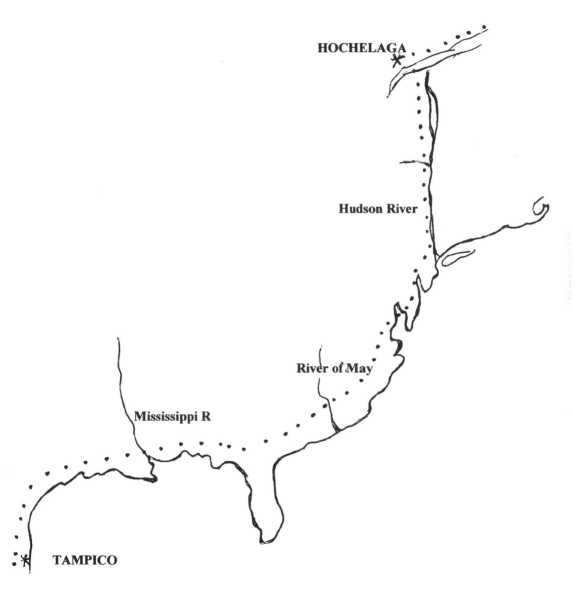

HOCHELAGA

Hudson River

River of May

Mississippi R

TAMPICO

such a long journey by water we can assume that this was not their route. And, if Ingram had seen Niagara Falls, surely there would have been mention of seeing such a wonder. So, it has to be believed that they did not walk along the western edge of New York, Lake Ontario or Lake Erie.

Ingram tells of Ochelega, which was Hochelaga, and today is Montreal. Logically the best way to reach Montreal, if the Great Lakes route is ruled out, is up the Hudson-Champlain Valley.

The Indians knew the trails near their villages and had knowledge of how to reach a far destination. These trails were used for trade, communication and warfare and were beaten by many feet to a foot, or so, below ground level. No doubt Ingram went the entire route at water level.

Today it is felt that Norumbega was on the Penobscot River. Champlain was the one who placed Norumbega on the Penobscot, but its latitude is 45 degrees according to the *Encyclopaedia Britannica* [or 44:30 in *Rand McNally*]. If this was the site of Norumbega, that would mean that Ingram would have had to turn westward, or backtrack, to reach Montreal.

Mercator placed Norumbega north of Manhattan, but south of Poughkeepsie. He used fairly correct latitude on his maps of the New World: his latitude of the area around New York City is 41 degrees. Consider that today in Putnam County there are many stone chambers: the county has the largest concentration of stone chambers in the northeast. Since there is a foot print, of these unexplained sites, could this area then be the location of Norumbega?

Gerard Mercator.

68

It is most likely that Ingram traveled to the Manhattan area and then up the Hudson River. At Fort Edward, he would have had the choice of going north by way of Lake George, or by Lake Champlain and then to Montreal.

David Ingram saw the land north of Albany well before Jogues, 1646. It remains to be proved if he saw Lake George. But, he definitely saw the Adirondacks and Lake Champlain well before Samuel de Champlain, 1609.

IRON

It has been stated that Ingram did not impart any new knowledge, that everything he related was available in print. Except for one important fact, "They have great plenty of iron," which could be bog iron. They also had iron swords and iron knives, could these have been trade goods, or did they forge them themselves? Until Arlington Mallery recently proved otherwise, it was assumed that iron was not known or worked by the Indians.

PROBLEMS

One problem to be found with his *Relations* is the tale about the, "Beasts with their heads on their breasts," which was a current belief. Early maps do show such a creature, and Ingram could have seen these drawings.

Such fantasy was rampart during this age. Hudson's log of 15 June 1608, reported a mermaid in the St Lawrence ...

This morning one of our company, looking overboard, saw a mermaid, and calling up some of the company to see her, once more come up, and by this time she had come close to the ship's side, looking earnestly on the men; a little after, a sea came and overturned her. From the navel upward her back and breasts were like a woman's (as they that saw her), her body as big as one of us: her skin was very white; and long hair hanging down behind of the colour black; in her going down they saw her tail, which was like the tail of a porpoise, and speckled like a mackerel.

Two other problems found with Ingram's *Relations* are, large birds and elephants, but these animals were also drawn on the maps of the day. Perhaps the large bird could have been a roc or the phoenix, both were part of the beliefs of the day, but today are considered to be fairy tales.

These few problems are not that bad considering all the things that he related. On that basis, and since he was believed by Walsingham, Ingram's trip has to be accepted as happening.

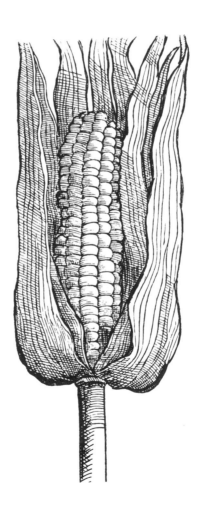

glossary

BARK THAT BITETH LIKE PEPPER ... John Hawkins wrote about Winter's bark (drimys winteri), which was used to prevent scurvy.

Aspirin, which is bitter, was first made from willow bark -- and willow bark has long been used by native peoples and herb doctors.

BASTARD ... is a sweet Spanish wine that tastes like muscatel. "Brown bastard is your only drink." Shakespeare. This wine was imported from Spain to Bristol during this time.

CASSAVA ... is a tropical American shrub cultivated for its edible roots. The peeled root is dried, to remove poison, and reduced to a flour. The flour is sprinkled onto a flat stone above a hot fire. No liquid is added. The flour is then patted with the hands and leveled with a wooden paddle to keep the thinness even. A taco, or a thin bread, is the result. The flour can also be used as a filler in soup.

CLOSE ... is a small enclosed field, surrounded by a wall, hedge, or fence of any kind.

CURETS ... probably a gorget, which was usually a crescent shaped plate hung around the neck.

DEVIL ... since their Gods were foreign to Ingram, they automatically became devils. Ward in his, *The Dutch And Swedes* wrote that they had, "Nor religion whatever, nor any divine worship, but serve the Devil, whom they called Menutto. This Menutto, however, one might easily identify with that Manitou, the Great Spirit, in whom many later observers saw the God of the Indians."

ELEPHANTS ... elephants are in Mayan art.

An elephant is featured on the, "Typus Cosmogra, Universalis Map" 1566; and several are drawn on the 1573 map of Abraham Ortelius, "A Representation Of The Empire Of Prester John." Ingram could have seen these maps and deducted that elephants were found world wide.

GRAIN ... maize was cultivated by mostly all the tribes of the Americas by this period.

GREAT RED LEAVES ... since Ingram did not state what color dye was produced we cannot be certain just what plants he saw.

Perhaps the leaves could have been: tobacco; annatto, but the seeds also had to be used; sumac; and amaranth which is currently used to color food and garments. In 1795, the *Elizabeth* docked at Bristol carrying, "100 bags of shumac."

During this period, the British Isles were producing many yards, or ells, of cloth, so a new source for dyes was an important factor.

GUYATHOS ... did he mean red raspberries, which grow wild even today and certainly have prickers?

HORSE TAIL ... because Ingram uses the words horse tails to describe an ensign does not mean that the hair came from a horse. There were animals that had long hair, buffalo, musk ox -- and Indians had the ability to strip grasses, leaves and even trees to form long fibers. Then too, it could be human hair.

71

Pale Ink, p 64, tells us that, "The skull of a horse unearthed by a team of professional archeologists in Wisconsin in 1936, and carbon-14 dated in 1964 as possibly as early as 490 AD. It is slowly being accepted that horses had been on the continent before the arrival of the Spanish.

IRON, they had short broad swords of black iron; darts headed with iron; crooked knives of iron; and great plenty of iron ... The Indians had tremendous trade routes that followed the great rivers of America. It is conceivable that iron goods from Mexico reached the northern tribes.

Arlington Mallery, and his associate James Howe, found at least 50 Nordic natural draft iron smelting furnaces along the Ohio, in the Roanoke Valley and in Newfoundland. It is also believed that the Indians knew how to find and work bog iron. Did the native Americans learn from the Norse or trade with them?

To learn more on this subject read Mallery's fascinating book, *Lost America*.

KINE ... is an archaic term for cattle.

LEAGUE ... is a measure of distance varying from about 2.42 to 4.6 English statute miles, of 5,280 feet. The marine league uses three geographic miles of 6,076.

MASSIVE SILVER ... silver is still mined in Mexico. But, how common was it in eastern North America? No doubt this was a ploy by Walsingham to attract settlers to settle on his lands.

OUNCES ... is the lynx.

PALMS ... naturally Ingram saw them at the beginning of his trek.

PLANTINE TREE ... plantain is a starchy food that has to be cooked. Resorts in the tropics like to slice and fry it as chips or cooked in long slices, boiled it tastes like a mild sweet potato.

Since Ingram says it was eaten raw, it has to be the banana. It used to be believed that the early Spanish brought this plant to the new world, but recent research has proved that it came from Africa.

POTTLE ... is a drinking vessel, pot, or tankard holding about half a gallon. It could also be a small basket that held fruit.

RUBIES ... Rebecca Baker, a graduate gemoligist stated that, "Rubies are still found in North Carolina. A 2" by 4" stone would probably would not be of gem quality today, but would make a good cabochon stone. Good gem quality stones certainly were available a few hundred years ago. Also Star Of Idaho, a type of garnet, is found all over -- and they go up to one pound in size."

The largest garnet mine in the world is in the Adirondacks at Gore Mountain, Warren County. It produces 90% of the world's industrial garnets, which are used as abrasives. This mine was discovered by Frank Hooper in the 1800s. Gemstones are found here, ranging up to a few feet across, according to the, *Encyclopaedia Britannica*. Garnet in matrix is so plentiful that fireplaces and walls in houses are built of it. On a sunny day the roads around the Gore Mountain area glisten red with the garnet grit imbedded in the black top. The Indians certainly must have known of this vast deposit and the many deposits nearby in the Adirondacks, which are not worked today.

Bakeless in his, *Eyes Of Discovery* simply could not believe that Ingram saw rubies, instead, he reasoned that the stones were turquoise and therefore concluded that the trio went through or near Pueblo country.

Most likely, Ingram saw hunks of garnet, which were probably found, by the Indians, just walking along, inspecting the ground.

SALT ... was not produced in England and had to be purchased from France or Portugal at great cost. Besides being used as a seasoning, salt was needed to preserve fish caught off the Great Banks, to preserve meat and to pickle. Etienne Bellenger explored the northern American coast, 1583, about the time that Ingram was questioned by Walsingham. Bellenger later told Richard Hakluyt that he thought, "Verilie that verie good salt may be made in great quantities in divers places along the Coast."

SHEEP... since Ingram said that he saw them near the Bay of St Marie, which was probably located near the mouth of the St Lawrence River, and that this animal was red, then, probably it was the seal. When the seal's coat is wet it does look reddish, and it has a fat layer to protect it from the cold. They do live in large colonies and are easily killed on land. Sheep were not in North America at that time.

SPECKLED DEER ... according to a newspaper article by Jean Hadden, in the *Adirondack Journal*, Kit Manzer, "Shot a most unusual spotted deer," in 1904. "Picture post cards showing the deer were made up, labeled 'The King of the Adirondacks'." The deer, "Was eventually taken to the State Education Building in Albany to be put on display."

SHIELDS ... according to Sagard, in his *Journal*, "They make ... shields which cover almost the whole body. [See glossary on Champlain, 1609.]

SWEET TURF TO BURN ... this is either tufa or marl, both are forms of calcium carbonate. Most likely it is marl. When vegetation builds up in a marsh or peat bog, lime secreted in organisms, forms a lens under the peat and under that lens marl is created.

Whereas tufa is found in clear springs or streams that have a high lime content.

geography

BALMA ... Certainly sounds like Alabama, which is a Choctaw word that means thicket clearers or vegetation gatherers. The Alabama River was named after a Creek tribe, the Alibamu. The Creek Nation lived in the southeast and central part, while the Choctaws were in the southwest part of the present state of Alabama.

In the early 1500s Spanish explorers were roaming the area, namely; de Pineda, de Narvaez, de las Bazares and de Soto. The region was well know to Europeans during this time.

CAPE BRITTON ... also known as Bretton/Briton/Brittayne. The Terre des Bretons,in the 16th century, according to some maps reached as far south as Florida. It appears on Jorge Reinel's map of c1519. In *New Voyages To North America*, p324 footnote 2, "Cape Breton was the name used first for the southern part of the island, now known by that name, because it was the haunt of certain fishers from Brittany."

GIRICKA ... as this was the first country that Ingram went through, it would be close to Tampico, Mexico.

STRAIGHT OF MAGELANE ... the Magdalen islands are in the Gulf of St Lawrence, so the straight was probably near.

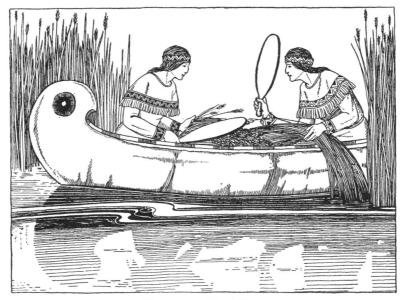

GATHERING WILD RICE

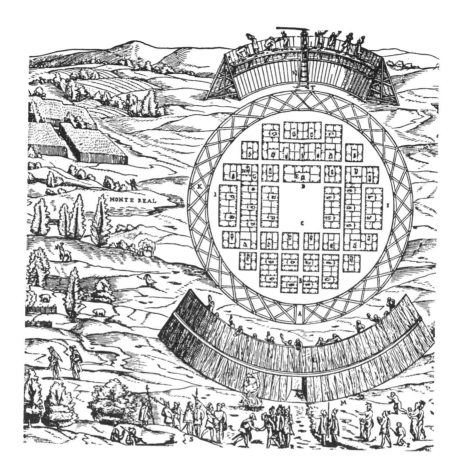

Hochelaga. Jacques Cartier is credited with discovering this stronghold during the fall of 1535/6, which was located a little to the west of present day Montreal. One thousand enthusiastic Indians greeted him. Due to war, the settlement was wiped out, so that when Champlain arrived there was nothing left. The St Lawrence River was also called Hochelaga.

Like many English, especially the Cockney, Ingram must have dropped his "H's". So Hochelaga became Ochala. HO-CHE-LA-GA was also known as Gahunda, according to Sylvester. Halsey in, *The Old New York Frontier* states that, "Gehunda, [is] the common word for river" in the Iroquois language.

Guinda was the most northerly town and river that Ingram visited. Is this a variation of Garinda? Since he dropped his "H's," as is seen in how he pronounced Hochelaga, it could be reasoned that Guinda is in reality Ga-hun-da, still another name for Hochelaga. Ingram also mentioned Gunda -- was this Guinda?

BEGA is really Norumbega ... also known as ...

NORAMBEGUE	ANOROBAGRA
NOREMBEGA	ARANBEGA
NOREMBEGUE	L'ANORMEE BERGE
	anormee means grand,vast, majestic
NOROMBEGA	LA TERRE D'ENORME BERGE
NORUMGEGU	LA TERRRE DE NORMEBERGE
ORANBEGA	LA TERRE DE NORUMBEGA
	LA TERRE DE NORE

Without accurate latitude and longitude, Norumbega can be made to fit anywhere in the northeast of North America. The next best thing to accurate latitude and longitude is another point of reference to determine location. Block Island, on early maps, was called Claudia and is east of the Hudson and south of Rhode Island. Thankfully there are a few maps that show Norumbega/Norumbega River with Claudia in just about the right location. These maps are in the right time frame of Ingram's trip.

It is surprising how inaccurate mapping was for the northeastern states -- Canada's maps are much more accurate for the period. Map makers cannot accept all the blame, they could only show information to which they had access. Even today latitude does not always agree in different sources: *Encyclopaedia Britannica* states that the Hudson River is 41:55 while Carmel, NY has a latitude of 41:25 -- rather surprising because Carmel is north of the mouth of the river; and Sandy Hook at 40:28. While *Rand McNally* lists, the Hudson River at 40:25, Carmel at 41:26, and Sandy Hook at 40:27.

Allefonsce wrote that he passed Cape Norembeague, 41 degrees latitude and that beyond descends the River of Norembeague about 80 miles [west]. If he sailed around Cape Cod and followed the shoreline of southern New England, the western tip of Long Island could be the Cape.

1527, Aranbega appears for the first time on a map of Hieronemus Verrazano, the brother of the explorer, Oranbega is shown south of Cape Race and Cape Breton.
1539, The whole eastern seaboard between Cape Breton and Florida was Norumbega.
1540, The Munster map depicts the Regio Giagantum [Hudson].
1545, Allefonsce's map is primitive, but it shows Riviere de Norombergue [Hudson]
1550, Gastaldi, of Venice, produced a map. The Hudson River is drawn up to the junction of the Mohawk. Norumbega is between the Hudson and Narragansett Bay
1556, Norumbega was now located between Cape Breton and New Jersey. Andre Thevet, a French geographer, said the French called the Grande River Norombegue and the Indians Aggone.
1568-69, Ingram saw Norumbega.
1583, Ingram sails with Sir Humprey Gilbert to return to Norumbega. Unfortunately they could not locate it.
1592, the Molineaux Globe shows the Rio Grande [Hudson] and about where Rensselaer is, Norumbega.

1605, Champlain sailed down the New England coast looking for Norumbega. Unfortunately he did not go far enough. He placed, Norumbega around the Penobscot River on his maps.

The Land Of The Grand Scarp, or The Land Of The Palisades, on the lower Hudson. Berge means the elevated border of a river, a scarp of a fortification, a steep side of a moat or road, or a designation for certain rocks elevated perpendicularly above water.

Furs being prepared and sewn in an old world fur shop.

FISH AND FUR

The unlimited fishing of the Great Banks was the primary reason for Europeans to cross the ocean.

Fishing was encouraged by European monarchs ...
- To bring much needed cash to poor fishermen
- To keep all boats busy
- Because fishermen would then be trained and able to operate their country's war ships in an emergency. Every ruler wanted to build a fleet to intimidate his neighbors and ultimately to dominate the seas.

The eating of fish had little to do with penance until the Catholic Church decided to encourage fishing, for the above reasons, and therefore ordered the abstinence of meat during Lent, Advent, plagues, natural disasters and on the eve of Holy Days.

Eventually the fishermen who sailed to North America began exchanging a simple trifle, or two, for a few pelts that were offered by the Indians. The women folk at home liked the luxury, so sailors started bringing back furs for friends and neighbors. Europe was colder and there was no central heating or glass in the window openings to keep out winter gales. Fur was a necessity to keep warm and the demand for it for garments, linings, hats and muffs was excessive. The continuance of wars kept the European supply of furs an iffy proposition. Soon fishermen started to carry cheap trinkets aboard just to acquire the desired skins: some sailors even bartered the ships sails, ropes, nails, ship stores -- whatever was not nailed down.

Early fishermen only came in contact with coastal Indians, so the fur trade was limited. In the beginning the interest was for fancy furs for trim. A new trade emerged slowly in America with great repercussions, the fur trade. Fur forever changed the Indians' life because it brought them a ready supply of iron. Fur replaced wampum as the currency of the period. Fur was the one item that Europeans wanted and were always willing to barter for, with the Indians. Fur was soft gold.

French, Basque And Portuguese Fishermen

The original name of Brittany means, "The Country of the Sea." Saint Malo was the center of the Newfoundland cod fisheries.
Anson

St Malo.

79

Parkman and others believe that Bretons started fishing the cod banks of Newfoundland long before Cabot's voyage of 1497. The French took the Canadian harbors as far south as Cape Breton, which was named after them. They fished far out on the Great Banks. Since they produced salt, they were able to heavily salt the catch aboard, while sailing back to Europe.

When Cabot arrived he found that the name Baccalaos was used by the natives for cod and came to the conclusion that Basques had been there before him, as Baccalaos is Basque for cod. The Basques had a monopoly on whaling and supplied Europe with oil for lamps and for the manufacture of broadcloth and tanning.

When whaling failed off the coast of Portugal, sometime during the 700s, the Portuguese and Basques were forced to fish farther and farther out into the Atlantic.

Eventually they reached Iceland, Greenland and Newfoundland. It is now accepted that the Portuguese reached Newfoundland before 1501. They took over the harbors from Cape Race north.

Whales did frequent the waters around Long Island, so the Portuguese and Basques must have found them. Since they were hunting whales, these fishermen would not be equipped to fish in rivers, therefore they can be discounted as having ventured up the Hudson.

Medieval seals of Biarritz and Motrico that show how important fishing and whaling were to the Basques.

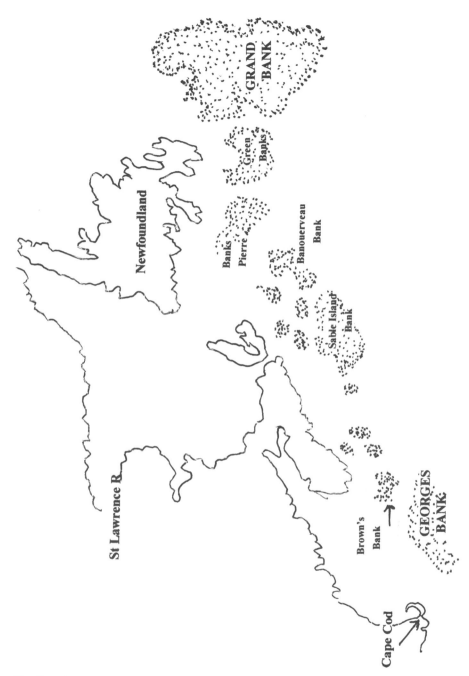

GRAND BANK

Green Banks

Newfoundland

Banks Pierre

Banouerveau Bank

Sable Island Bank

St Lawrence R.

Brown's Bank

GEORGES BANK

Cape Cod

The Great Banks of Newfoundland were accidentally found and probably kept secret for many years. Somehow the secret was discovered and boats of various European countries were found there for the summer fishing. Fishermen were pushed south by storms, winds, currents and especially by pirates until some were fishing as far south as the Georges Bank, off Cape Cod.

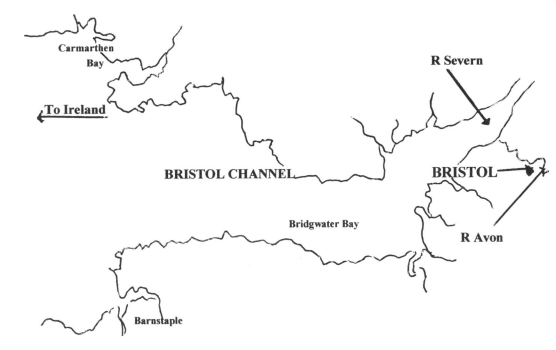

Bristol Fishermen

Bristol Harbor is on the Avon River that flows, into the Severn Estuary which flows, into the fierce Atlantic. Due to this protected location she became the second largest port of the British Kingdom in the 15th century. Bristol merchants, frustrated in the Icelandic trade by Danish competition, were searching for new fishing grounds.

Bristol faces Ireland and it is believed that Bristol fishermen watched the Irish, who were fearless, sailing their small craft out into the Atlantic instead of hugging the coast. The Bristolmen then decided to follow the Irish curraghs and then they too were fishing far into the Atlantic. Records of the Bristol Harbor Masters prove that local ships were bringing back Newfoundland cod in the early 1480s: and it is beginning to be believed that they just might have reached the Great Banks before that.

The Bristol merchants had updated charts by 1480, showing the future discoveries of Columbus. The city believes that Thomas Jay [not John Jay] of Bristol, along with a friend, Thomas Lloyd sailed westward on 15 July 1480, looking for the fabled Isles of Brasylle. The burden of their vessel was only 80 tons. The duo sailed north and south, but the expedition ended when Jay died in his ship off Ireland. Their voyage was backed up when L Vigneras found a letter in Spain during 1955. This letter dated December 1497, or January 1498, from the London merchant John Day, the alias of Hugh Say, to Columbus, and gave a detailed account of John Cabot's successful voyage to the east coast of North America, with a surprising date of 1494, adding the comment that they found this land before, "En otros tiempos [in times past] as your lordship knows." This raises the question whether the 1480 expedition of Jay and Lloyd, or some voyage between 1480 and 1492, had found land in the west before Columbus did.

John Cabot, Master of the *Matthew* in 1497, announced that the sea off Newfoundland was, "Swarming with fish, which can be taken not only with the net, but in baskets let down with a stone." From Cabot's time, the shores of Newfoundland were a familiar landfall for European fishermen. Each year the island's coasts and offshore fishing banks provided cargoes for hundreds of vessels from Portugal, Spain, France and England. Cod, from the Great Banks, soon became a European staple. These fishing grounds are called the silver mines of the Atlantic and yielded more wealth than the gold of Mezzo America, the Indies and South America. The English concentrated on inshore fishing and only lightly salted the cod before they laid them out to dry on flakes or stages. Later, the Dutch would sail to the banks to buy fresh fish, which they sold to Mediterranean countries.

The current thinking is that a great deal of Bristol's early shipping was illegal and therefore does not appear in the port records. This was done for various reasons: to avoid port charges; to avoid taxation on cargo, including fish and fish oil; and to keep the knowledge of the rich fishing banks to themselves.

In pursuing the port records of the city it becomes apparent that some ships were leaving Bristol with unusually large amounts of salt. Salt was not produced in the country and had to be purchased, usually from France or Portugal, for a stiff price. It can therefore be concluded that these ships were not be going to sell this salt to other ports, because of what the Bristolmen would have had to have charged for it. In other words, a cargo of salt leaving Bristol, was meant to preserve fish caught in the waters off North America.

During Elizabeth's day more than 10,000 worked in the fishing trade and more than half of Britain's revenue came directly from it.

Bristol ships were small, the largest was 400 tons and the smallest ones were only 25 tons, the majority was usually under 100 tons. Tonnage was determined by the number of wine casks that a ship could carry, so that a ship of 400 tons meant that that ship could carry 400 wine casks. A ton/tun of wine usually weighed 2,000 pounds.

Pirates

The fishermen of Newfoundland were cruelly harassed by pirates.
Brown

Pirating has been a scourge for many centuries. It has not left us, today ships sailing the Strait of Malacca, and off the coasts of Africa and South America have to be extremely careful and even then there is a possibility that they could be boarded by pirates.

The Great Banks were being fished in the 1400s and possibly before. The catch was unbelievable. A ship brimming full of fish could sell for a few thousand pounds -- this was in the period when one pound was a good salary for a month.

This was a great temptation to unscrupulous seafarers. All that was needed was one strong ship, a pilot or navigator and a group of hungry adventurers. Then too, there were masters of ships, who were clever enough to cover their tracks, but were in reality full time or part time pirates.

Pirates would attack the ships of: former enemies; any nation; their country; or those that belonged to a different religion. All fishing boats carried a few cannon because their cargo was so valuable -- but the sheer number of the cutthroats was too much for the fishermen. If there was anything of value aboard the ship, the pirates took that too.

A pirate.

One of the best known seafarers of all times was Sir Francis Drake: his exploits, under Elizabeth are open to the question of piracy. It was during this period when privateering turned into pirating for a good number of seafarers. England was most

84

A fishing stage used at the banks to split and dry cod.

pleased with her pirates, who sometimes numbered 400 strong, for a simple reason, the pirates took the place of a large standing navy.

James Easton, as Admiral during Elizabeth's reign, conveyed English fishing boats to and from the banks. Later, he obtained permission to requisition stores, munitions and even to press seamen from the fishing fleet at Newfoundland's Great Banks. He became such a notorious pirate, during the reign of James I, that ships quailed before him and surrendered without firing a shot. Easton had between 10 to 20 ships under his command and during the winter months sailed south to the Caribbean. There is a long list of English pirates after him.

Pirates were such a threat that English Vice Admiral Fitzwilliam urged Cardinal Woolsey that warships on the west coast, "Be sent for the commyng home of the new found Isle lands fleet."

Admiral Jean Ango of Dieppe sailed his pirate ship into Newfoundland waters in 1520 and destroyed many non French fishing ships, stages and flakes. He amassed enough money to retire and build a castle in France.

Not all pirating was done at the banks, some lazy fellows preferred to stop fishing ships close to their home ports. The pirating season was year round: in the summer, they went to northern waters, during the winter they would sail off Morocco.

Fishing In The Hudson

Shad is an anadromous fish that spends half of its life in the ocean only to return to freshwater to spawn. Each year they return, migrating up large rivers in huge runs.

Up to and shortly after WW II, the fishing industry was very lucrative on the Hudson. Shad is a large anadromous fish that runs up the river, in the spring, when the shadbush tree blooms in the woods. This is a mushy fish full of bones and particularly noted for its roe. Not too long ago, fishmongers near the river, sold this fish in large quantities. Holden in his, *History Of Queensbury* noted that, "Until the erection of dams and mills, shad ran up in the spring as far north as the Falls [Glens Falls?] where they were caught in considerable quantities and were to some extent an article of commerce." Sadly their numbers have been reduced due to pollution of the pristine waterway caused by decades of dumping of sewerage and PCBs, plus the leakage of phosphates from commercial fertilizer. Shad are making a slow comeback due to the partial cleanup of the river.

There were numerous other fish to be caught in the Hudson. The Patroon wrote that, "Opposite Fort Orange ... the sturgeon are smaller than at the Manhattans. One can be bought ... for a knife." Sturgeon was also referred to as Albany beef because so much was sold and shipped from there. Herring ran up the west side of the Hudson, "In such shoals [schools] that it was hardly credible."

conclusion

There are rumors that fishermen had reached the Hudson River before 1609.

If the Vikings had found the river, then knowledge of their catching salmon must have trickled into different European ports. It is a known fact that sailors like to gossip and compare adventures: then too there is always the urge to brag.

Piracy would be the strongest argument that the Hudson was discovered before Gomez, Verrazano and Hudson. Consider the angry fisherman who had his entire catch stolen and possibly things of value. He would have laid out cash to outfit the ship and wasted an entire season -- for nothing. Frustration could have driven him, and others like him, to discover another fishing bank a little to the south of the Great Banks, and yet another, until they ultimately beat down the coast to fish the banks off Cape Cod. Imagine a fierce storm blowing, which is quite an ordinary happening on the New England coast: such a storm would blow the tiny barks into Long Island Sound, bringing them to the fishing riches of the Hudson.

The majestic Hudson had an abundance of fish and shellfish: someone from hungry Europe had to have discovered that fact before the Dutch.

Below Glens Falls.

Manhattan Island in the sixteenth century.

The GREENLAND COMPANY, 1598

They erected two little forts on the North and South River.
Dutch West India Company

Several Greenland Company vessels were sent from Amsterdam to the West Indies during 1598. For reasons not made clear, some of the traders of the company decided to make a temporary winter settlement around New York Harbor. It could have been because they realized that it was too late in the sailing season to return to Holland, or that they had found a lucrative source for furs. Or, they were there to learn the lay of the land to establish a future trading outpost at the mouth of the Hudson River.

That these persons were there is apparent from this report ...

New Netherland, situated in America, between English Virginia and New England, extending from the South River [Delaware] lying in 34.5 degrees, to Cape Malabar (New England), in the latitude of 41.5 degrees was first settled by the inhabitants of this country in the year 1598, and especially by those of the Greenland Company, but without making any fixed settlements, only as a shelter in the winter. For which purpose they erected two little forts on the North [Hudson] and South Rivers against the attacks of the Indians.
Dutch West India Company Report; Assembly of the XIX
15 December 1644

During 1627, Governor Bradford, of the Plymouth Plantation, wrote that the Dutch, "Have used trading there (on the Hudson) this six-or seven-and-twenty years." Bradford meant that the Dutch were there 1600-1601, just a couple of years off from 1598.

Isaac Joques noted on 3 August 1646, that the Dutch were in New York City about 50 years before, but they only began to scttle permanently about 20 years ago. That too, just about goes back to 1598.

conclusion

Since the traders built two forts more than a few miles apart, one on the Hudson River and the other on the Delaware, it would seem that a ship stayed at each location. There had to be at least 20 to 30 men aboard each vessel, so there could have been at least 40 men wintering in the area and there is a faint possibility that someone of the group might have wandered north of the mouth of the Hudson. The fort on the Hudson was the first one built in New York State: Fort Nassau, on Castle Island, would not be built until 1614.

What is more important, the Greenland Company men and sailors could have influenced traders and fishermen to travel up the Hudson at a later date. Since this company had headquarters in Holland, the Dutch East India Company, merchants, or Henry Hudson might have examined their records -- or at least have heard about the Greenland Company's winter venture.

The men who wrote about this early stay have to be believed. Bradford was English and Jogues was French, both of whom were trained observers and would have no interest in creating false propaganda for the Dutch.

The Hudson River, and its location, was known in Europe during the late 1590s.

glossary

THE GREENLAND COMPANY ... was a Dutch company thought to have been founded to trade with Spitzbergen, known as Greenland.

New Amsterdam c1642.

90

The Typus Orbis Terrarum Map, in *Discours Of Voyages Into Y East & West* Indies. This book, which describes the voyages of Jan van Linschoten, was first printed in Dutch during 1596 and later in Latin, 1599. The map shows a dotted line from around the Delaware area north to Hudson Bay. Wilson in his, *Memorial History Of The City Of New York* jumped to the erroneous conclusion that this dotted line was a trail leading from the Hudson River to the St Lawrence. He further assumed that it was this trail that drew the Greenland men to the area. However, a careful study of this map, plus others in the 1598 English edition, shows that the dotted lines are territory boundaries.

It is more reasonable to believe that maps showing the location of the town of Norumbega on the Norumbega River drew these adventurers to the lower Hudson and Delaware Rivers to search for fabulous treasure believed to be there.

91

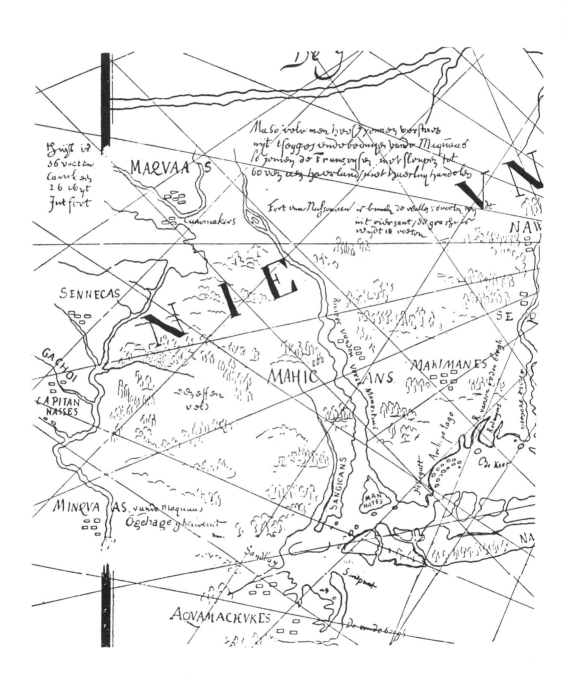

The Figurative Map of 1616, was found in 1841, by J Brodhead, NYS Historian, in the Royal Archives at the Hague. It shows discoveries made by Cornelis Hendricx, Master of the *Onrust*.

CASTLE ISLAND, before 1609

Someone was on Castle Island before 1609. Who?

Spanish

A journal kept by the Labadist, Jasper Danckaerts, who traveled around the Northeast during 1680, to determine where this religious sect should settle, contains two very interesting statements. That when he and his companion visited Long Island the Indians told them that the first strangers, "Seen in these parts" were "Spaniards or Portuguese," but that they did not remain long and that, "afterwards" the Dutch came.

Jasper also wrote that they later visited Castle Island, near the west bank and a little below early Albany. Here they were shown earthen mounds that had been foundations of a fort, and were told by their guide, that the structure had been built by the Spanish.

De Costa raised an interesting premise: he felt that Estevan Gomez, who sailed for Spain in 1525, ascended the Hudson as far as he could. De Costa's reasoning was that because the explorer was searching for a passage to the Indies, he would investigate such a broad river to determine if it connected with an inland sea and thence to the Pacific. If De Costa is correct, then Gomez went up to the Albany Troy-Waterford area.

French

There are two "Figurative Maps" created by a group of Dutch merchants and presented by them to the States General Of The United Netherlands on 11 October 1614, and again on 18 August 1616. The merchants desired to secure a trading monopoly for New Netherland. The second map relates a bit of startling information, "But as far as one can understand by what the Maquaas [Mohawks] say and show, the French came with sloops as high up as their country to trade with them." (Ma so vele men heeft connen verstaen uyt i seggen ende beduyen van de Maquaas so comen de Francoysen met sloupen tot bovem aen haer land met haerluy handeln.)

This notation was written a little northeast of the present city of Albany -- does this mean that they traded at the meeting of the Mohawk and Hudson Rivers? Or did they trade a little to the south on Castle Island?

Just how far north did the French sloops go up the Hudson? When?

conclusion

Van der Donck wrote that the Indians claimed that they had never seen any whitemen before the Dutch came. It must be remembered that Van der Donck was a lawyer, who was trying to prove that the Dutch had a legal title to New Netherland, because technically the Dutch had squatted on English territory. Van der Donck's statement has to be ignored, especially when the Indians of Long Island said that

Spaniards or Portuguese had been there, and the Albany Indians stated that the Spanish had built a fort on Castle Island.

It can be assumed that the Indians saw men who were probably short and swarthy, whether they were Spanish, or French, or even Portuguese remains to be proved. The three groups had been near the Hudson. De Costa stated that, "Verrazano, Estevan Gomez and the Dutch [The Greenland Company] of 1598 all rise up to claim a long priority [of discovering the Hudson River] thus the old Labadist tradition takes life and meaning." And Gomez was a Portuguese, sailing for Spain.

Then the "Figurative Map" has to be addressed. The Dutch wrote on it that the French had ascended in their sloops; did they build a trading post on Castle Island? Many Indian bones were found there, indicating that the Indians favored the site. Or did the French trade with the Indians who were living on The Flatts, just north of Albany?

Since there are mentions of: Spanish or Portuguese on Long Island; Spanish on Castle Island; French trading in the Albany area before the Dutch -- it has to be accepted that Europeans had ascended to the head of navigation before 1609.

Jehan Fonteneau dit Allefonsce, c1543
Was he the one who built on Castle Island?

There are those who place Allefonsce [Jean; Allepfonsce/Afonse/Alphonse] on Castle Island, building a chateau and then leading French fur traders into the Hoosick Valley in Rensselaer County, all in the year 1640.

Jean Fonteneau was born in Saintonge, France. He became a sailor, head of a pirate fleet and married Valentine Alfonse, a Portuguese girl, whose name he decided to adopt.

The Sieur de Roberval and Jacques Cartier, received a patent from Francis I, in 1540, to establish a colony on the St Lawrence. Roberval left France on 22 April 1541 and took with him as pilot, Jean Allefonsce. Within a year or two, Allefonsce sailed from the St Lawrence down the Atlantic coast for a considerable distance and made a crude map.

Weise used this translation of Allefonsce's three page manuscript ...

Beyond the Cape of Norombegue [Cape Cod], the river of the Norombegue descends about 25 leagues [75 miles] from the cape. This river is wider than 40 leagues at its mouth [entrance of Long Island Sound.] And within, this width is as much as 30 or 40 leagues. It is full of isles which stretch out 10 or 12 leagues in the sea [or sound?] and are very dangerous on account of rocks and swashings. The river is in 42 degrees of the height of the arctic circle.

Up the river, 15 leagues, there is a town which is called Norombegue, and there is in it a good people, and they have many peltries of all kinds of animals. The inhabitants of the town are dressed in skins, wearing mantles of martens. I think that the river runs into the river Hochelaga [St Lawrence], for it is salt for more than 40 leagues up, according to the statement of the people of the town. The people use many words which resemble Latin and they

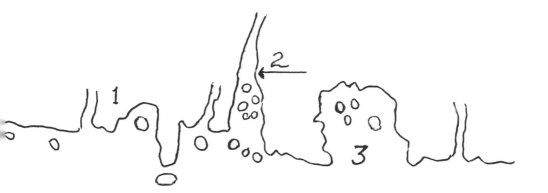

The location of Norumbega according to Allefonsce's 1545 map.

1) Cap de laFrancisane [Cape May]
2) Riviere de Norombergue [Hudson River]
3) Baye des Isles [Jamaica Bay]

worship the sun. They are a handsome people and are large framed. The land of Norumbegue is high and good.

And on the west side of the town there are many rocks [the Palisades] which extend to the sea, about 15 leagues. And north of it [the sea] there is a bay, in which there is a small island which is often subject to tempests and cannot be inhabited [Governor's Island?].
Discovery Of America

In giving a description of the shoreline between the River of Norumbega and a cape presumed to be Hatteras, he mentions, "A large river of sweet water," at the mouth of which is an island of sand. This island is believed to be Sandy Hook, off the New Jersey coast.

conclusion

Allefonsce wrote of an exploration trip along the northeastern coast of North America and said that the Hudson was salty for about 120 miles, "According to the inhabitants of the town," of Norumbega. It is this mention of the river being salty that made Weise, who apparently did not pay attention to what he had inserted in his book, jump to the conclusion that Allefonsce sailed up the Hudson to Albany-Troy. Several writers, who evidently read Weise, copied his conclusion and added a bit more: that he built a "chateau" on Castle Island at Albany; wandered with fur traders into the Hoosick Valley and built there. All of these writers have made Allefonsce into a superman, who would have had to work at least 36 hours a day, to accomplish so much in such a short period of time. They also have him in the Albany area 1640, a year before he sailed with Roberval: it is extremely hard to pinpoint dates for Allefonsce.

Some even claim that Allefonsce brought along a Jesuit. The Jesuit Society was founded in 1540 -- would they have been in a position only a year or so later to send a priest to the new world? They state that the first, of their order, went to Canada about 1625 at the invitation of the Recollects. Isaac Jogues was the first recorded Jesuit to appear in New York, 1642.

Allefonsce noted that Norumbega was 15 leagues up the Hudson. A league is equal to about three miles, so this would place the legendary town about 45 miles above the tip of Manhattan. Putnam County is a bit further north, but it does have a foot print of many stone chambers that have not been explained.

The biggest clue of the location of the town and river, besides the given latitude, was the belief that the Norumbega River entered into the St Lawrence. The only north-south river that can fit this description is the Hudson. This was even believed to be true after the Dutch arrived. Based on the assumption that the Hudson River was the Norumbega, then the location of the town of Norumbega would indeed be a bit north of Manhattan..

[*See the chapter on David Ingram for more information on Norumbega.*]

glossary

JESUITS ... a male Catholic religious order founded in 1540, by St Ignatius of Loyola. Their formal name is The Society of Jesus.

LABADISTS ... Jean de la Badie was born in Bourg, France on 13 February 1610. He preached in a Separist church and was the founder of the Labadists. One of his disciples, Anna Maria Schurman wrote *Eucleria*, expounding his ideas -- which includes community of goods within the church, the continuance of prophecy, the sanctity of marriage between two believers, the continuous Sabbath, etc. The life and separatism of the community brought them into frequent heated arguments with their neighbors and with the magistrates. The group migrated to Bremen in 1672, and afterward to Altona, where they were dispersed on the death of their leaders. There were also small communities in the Rhineland and a missionary settlement in New York.

SIEUR ... an old French title of respect that means sir or master.

~ Calendar For Allefonsce ~

22 April 1641, he left France as pilot for Roberval.
  "Alfonse seriat parti de I lonfleur le 22 Aout 1541, oonduicant Canada les deux navires que Roberval amenait a Jacques Cartier."
11 September 1643, he is home again in France.
  "M Harrisse fait revenir Alfonce a la Rochelle avec d'Auxihon de Senneterre, lieu tentant de Roberval apres le 11 Septembre 1543, et non avec Cartier le 21 Octo bre 1542."

A sloop.

Sixty Algonquins and Hurons, in 24 canoes looking for their enemy, the Iroquois on Lake Champlain. While this is a dramatic rendering, would a bark canoe be able to carry so many and would it be able to support a standing man?

SAMUEL de CHAMPLAIN, 1609
Was he a sloppy reporter and mapper?

CHAMPLAIN'S ACCOUNT OF HIS VOYAGE UP LAKE CHAMPLAIN ...

2 July or 12 July
Historians argue about Champlain's dates because he wrote -- 28 June left Quebec, 1 June went 15 leagues, 3 June at Three Rivers, 2 July left Chambly Rapids, 14 July reached the lake.

We left next day, continuing our route along the river (Richelieu) as far as the mouth of the lake [Champlain]. Here are a number of beautiful, but low islands with very fine woods and prairies. There is a quantity of game and wild animals, such as stags, deer, fawns, roebucks, bears and other sorts of animals that come from the main land to the islands. We caught a quantity of them. There is quite a number of beaver, in the river as in several other streams which empty into it. These parts, though agreeable, are not inhabited by any Indians because of their wars; they retire from the rivers as far as possible, deep into the country, in order not to be discovered.

14 July
Next day we entered the lake, which is of considerable extent; some 50 or 60 leagues, where I saw four beautiful islands 10, 12 and 15 leagues in length, formerly inhabited by Indians, as well as the Iroquois River. Several rivers discharge into the lake, surrounded by a number of fine trees similar to those we have in France, with a quantity of vines handsomer than any I ever saw and many chestnuts.

Champlain sketched a chaousarou, swimming in the Great Lakes, on his 1612 map. This is the gar pike, which is still found in Lake Champlain. There is an almost identical description about a causar, in the 1610 *Jesuit Relations*, printed in 1613. Did one writer copy from the other?

I have only seen the margin of the lake, where there is a large abundance of different species of fish. There is one that is called chaousarou by the Indians, the largest, I was informed by the people, are eight to ten feet. I saw one that was five feet, as thick as a thigh, with a head as big as two fists, jaws two feet and a half long, and a double set of very sharp and danger-ous teeth. The form of the body resembles the pike, is armed with scales that a thrust of a poniard cannot pierce, and is a silver gray color. The point of its snout is like that of a hog. This fish makes war on all the others in the lakes and rivers. It possesses, as those people assure me, a wonderful instinct: it goes among the rushes or reeds that border the lake, in many places, and keeps its half opened beak out of the water. When birds perch on the beak, they imagine it is a limb of a tree, then the fish subtly closes its jaws, pulling the birds under water by the feet. The Indians gave me a head of it, which they prize highly, saying that when

they have a headache they draw blood with its teeth, at the seat of the pain. The pain immediately goes away.

Continuing our route along the west side of the lake, I saw very high mountains capped with snow on the east side. I asked the Indians if those parts were inhabited? They answered me, Yes, by the Iroquois. There were beautiful valleys and fields fertile in corn as good as I had ever eaten in the country, with an infinitude of other fruits. The lake extended close to the mountains, which were, according to my judgment, 15 leagues from us. I saw others, to the south, not less high than the former, only they were without snow. The Indians told me it was there that we were to go to meet their enemies: and that it was thickly inhabited.

We must pass by a waterfall, which I afterwards saw: and then enter another lake [George] three or four leagues long. After arriving at its head, there were four leagues overland to be traveled to reach a river [Hudson], that flows towards the coast of the Almouchiquois (Indians west of the Kennebec River). Some prisoners, we had taken, conversed freely with me about all they had noticed and that it only had taken them two days in their canoes [to travel the length of Lake George?].

Now, on coming within two or three days journey of the enemy's quarters, we traveled only by night and rested by day. Nevertheless, they never omitted their usual superstitions to ask if this enterprise would be successful, and often asked me whether I had dreamed and seen their enemies. I answered, No, but encouraged them and gave them good hopes.

Night fell, and we continued our journey until morning, when we withdrew into the picket fort to pass the remainder of the day. About 10 or 11 o'clock, I lay down after having walked some time around our quarters. Falling asleep, I thought I beheld our enemies, the Iroquois drowning in the lake near a mountain. Being desirous to save them, our savage allies told me that I must let them all perish as they were good for nothing. On awaking, they did not omit, as usual to ask me, if I had a dream. I did tell them in fact that I had dreamed. It gained much credit among them and they no longer doubted that they should meet with success.

29 July

At nightfall we embarked in our canoes to continue our journey. We advanced very softly and noiselessly. We encountered a war party of Iroquois, on the 29th of the month, about 10 o'clock at night, at the point of a cape which juts into the lake on the west side. They and we began to shout, each seizing his arms. We withdrew towards the water. The Iroquois repaired on shore and arranged all their canoes, one beside the other They began to hew down trees with villainous axes, which they sometimes got in war, and others of stone Some fortified themselves very securely.

Our party, likewise, kept their canoes arranged one alongside the other, tied to poles so as not to run adrift, in order to fight all together should need be. We were on the water about an arrow shot from their barricades

When they were armed and in order, they sent two canoes from the fleet to know if their enemies wished to fight, who answered they desired nothing else. But that just then, there was not much light so we must wait for day to distinguish each other and that they would battle us at sunrise. This was agreed to by our party. The whole night was spent in dancing and singing, as well on one side as on the other, mingled with an infinitude of insults and other taunts, with the little courage they had; how powerless their resistance against their arms [did he mean "our" instead of "their arms"?] When day broke, they should experience

their ruin. Ours, likewise, did not fail in repartee; telling them they should witness t
of arms they had never seen before. Then with a multitude of other speeches, as is u.
siege of a town, one or the other sang, danced and parliamented.

30 July

Day broke. My companions and I were always concealed for fear the enemy should see us preparing our arms the best we could, each in one of the canoes belonging to the savage Montagnars.

After being equipped with light armor, we each took an arquebus and went ashore. I saw the enemy leave their barricade. They were about 200 men, of strong and robust appearance, who were coming slowly towards us, with a gravity and assurance which greatly pleased me, led on by three chiefs. Ours were marching in similar order and told me that those who bore three lofty plumes were the chiefs, these plumes were considerably larger than those of their companions -- and that I must do all I could to kill them. I promised to do what I could. I was very sorry they could not clearly understand me, so as to give them the order and plan of attacking their enemies, as we should indubitably defeat them all: but there was no help for that. I was very glad to encourage them and to manifest to them my good will when we should be engaged.

The moment we landed they began to run about 200 paces towards their enemies, who stood firm, and had not yet perceived my companions, who went into the bush with some savages. Ours commenced calling me in a loud voice, and making way for me, opened In two and placed me at their head, marching about 20 paces in advance until I was within 30 paces of the enemy.

The moment they saw me, they halted, gazing at me and I at them. When I saw them preparing to shoot at us, I raised my arquebus and aimed directly at one of the three chiefs. Two of them fell to the ground by this shot and one of their companions received a wound, of which he died afterwards. I had put four balls in my arquebus. Ours, on witnessing a shot so favorable for them, set up such tremendous shouts that thunder could not have been heard: and yet, there was no lack of arrows on one side or the other. The Iroquois were greatly astonished seeing two men killed so instantaneously, notwithstanding they were provided with arrowproof armor woven of cotton thread and wood. This frightened them very much.

Whilst I was re-loading, one of my companions in the bush fired a shot, which again astonished them. Seeing their chiefs slain, they lost courage, took flight and abandoned the field and their fort, hiding themselves in the depths of the forest. Pursuing them, I killed some others. Our savages also killed several of them and took 10 or 12 prisoners. The rest carried off the wounded. Fifteen or 16 of ours were wounded by arrows: they quickly recovered.

After having gained victory, they amused themselves plundering Indian corn and meal from the enemy, and their arms which they had thrown away, in order to run better. Having feasted, danced and sung, we returned three hours afterwards with the prisoners.

The place where this battle was fought is 43 degrees some minutes latitude, and I named it Lake Champlain.

The Documentary History Of The State Of New York Vol 3.
E O'Callaghan

conclusion
There are problems with Champlain's account of his trip up Lake Champlain.

WHAT CHAMPLAIN TELLS US ...
- He arrived at the northern edge of the lake on 14 July
- Mountains are to the south, the ones to the east are capped with snow
- He saw a waterfall from Lake George
- That they went as far south as two or three days journey from the enemy's quarters
- The enemy was encounted on 29 July, at 43 degrees some minutes
- A battle occurred the next day
- He killed two chiefs and mortally wounded a third -- with one shot!
- And three hours later, the party turned and swiftly paddled home.

WHY DID CHAMPLAIN TAKE THIS TRIP?
 Why did a man, who professed to be religious, take this trip into enemy territory? Was it simply to incite the ire of the Iroquois? Was Champlain forced to fight the Iroquois to prove to his Indian allies that he was on their side? Thomas Campbell SJ, in his "Address" for Nicolet Day on Mackinac Island, said that Champlain, "Was in the relentless grip of a fur company that not only owned the colony, but had determined to defeat the magnificent project of making it a mighty appendage of the crown of France, and of increasing the glory and power of the mother country in the New World."
 Or put simply, the reason was greed. Greed for precious furs to be sent to Europe. Greed for new territory for France.

WHY WAS THE TRIP SO LONG?
 Just what did Champlain do that it took his party 15 days to go up the lake to Crown Point or to Fort Ticonderoga? He must have had experienced paddlers and guides who could travel fast -- his party consisted of himself, two Frenchmen, 60 Algonguins and Hurons in 24 canoes. In 1644, Bressani's trip up Lake Champlain only took five or six days, and that party was dragging prisoners, so one might assume that they could have gone a bit faster if they had not been not so encumbered. And probably Bressani went as far as Whitehall, a few miles farther south.
 After the decisive battle it only took Champlain three or four days to reach the mouth of the Richelieu.
 If Champlain had paddled an average of 60 miles a day, he could have gone 840 miles. Lake Champlain is 125 miles long and if they went its entire length, or to Whitehall, they would only have averaged 8.9 miles a day.

HOW FAR UP THE LAKE DID HE GO?
 Going south, the mountains, on both sides, of the lake can be viewed from Plattsburg or Burlington: several large islands lie between these two cities. Did Champlain only go as far as Burlington and fudge the rest? He was supposed to claim territory for France, so it would be plausible to exaggerate the latitude to claim a larger territory.

102

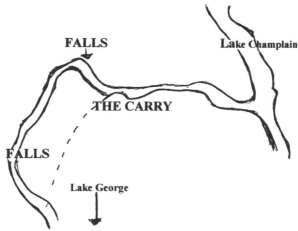

The portage from the La Chute River waterfall to Ti Creek.

Champlain wrote that he saw a "waterfall" of another lake. This statement needs to be examined because Lake George drops into the La Chute River with a waterfall Further northeast or downstream there is a second, wider waterfall, and from that point the La Chute soon flows into Lake Champlain. Near the second waterfall, it is believed, the Indians would leave the river and pick up their canoes to begin the portage to Lake George. Champlain does not say if he paddled to the waterfall, or walked; it could be an important distinction.

If he did see the waterfall, logically he saw it before the battle. That should mean that the battle occurred by the mouth of the La Chute or farther south. Not necessarily, the party could have backtracked north after viewing the waterfall -- then the battle could have occurred some time later and at another location.

In his later map of 1632, he labels the battle site: but, this was done some 20 years after the fact. Noting how faulty his memory was on recent events, how accurate was his memory after so long a period?

The most puzzling statement that he made is that they were only two or three days from the enemy's territory ... then they only traveled at night ... and they continued traveling south. But for how many days? He wrote that there were no Indians living on the shores of Lake Champlain, so the nearest enemy villages, or Iroquois, would be located on the Mohawk River.

A rough guide to the time involved to travel from Fort Ticonderoga to the Mohawk villages ... it would take at least a day to paddle the La Chute River to the portage, drag their canoes out, carry them and then place them in Lake George ... two days to transverse the lake, according to what the captive Indians had related ... at least a day for the Great Carry to Fort Edward ... and a day to paddle south on the Hudson to the carry at the Mohawk River then probably another two days to the beginnings of the Iroquois villages. That is a minimum of six days -- not two or three.

Champlain's Map of 1612, raises the question as how far south of Burlington did he venture? His rendition abruptly closes the lake about there, but the lake has a long neck that goes south from about Essex to Whitehall. He has the lake running SE to SW, whereas the lake has a NS axis. On the 1632 map Lake George is a round blurb. Both lakes are depicted too close to the Atlantic. It will be during the French and Indian Wars before the two lakes will assume their correct location.

Around the late 1800s, a local historian, Austin Holden believed that, "The battle was fought on the shores of Lake George and not Lake Champlain. The place is stated to have been, '43 degrees and some minutes of latitude' that is nearly that of the present village of Caldwells [Lake George]; perhaps near the moldering ruins of Fort William Henry."

Perhaps the local historians, around the end of the 19th century, who claimed that the battle was fought on the southern shore of Lake George were not daft after all!

And so the argument swirls.

104

SNOW ON THE MOUNTAINS

Seeing snow on mountains in July is a bit of a stretch. Granted there is snow year round in Tuckerman's Ravine and skiers go there in the summer: but, this ravine cannot be seen from Lake Champlain. If there was a summerless year in 1609, such as the one in 1816, Champlain would have related this information ... also Juet, writing the ship's log for the *Half Moon*, only a few months later, would have written about the terrible cold when ascending the Hudson. So, this possibility can be forgotten. The tops of some of the Green Mountains are bare and when the western sun strikes them, it does resemble snow. As Champlain was on the lake for so many days, why didn't he, or some of his large party, notice the difference? However Sullivan wrote, "That on one or more occasions snow has been seen on Mount Mansfield in the summer months." The Clinton County Historian claims that she has seen snow from her home on the western shore of the lake.

The first settlers of Jamestown, 1607, experienced one of the worse droughts in the past 800 years. This recent conclusion was reached by taking core samples from bald cypress trees in the area that showed severe drought for seven years [1607-1612.] Could this drought have affected the Champlain area for the same time period? If so, snow in the summer of 1609, probably was not possible.

WHY WERE THERE SO MANY IROQUOIS?

The Clinton County Historical Museum printed an interesting book, *The Original People*. They proposed some original ideas about the battle, that are worth considering. That ...

The party of Mohawks was too large to be a hunting or fishing party. The Great Law of the Iroquois prohibits a chief from going to war. If he does, he must leave his office and title behind and go as a warrior. War parties are lead by chiefs but it is highly unlikely that three of them would lead one war party. If combat were imminent, the three chiefs would not have been so close together but scattered among their warriors to encourage them and to prevent the leadership from being eliminated, as apparently happened. It is also unlikely that the warriors would have marched directly into an impeding shower of arrows without protection from a wall of shields. The Iroquois were brave warriors ... but they were not foolhardy. This group did not act as a war party, nor did they appear to be one.

The remaining possibility is that they were on a diplomatic mission of some sort, perhaps to meet with another northern tribe to negotiate opening a trade link to the growing and important fur trade on the St Lawrence River.

If it had been a peace party, surely the Iroquois would have passed down that information when they told and retold about the battle, which was recorded by them on a historic wampum belt.

A party of 200 moving down the lake makes one wonder if he made a correct count. Champlain might have written that he encountered a group of fierce Iroquois, twice the size of his party, to show how brave he was. He probably thought that this reporting would loosen much needed funds from stingy officials. This argument has to be considered because recently it has been determined that the French, after the battle of Fort William Henry, sent reports back to France that exaggerated the number of enemy they killed.

THE KILLING OF THE CHIEFS

Champlain probably wrote that he killed two chiefs and mortally wounded a third with one blast, to show how necessary arms were, in the right hands of course.

This incident seems to be the forerunner of various tall tales circulating in the Adirondacks. For example, *The Warrensburg Lake George News*, 11 September 1902, wrote this one ...

George Little, of the Adirondacks, went out hunting one day near Raquette Lake, saw a flock of geese flying overhead and fired his muzzle loader so quickly, that he did not have time to remove the ramrod. Well, to make a long story short -- he shot a deer, but behind the deer, 17 geese were speared by the ramrod, which was embedded in a tree. Oh by the way, when he waded through Raquette Lake, to retrieve the deer, he also picked up 70 pounds of fish in his pantaloons.

Rather like Champlain's tale.

The arquebus was a muzzle loader, the hottest weapon of the 16th century. Champlain's sketch of the battle shows that the gun had been modified to fire from the shoulder, a decided advance over firing from a forked rest or the chest. It featured the serpentine, a device attached to the trigger. Before battle, the serpentine was lit by a punk stick or match, blown upon until it turned cherry red, then the arquebusier was able to pull the trigger. Champlain stated that he used balls, but powder could also be used. It was the forerunner of the musket.

DID HIS ARQUEBUS START THE FRENCH AND INDIAN WAR?

Even though the Iroquois and the St Lawrence tribes had been harassing, torturing and killing each other for over 100 years, the question arises -- what effect did Champlain's trip have on future history? If he had never shot the three Iroquois "chiefs" and had never ventured into the Oneida Lake area, would the First World War, aka the French and Indian War have occurred?.

An interesting thought to ponder.

ERRORS

His reporting of the latitude for Lake Champlain is off by a few miles. He owned an astrolabe; had he taken it? Admiral Morison believed that he could have used a simple method of figuring latitude, just by using a small piece of oak attached to a knotted rope [see pages 10 & 11.]

Parkman in his, *Pioneers Of France In The New World* points out that Champlain was, "Exceedingly careless and confused," about dates in his 1609 narrative. In other words he arrived at Lake Champlain earlier than the day he left Quebec. Parkman felt that he made too many latitude errors in his reports.

John Wagner wrote that Ray and John Fadden, Mohawks of the Wolf Clan who are connected with the Six Nations Museum at Onchiota, claim that Champlain's drawing of the 1609 battle contains these errors ...

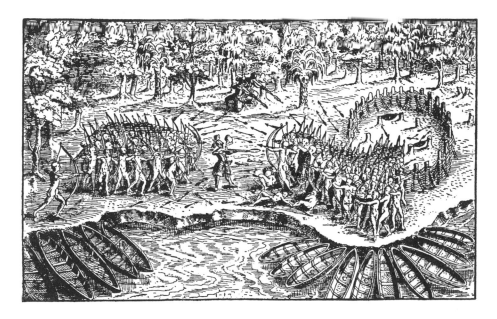

- The canoes are incorrectly depicted of sawn lumber, with flat bottoms -- instead they should be made of bark with a "v" bottom.

- The arrows should have feathers attached to, "Form a wrap around a figure eight on the shaft."

- The men killed, "Might have been war captains." A chief would not wear plumes [feathers], but rather a head dress of deer antlers.

The canoes labeled "C" are Iroquois, those marked "H" and "I" belong to Champlain's group. Note the palms, which certainly do not grow in New York State.

Bishop wondered if Champlain ever went to the Caribbean because his account of the voyage is so full of errors. Bishop also questioned the reporting about the Chagres River in Central America and concluded that the errors of the 1609 venture were not the only ones that he had made.

Bishop stated that Champlain sketched as he traveled and wrote later -- relying on his sketches to nudge his memory. So when did Champlain do his sketch of the battle? He had no time after the battle or during the return flight to Quebec. How much later did he write his account? Evidently it was done when details had escaped his memory. The map was drawn in 1612 and published a year later. Why did he correct it in 1632?

Champlain's reporting of the hour that he met the Iroquois on Lake Champlain has to be incorrect. He stated that it occurred at 10 in the evening: then the Indians proceeded to: cut down trees, built defenses and arranged their canoes -- which must have taken at least two hours, or even longer. He added that after all this preparation was done that, "There was not much light." Of course there would not be much light, it had to have been midnight, probably later. During July, it is dark at nine and pitch black at midnight. Unless, there was a full moon that rose during that time.

Considering his problems with latitude, it is just about impossible to determine just where this battle occurred. All the arguments for a specific site are just that, arguments. Just believe that Champlain was on a lake, possibly even Lake George, and that the battle occurred on a point somewhere south of Plattsburgh.

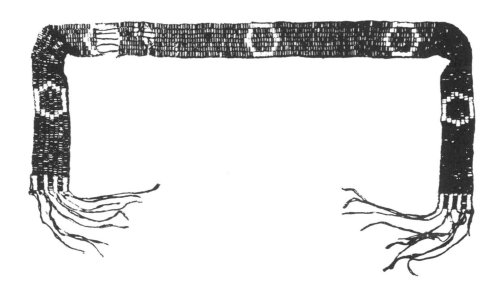

The Champlain wampum belt.

glossary

COTTON ... in the *History Of Warren County*, by H Smith, a footnote on page 53 states that, "The allusion to this armor presents an interesting and suggestive inquiry. We know of the product of no indigenous plant, which Champlain might have mistaken for cotton. He must have been familiar with that plant. That he mentions cotton infers either the existence of a common intercourse between the natives of the north and south; or perhaps the Mohawks may have secured the cotton as a trophy in some of their southern incursions." Watson's *Essex County*, has the same wording about obtaining cotton from southern tribes but adds, "That it is doubtful if the Indians could at that early date, have obtained cotton upon any southern incursion."

But, Sagard in his *Journal* wrote, "They wear a sort of armor and curass which they call Aquientor, on their back and legs and other parts of the body to get protection from arrow shots; for it is made proof against those sharp pointed stones, yet not against our Quebec iron heads when the arrows fitted with them are shot by a stout and powerful arm such as that of a savage. The cuirasses are made of white rods cut to the same length and pressed against one another, sewn and interlaced with little cords, very tightly and neatly." Champlain must have thought those rods were cotton.

geography

43 DEGREES SOME MINUTES ... this is not the latitude of Fort Ticonderoga. Just where did this battle occur? There are 60 miles between 43 and 44 degrees.

43 degrees, 25 minutes, 0229 seconds. Lake George Village, Holden placed the battle there.
43 degrees, 40 ? minutes. The Town of Putnam says that the battle was fought on their soil.
43 degrees, 50 minutes, 28 seconds. Fort Ticonderoga, some historians feel the battle was just
    north of the fort.
44 degrees, 1 minute, 49 seconds. Crown Point, some believe that the battle was here.

OTHER NAMES FOR LAKE CHAMPLAIN ...
- Canieadare-quaront/Caniaderiguarunte, [the lake that is the gateway to the country]
- Caniaderi-Guarunte [the mouth or door to the country]
- Corlear, in honor of Van Curler
- Rod-si-o-Ca-ny-a-ta-re
- Ska-ne-togh-ro-wa [large lake]
- O-ne-a-da-lote
- Lake of the Iroquois
- Lake Rod-si-o

UP LAKE CHAMPLAIN ... as this lake eventually empties into the Atlantic -- north becomes down and south becomes up, so when Champlain writes, "Up the lake" he is going south.

Verrazano.

Captain John Smith.

Henry Hudson.

110

HENRY HUDSON, 1609

How far up the Hudson did the Half Moon go?

Less than 100 miles south of Champlain's battle site, and about a month later, another explorer would view upper New York State. But Henry Hudson was not the first to see this river. Probably around 1010, Thorfinn Karlsefni sailed up the river to Albany. De Costa believed that Giovanni da Verrazano ventured into New York Harbor in 1524 and charted it -- but that Estevan Gomez named the river. Then in 1568, David Ingram and his companions wandered northward through the valley.

Hudson had to have heard of Verrazano and Gomez: and he must have known that the Greenland Company had wintered near the river during 1598. Most importantly, he had met and conferred with Plancius, the cosmographer, shortly before this voyage. Hudson showed him a letter and maps from his friend, Captain John Smith of Jamestown fame. Hudson and Plancius agreed with Smith's deduction that a passage to the Orient would be found just north of Chesapeake Bay. Plancius either gave to Hudson, or allowed him to look at, George Weymouth's Journals of his 1602, and 1605, voyages to the entrance of the Hudson Strait and as far south as 41 degrees. By the time Hudson had left Plancius, he must have concluded that an "opening" to the Orient would be found between Weymouth's 41 degrees 30 minutes 38 seconds, and the coastline that the Virginia Company had explored -- a void of some 200 unexplored coastal miles.

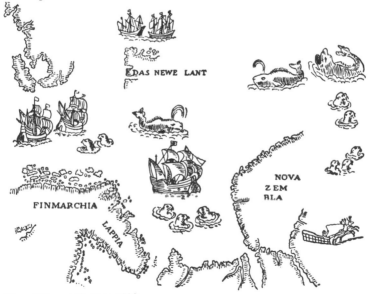

EDAS NEWE LANT

NOVA ZEM BLA

FINMARCHIA

LAPPIA

DeBrey's Map of Novaya Zemlya, 1598.

Hudson had a contract from the Dutch East India Company to go north of Novaya Zemyla, turn east and sail until he found a passageway to fabled Cathay. His pay for the venture would be 800 guilders. He left Holland on 6 April 1609, in a flat bottomed yacht with a shallow keel, which certainly could help her glide over reefs and sand bars. She was only 65' long and 17' wide with a crew of 20.

He did sail towards Novaya Zemlya, as his contract stipulated, but claimed that ice and snow forced him to stop. He then turned around, without permission of the company, and headed toward that enticing 200 mile stretch of Atlantic shoreline. There was almost mutiny aboard.

The *Half Moon* started up the great river on 12 September. By taking advantage of the tides, she was able to reach the vicinity of Albany and head back to New York Harbor in 23 days.

17 September
They went six leagues as soon as the sun appeared. There were shoals in the middle of the channel and small islands. Towards night, they tacked too close to shore and became grounded, but managed to heave off when the tide lifted the ship. They anchored all night.

18 September
They rode still.

19 September
The tide was at 11 and they ran two leagues, or 4.8 miles, above the shoals or the Overslaag.

20 September
Hudson sent his mate along with four men, in the ship's boat, to take soundings to determine if the *Half Moon* could sail farther upriver. The men returned and related that two leagues above them it was only two fathoms and narrow, but above that was seven or eight fathoms. They anchored.

21 September
The ship did not move.

22 September
The two and twentieth, was faire weather: in the morning our Masters Mate and foure more of the companie went up with our boat to sound the river higher up. The people of the countrey came not aboard till noone: but when they came, and saw the savages well, they were glad. So at three of the clocke in the after-noone they came aboard, and brought tabacco, and more beades, and gave them to our Master, and made an oration, and shewed him all the countrey round about. Then they sent one of their companie on land, who presently returned, and brought a great platter full of venison dressed by themselves; and they caused him to eate with them: then they made him reverence, and departed all save the old man that lay aboord. This night at 10 of the clocke, our boat returned in a showre of raine from the sounding of the river; and found it to bee at an end for shipping to goe in. For they had beene up eight [19.2 miles] or nine [21.6 miles] leagues, and found but seven foot water, and unconstant soundings.

112

23 September

The Half Moon turned and headed down the river.

conclusion

Henry Hudson was not the first European to see the river, neither was he the first to sail up it to the Albany area. What is important, is that the Netherlands started fur trading with the Indians and later established a colony.

The tide, which was at least 4' 8", easily could have floated the flat bottomed small ship over the Overslaag. Juet's *Journal* states that on 19 September, the ship went 4.8 miles further north. This would bring the ship to the area somewhere between the Dunn Memorial Bridge and the former New York Central Railroad Station. It agrees with Emanuel van Merten, who wrote in 1610, that the *Half Moon* reached 42 degrees 40 minutes: Steuben Street, in Albany, is 42 degrees 39 minutes and 6.4 seconds.

The mate plus four others ascended 19.2 or 21.6 miles. The dams around Cohoes, Lansingburg and Troy had not been built, so it is possible that the tide flowed as far as the Riffs. The tide could have lifted the ship's boat over them. They left in the morning, probably with the incoming tide, say around eight o'clock and returned at 10 in the evening -- that would give them approximately 14 hours. It is about eight miles from Hudson's anchorage, in the center of Albany, to the Riffs. A round trip to the Riffs would only be 16 miles and certainly not take 14 hours, even with sounding. Especially when the 1732, "Map Of Lake Champlain," in *The Documentary History Of The State Of New York* Vol I, is considered: this map states that it is five hours from Fort Edward to Albany by canoe.

During the 300th Anniversary of Hudson's ascent, Cohoes produced a booklet, "The Saga Of The Half Moon" and included a map showing the latitude of Lock One, at the Riffs, at 42:48. The Anniversary Committee wrote that, "The mate with four men in a small boat ... [went] eight or nine leagues 'higher up' [and landed] at a point near the confluence of the Hudson." They must have assumed that a league was equal to a mile. In 1959, probably based on that assumption of a league is a mile, a New York State Education Department historic marker was placed on Route 4, opposite Lock One in Waterford, stating that, "Henry Hudson stopped near here in shallow water in the Hudson River." [Which of course is a bit off target, the Master's Mate in the ship's boat, was who and what had reached this point, not the *Half Moon*. Hudson had remained on board the *Half Moon*, anchored at Albany.]

How far did the ship's boat go? Mechanicsville is 42 degrees 55 minutes, subtract Albany's latitude and you get about 16 miles, a bit short of 19.2 or 21.6 miles.

The *Half Moon* sat at anchor for many hours at Albany and the Indians were coming and going. Hudson was eager to find a route to the Orient, so he had to have spent quite a bit of time with them, and the other Indians he had met on the way upriver, inquiring about what lay ahead. The Indians, who knew the area well, must have told him and drew sketches of: the Mohawk with the large falls at Cohoes; the Riffs; and the direction of the Hudson at the Great Carry, at Fort Edward.

It is plausible to consider that the destination of the ship's boat could be the Great Carry. Then Hudson would know if this river was the answer to finding a passage to the Orient. Fort Edward has a latitude of 43 degrees 15 minutes, therefore a 14 hour trip would be about right to reach the Great Carry.

Did the small boat head for Fort Edward? Did it reach it? They certainly had enough time. Or did it stop at Mechanicsville? Or further south? When the time spent away from the *Half Moon* is considered -- about 14 hours with a distance rowed of 19.2 to 21.6 miles -- it becomes apparent that the ship's boat definitely went north of the Riffs.

glossary

DUTCH WEST INDIA COMPANY ... was a Dutch stock company that was subscribed to until 1 December 1621. This new company granted a monopoly to Dutch trade along the Atlantic coasts of Africa and the New World. The company stated that its New Netherland operation went back to the building of Fort Nassau. In the beginning, its primary business was commerce -- later it became interested in colonization and created the Patroon system in 1629. It ruled New Netherland until the English arrived in 1664.

JUET, Robert ... of Limehouse, England. There is no agreement among historians as to his duty aboard the Half Moon. He had served as chief mate on Hudson's previous voyage and would hold that title for Hudson's venture to Hudson Bay. Since a Dutchman was mate on the 1609 trip, it has been suggested that Juet was just an observer. However, that does not seem reasonable due to the smallness of the crew, and the size of the vessel, all aboard would have to work.

Why did Juet keep a journal? Probably we will never know, but should be thankful that he did. Combining the known fragments of Hudson's Log with Juet's *Journal*, we have a more rounded account of this voyage.

geography

EARLIER NAMES FOR THE HUDSON RIVER ...

~Indian Names~

- Cohahatated, Cohatatea, Cohaohatatea, Cahohatatea, Shatemuc, Shatemuck, Mahicanituk, Mohicannituck, Mohicanhittuchi, Mohegan, Mahakaneghtue, Ologue, Shatemuc, Sanatatea, Shenahtahde, Shawnataty

~Other names~

- Rio San Antonio
- Rio de Gamas, Rio de Gomez
- Grande River de Montagnes, Montague, Groote, The Great River
- Norumbega which means the River of the Steep Hills
- Great River of the Manhattans, Mahattas, Manhattes, Manhattos River after the tribe that lived there
- Hudson's River
- Noort, Noordt, North River, The Great North River of the New Netherland
- Rio de Montaigue, Montague, De Riviere van den Vorst Mauritius, Mauritis, Mauritz, Maurice, Riviere d'Orange, Nassau after Prince Maurice of Nassau, The Netherlands
- Riviere des Trettes [meaning unknown], San Germano.

How far up the river did Hudson go **?**

___ 43 degrees 15 min, FT EDWARD

___ 42 degrees 55 min, Mechanicsville

The Riffs were located close to Lock One on the Hudson, north of Albany. This was the stopping place for all sloops.

___ 42 degrees 48 min, Lock One - Riffs

___ 42 degrees 40 min, *Half Moon*
___ 42 degrees 39 min, Steuben St

___ 35 degrees

The Overslaag/Overslaugh, was located near Van Weis Point, south of Albany. These sand bars were formed by the Normanskill spewing out sand, gravel and soil. The pattern of the bars changed after each flood, heavy storms and from year to year. The situation became worse after land along the creek and the river began to be plowed. The sloops had to wait at the Overslaag for the tide to lift them over the barrier. With constant dredging for decades, and less land being plowed above stream, the situation has been corrected. Now, ships from all over the world sail up to the Port of Albany to load and unload.

___ 34 degrees 59? min, Van Weis Point
                            Overslaag

116

1610 found Hudson, in command of a ship, in Hudson Bay. His crew apparently had had enough of him for they put him, his young son and seven others in a small boat in the bay, and that was the last time anyone ever saw Henry Hudson.

117

Fort Nassau was on Castle Island 1614, but abandoned c1618, after severe floods.

OTHER NAMES FOR ALBANY

~Indian Names~

- Schaughnaughtada/Scho-negh-ta-da/Skenectadea, means over the plains. The Dutch later used this Indian name for Van Curler's settlement of Schenectady.

~Dutch Names~

- Fort Orange/Fort Aurania, replaced Fort Nassau in 1623 or 1624, and was built further north in the new settlement of the Fuyck.
- The Fuyck [pronounced fowk] was the earliest name for the city. The word means a hoop net and the settlement was laid out in this shape.
- Beversfuyck/Beverswyck/Beverwyck, still meant a hoop net, but beaver, the settlement's chief export was added to Fuyck. It was first written in 1634, and continued to be used until 1681, after the English came.
- Willemstadt.

THE DUTCH FUR TRADE, started in 1609

The beaver does everything to perfection. He makes for us kettles, axes, swords, knives and give us drink and food without the trouble of cultivating the ground.
Lescarbot

The beginnings of the Dutch fur trade started when local Indians boarded the *Half Moon*. Hudson himself traded for beaver and other pelts in the region of present day Albany.

Up to that time, Dutch merchants had depended upon Russia as a source for furs. The Russian trade was hampered by a five percent tax imposed by the government on all imports and exports. The Dutch merchants responded immediately and each year after 1609, one or more Dutch ships were trading on the Hudson River.

Hendrick [Hendrik] Christiaensen [Christians/Christiaens/Chrystiaense] accompanied by Adriaen Block, sailed the *Fortune* up the Hudson River to the head of navigation in 1614. Here, near the junction of the Mohawk and the Hudson, was the place where Indian trade routes met. The Mohawk Valley formed a natural highway between the Great Lakes and the Hudson, while Lake Champlain and Lake George were the funnel to the south

So advantageous was the Albany site, that after the first winter, Christiaensen built Fort Nassau on Castle Island -- the second Dutch fort in New York. It was probably not much more than a stockade with a breastwork surrounding the most important part, a warehouse. The entire structure, including an 18' moat, covered a rather small space of 100 square feet. Two cannon and 11 swivel guns were taken from the *Fortune* and mounted upon the walls of the fort and 10 or 12 men were detailed to garrison it. After the fort was completed, Christiaensen sailed downriver to the Manhattan trading post.

Stacking bundles of furs and moving rum barrels in the warehouse at Fort Nassau.

Jacob Eelkens [Eelckens] was put in command of the primitive fort and is believed to have dealt in furs. A flash flood in 1617, washed away everything. Eelkens promptly selected a more protected location for a new fort, in 1618, below Albany where the Normanskill joins the Hudson. The Iroquois called this creek, Tawasentha. Since there is no indication of a new name given to the fort, it can be assumed that it too, went by the name of Fort Nassau.

Quickly a new breed of traders emerged, the independant fur traders who were called bosloopers [bosch-loopers]. The Dutch in New Netherland wrote back to Holland complaining that, "Petty traders who swarm hither with great industry; reap immense profit and exhaust the country without adding to its population or security, while agriculture and many necessary matters remain neglected." These woodsrunners ranged far, even into French territory. They bought trading goods, guns and liquor from the Dutch, or from smugglers of different nationalities, and exchanged these goods for pelts illegally obtained from the Indians. They then sold the very same pelts to the Dutch. The bosloopers were blamed for the Indian War of 1643.

One well-known boslooper was Cornelis Van Slyck, who married a Mohawk, and was called by the Indians, Broer Cornelis. He lived near the Cohoes Falls around 1640, and was given a large land grant in Catskill, six years later, in appreciation for services to Governor Kieft.

The beaver is a medium sized animal with dark brown fur. He lives in ponds and fells trees, with his strong orange teeth, to build dams. In New York State, this busy fellow almost became extinct because of the demand for his fur. But, recently he has made a come back. They were about four feet and weighed up to 60 pounds, when they were first trapped. Their size soon decreased to three feet and weighed only 25 to 30 pounds. Beaver pelts have coarse unwanted guard hairs that had to be plucked by hand. The traders soon realized that if they bought used fur garments, all or mostly all, the guard hairs were rubbed off -- because the Indians placed the fur side next to their bodies during the winter.

Someone discovered that fur shaved off a pelt could be beaten into felt -- and beaver was in demand. A hat made out of beaver was the height of style. A beaver hat can have a pile up to and exceeding an inch, can be blocked into any shape and dyed any color. The demand for beaver skins soon depleted New York's resource so the Iroquois tried to move in on western sources, which heightened bitter feelings among the Hurons and their neighbors. Beaver hats and furs were so valued that they were left to heirs in wills.

For most uses guard hairs are still not wanted, so beaver is currently sheared by machine. The fur can be bleached and dyed in exotic colors. The price of a beaver hat, today, is quite expensive, but they can last for more than 40 years.

The newly formed Dutch West India Company sent 30 Walloon families, plus some single men, to the new colony: but only 18 families settled in the Albany area. This was during 1624, or possibly a year earlier. The families were to start a farmng community but were forbidden to engage in the fur trade. The single men were to establish the fur trade, until the Company could send permanent personnel.

When their ship reached New York Harbor, they encountered a French vessel bent on planting settlers. Fortunately, the *Mackarel* appeared and escorted the French-man out into the Atlantic. Why was this French ship going to drop settlers in the Manhattan area? Could it be related to the information written on "The Figurative Map of 1616," which stated that the French had been there before the Dutch? Did the French have a memory of going to the Hudson River?

The landing of the Walloons at Albany. These French speaking Protestants had sought refuge in Belgium, until Catholic Spain made it uncomfortable for them. They then moved to Holland, but unfortunately this small country could not provide enough work. Next they petitioned King James of England, to settle in Virginia, where they hoped to set up a feudal colony and live like royalty.

The Dutch West India Company learned of their plight and sent 30 families, most of whom were Walloons, plus some single men on the *New Netherland*. The ship dropped a couple of families and men off at the Connecticut River; four couples who had been married at sea on the Delaware River; a few men at Manhattan; and 18 families at Albany under the care of Cornelius May.

The community of Walloomsac and the Wallomsac River in northeastern Rensselaer County are named after the Walloons who settled there.

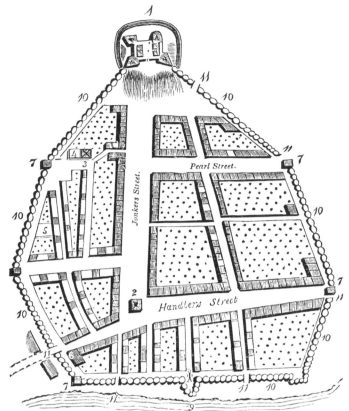

The Fuyck. This print shows that the shape of the new settlement was indeed like a fishnet. 1) The fort; 2) Dutch Calvinistic Church; 3) German Lutheran Church; 4) Lutheran cemetery; 5) Dutch Church cemetery; 6) [not identified]; 7) Blockhouses; 8) Stadt House; 9) A great gun to clear a gully; 10) City gates, six in number.

In 1624, the Dutch West India Company erected a more permanent post, Fort Orange, north of the ruined Fort Nassau. Twenty years later the company closed this trading house. The fort continued to be maintained as a company outpost, but it became increasingly a place of rendezvous and settlement for private traders who congregated in the village of Beverwyck located to the north of the wooden palisade.

conclusion

The Dutch had no desire to fish the Great Banks because they more or less controlled fishing in the North Sea off Holland. But when the well-to-do merchants learned about the rich pelts that could be had in New Netherland, they decided to move. They quickly set up the Dutch West India Company to absolutely control the entire area. Nothing, in the new colony, could be done without their authority and no one was permitted to trade in furs unless employed by the company.

The single Walloon men who came to the Albany area established the fur trade for the Company. They could have been the same fur traders who built rude huts on Halfmoon Point at Waterford.

122

glossary

HIAWATHA ... yes, there was an Indian chief with the name of Hiawatha. He lived in the 16th century and belonged to the Turtle Clan of the Mohawks. Hiawatha traveled through the Mohawk Valley preaching to the Indians that they should not kill; be at war with one another; or eat humans. It was through his efforts that the Iroquois Confederacy was formed in the Vale of Tawasentha. This strong grouping enabled them to fight as a team and promoted trade routes -- especially across the Mohawk Valley. This league was at first composed of only five Nations, the Mohawks, Senecas, Cayuga, Oneidas and Onondagas.

The Song Of Hiawatha
Longfellow

In the Vale of Tawasentha,
In the green and silent valley,
By the pleasant watercourses,
Dwelt the singer Nawadaha.
Round about the Indian village
Spread the meadows and the cornfields,
And beyond then stood the forest,
Stood the groves of singing pinetrees;
Green in Summer, white in Winter,
Ever sighing, ever singing.
And the pleasant watercourses,
You could trace them through the valley,
By the rushing in the Spring-time,
By the alders in the Summer,
By the black line in the Winter;
And beside them dwelt the singer,
In the vale of Tawasentha,
In the green and silent valley.
There he sang of Hiawatha ...

Longfellow's poem created a myth -- he had picked up Schoolcraft's mistake, which combined Hiawatha of the Mohawks and a Chippewa deity. The name Hiawatha and the Vale Of Tawasentha are true for the Mohawk-Hudson Valleys.

geography
CASTLE ISLAND ... other names were, Kasteel/Rensselaer/West/Westerlo/Brandpylen's/The Island of Brant Peelen/Boyds.
KILL ... means creek. Therefore, it is redundant to say Normanskill Creek.
NORMANSKILL ... this creek was named after Albert Adriaensen Bradt de Norman. It was also written, Norman's Kill/Tawasentha, the place of the many dead/Ta-wa-sent-ha.

After the *Tiger* burned, Captain Block built a log house for his crew and began to build the *Onrust*. The new ship was 16 tons burden and was launched during 1614 in the Upper Bay, of Manhattan.

KLEYNTIES, c1614

Dutch merchants desirous to learn about the land, its resources and the various peoples living in New Netherland decided to send five ships and men to explore. There are three versions of a few Dutchmen who left Albany about 1614, and what later happened to them.

1) Sometime around 1614, a ship ascended the Hudson River and dropped off some men. at Fort Orange. The second, "Figurative Map" of 1616, states that a man named, "Kleynties" first name unknown and his comrade set out to explore and to report back what they had seen. Kleynties and a comrade make two men.

2) About 1615-1616, Cornelis Hendricx [Hendricksen] left the Manhattan area on the *Onrust* trying to discover what the new colony offered. He came across, "Three persons ... belonging to this company" supposedly around the Schuylkill, "and traded for and bought from the inhabitants, the Minquaes," these same men who had been, "Employed in the service of the Mohawks and Machicans [Mohicans]." *New York Colonial Manuscripts* Vol 1, p 14.

3) Champlain wrote that in 1615, three Dutchmen were trading around 40 degrees latitude, [Philadelphia's latitude] and were captured by, "Canadian Indians." The Indians realized that they spoke French and brought them to Canada. Sullivan In his history of New York, added to this version by assuming that they were Walloons, because they spoke French instead of Dutch.

conclusion

It can be assumed that the three versions refer to the same men: whether they were two or three can not be proved at this time.

Since the Mohawks and the Mohicans were involved, it would appear that the men were captured near Albany. Which tribe captured them? Surely not both, because the Mohawks could not get along with the Mohicans. It does not seem reasonable that the men "worked" for both tribes.

The tribe that captured them must have used the men as slaves but quickly sold them to the Minquaes. Did the Minquaes know that the Dutch were in the Manhattan area and decided that the men could be an item of trade?

The, "Figurative Map" states that the "expedition" found, "The locality of the rivers and the position of the tribes ... from the Maquaas into the interior and along the New River downward to Ogehage (that is the enemies of the aforesaid northern tribes.)"

Since there is no information given, on the map, about the terrain north of Albany, it can be assumed that the men did not go north. The little information presented about the east could have been learned from the Indians around Fort Nassau. The map makes it apparent that they went west of Albany because the bulk of the information shown is to the south and southwest of Albany: they could have followed the Normanskill westward, but it is more plausible that they walked through the Pine

Bush, west of Albany, and hit the Mohawk River about where the current bridge connects Schenectady to Scotia. They would have used the Mohawk as their guide for a few miles and then turn south to the Susquehanna River. Or, perhaps they went a few miles further west along the Mohawk and headed back, or southeast, to the Susquehanna. Whatever route they took, the map makes it clear that the men wandered down the Susquehanna.

Considering Champlain's sloppiness regarding latitude and other details, his reporting of this incident seems questionable. What were Canadian Indians doing so far south? Why did he say that the men had been returned to Canada?

Officially, the Walloons would not be in New Netherland until years later.

Knowing the comparative accuracy of Dutch records, the "Figurative Map" and Hendricx's version are probably correct.

Burning of the _Tiger_.

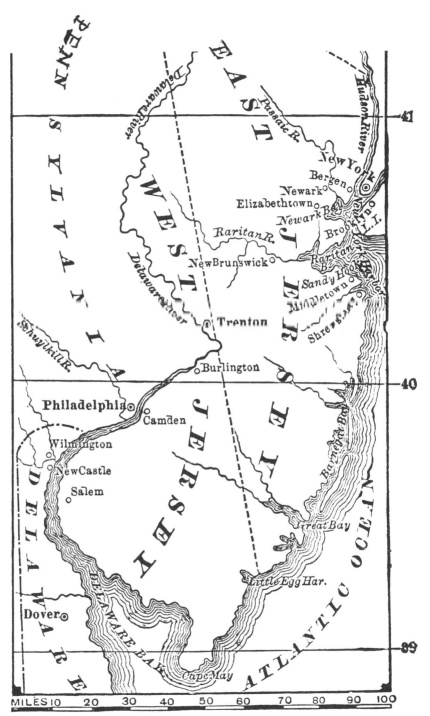

The Schuylkill area.

ETIENNE BRULE, 1615

The explorer of explorers.
Francis Parkman

It is thought that Etienne Brule was born 1592, in Champigny, France. The 16 year old sailed, into a life of unbelievable adventure, with Champlain during 1608. He was one of the fortunate few who survived the following harsh winter in Quebec.

A few historians have suggested that he accompanied Champlain, on his 1609 venture, to fight the Iroquois. It would be nice to believe this, but there is not a shred of evidence to back this conjecture. The next year, Champlain sent him, with Chief Iroquet, to live among the Iroquets to learn their language and ways. Brule throve and became more Indian than the Indians

All of Champlain's young men were able to read and write, so why didn't Brule keep a journal? Did he write one only to have it destroyed, after his death, by: Champlain, the Hurons or the Jesuits? A personal record would have told us so much: told of his numerous discoveries; told how he learned to accept the Indian lifestyle, and told how he managed to learn the Huron languages so readily. Because he left no personal record, he was almost forgotten.

It has been suggested that Brule did send written reports to Champlain, who used them in his writings; and that he took credit for some of Brule's explorations. It is believed that Champlain did this to enhance his image and to reinforce how necessary he was to the fledgling colony.

Brule was an advance agent who reported to Champlain the location of Indian mines and anything that was rare or valuable. Without his ability to become a part of the tribes, the Canadian fur trade would have floundered. He was the ultimate diplomat with the Hurons, the Algonquins and the Montagnais. He was the first white person to see: Lake Nipissing, four of the Great Lakes, the Susquehanna River, the first to ascend the Ottawa River and the first to descend the Lachine Rapids.

His free life style, especially with young Indian women, turned opinion against him. Champlain, who had referred to him as "my lad" or "my young man," bowed to the growing hatred against him, stopped writing his name in reports; but, continued to pay him a generous salary for his necessary services. Brule was labeled a scoundrel and worse first by the Recollects and later by the Jesuits and the adjectives have stuck through the years; but he was a hero to the Hurons.

Twice Champlain had been successful fighting the Iroquois and therefore decided again to go to war against them. Champlain had no doubt that this third battle too, would be successful. He went about 1,000 miles out of his way to reach the Onondaga fort to visit six or seven Huron villages. Brule accompanied him to harangue the warriors into joining, but only 500 decided to accompany them. The Indians further frustrated Champlain with their delay of feasting and dancing before the battle.

On 8 September 1615, Brule, along with 12 Indians, left Lake Simcoe in two canoes and headed south through dangerous enemy, or Iroquois country, to Carantouan to ask the Andastes for their support. And, to tell them that they should hurry because Champlain was on his way to the fort. The Andastes warriors also were in no

ave the pre-battle festivities in their village. Therefore Brule and the Indi-
two days late, because Champlain, in defeat, had left the battle scene. It
three years before the two would meet again and Brule could tell
Champlain of his adventures.

Brule and the Andastes returned to Carantouan, where he spent the winter. Naturally he explored the surrounding country and supposedly went down the Susquehanna River to its mouth. He returned to the village the following spring and six
Andastes offered to guide him back to Canada. On the trail, they met some Iroquois,
the Andastes scattered and Brule ran for his life. After several days, hungry and lost,
he finally found a trail that he followed. He surprised three Iroquois who had been
fishing. The Indians were so stunned by his sudden appearance that they started to
run away, so Brule threw down his weapons to show that he meant no harm.

They took him to their village, where he told them that he was Dutch and therefore
their friend. They did not believe this, and against the wishes of the chief, tied him
to a tree and proceeded to torture him. They pulled out his beard, hair by hair, tore
off his fingernails with their teeth and applied burning sticks to his body.

He wore an Agnus Dei around his neck. When an Indian tried to pull it off, he
cried, "If you touch it, you and all your race will die." Just then a sudden thunder
storm occurred: the petrified Indians tore into the woods. He was eventually cut
down by the chief. After that event, Brule was a guest of honor at all their festivities.
Finally, the Iroquois guided him back to the Hurons.

English Admiral David Kirke managed to capture Quebec, in 1629, without a shot
being fired, Brule then turned coat and gave his allegiance to England.

Champlain returned to New France during 1632. A year later, the Huron Bear
Tribe, labeled Brule a traitor -- and killed him, in Toanche, at the age of 41. They
went on to quarter him, boil him and finally ate him with gusto. The Jesuits, even
though they had not approved of his life style, were in a state of shock and wrote,
and wrote about his horrible death. They sometimes called him Estienne Brusle.

Champlain did not retaliate Brule's murder because, to his thinking, Brule's de-
sertion to the English had lost him his French citizenship.

conclusion

Brule definitely was in upstate New York, although a bit tardy, when he arrived at
the site of Champlain's battle.

Later, on his return to the Hurons, he was captured by the Iroquois. Unfortunately,
the location of their village is not known. Butterfield thought it was on the Genesee
River in Livingston County. Because there is a chance that this village was to the
east, the tale of his capture has been included in this book. Brule might have made
up the Agnus Dei story to poke fun at Champlain, feeling that this tale would be accepted with much rejoicing from such a devil.

Times and mores change so that if Brule were alive today he would be applauded
for his attempts to live as the Indians. But back in the 1600s, there was a far different code and Brule made no attempt to follow French guidelines, which were really
Catholic. He loved the Indian women far too much; ate meat on Friday; was not

pious; and probably poked fun at the establishment. The Recollect hatred of him was passed along to the Jesuits and the Jesuits set the moral standard for the entire colony. It was a strict unforgiving standard and Brule did not even begin to adhere: he lived the life of a free wheeling son of the forest.

Strangely, the Recollects or the Jesuits did not criticize Champlain who avoided matrimony for many years. This was when society, the church and family expected a man to marry; and marry early in life. The Indians were amazed that he was able to resist their fair maidens. Finally, in his 40s, he married a 12 year old child, and waited two more years before the union was consummated: but no criticism from the clergy. Certainly a double standard

It is felt that if it had not been for Brule, Champlain would not have done, or even attempted so much exploration. He was the first white man to see much of northern North America and nothing was impossible for him.

Hollywood would have loved him, a James Bond coureur de bois, 007.

The Susquehanna at Monocasy Island.

131

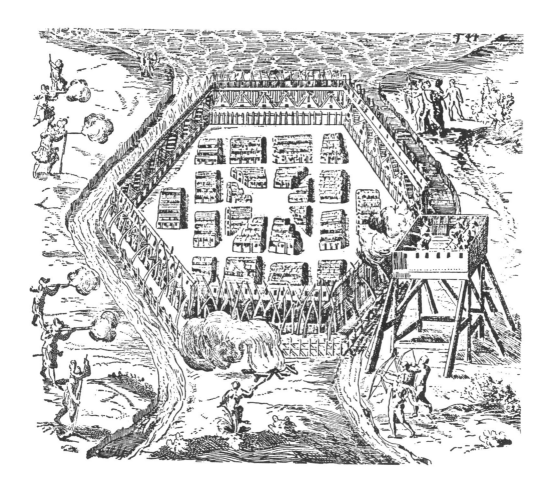

The Battle of 1615. Consul Butterfield noted that there are differences between Champlain's text and this sketch and stated therefore Champlain did not draw it. For instance: Champlain said that there were only two Frenchmen, himself and his servant, there are five shown on land and seven in the tower; and where would they have found sawn lumber to construct the tower?

132

SAMUEL DE CHAMPLAIN, 1615

I shewed them what they never saw nor heard before.
Champlain

In the summer of 1615, a great number of Hurons and Algonquins gathered at Montreal for the yearly fur trade. They asked Champlain to come with them to fight their enemy, the Onondagas [it is currently felt that the enemy was the Oneidas] and promised that many warriors would join them: they would be an army of some 2,500.

Champlain could not resist the temptation of the battle and the chance to see the vast territory to the west. So on 9 July, Champlain, his servant and Brule headed west. They went extra miles out of their way to visit more villages. At each village the pair would exhort the braves into joining their war party, but the Indians were not that eager to follow.

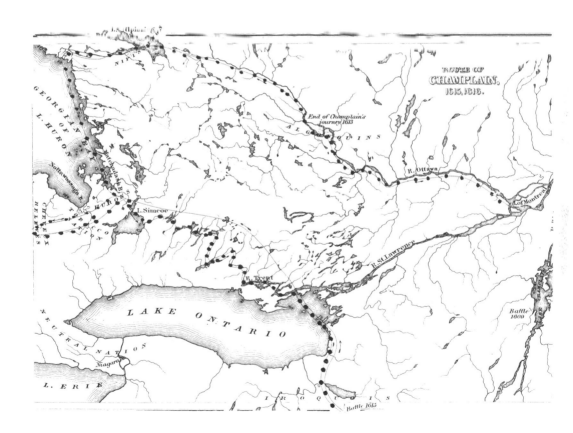

A possible route for Champlain's trip.

...continued along the border of the lake of the Entouhonorons [Lake Ontario], always hunting. We crossed over at one of the extremities, tending eastward, which is the beginning of the River Saint Lawrence, in 43 degrees latitude. There are some beautiful and very large islands in this passage and it is about 14 leagues to cross to the other side of the lake. We proceeded southward, towards the enemy's country. The Indians concealed all their canoes in the woods near the lake. We traveled by land about four leagues over a sandy plain, where I observed a very pleasing and fine country, watered by numerous small streams, two little rivers which empty into said lake, and a number of ponds and prairies. There was an infinite quantity of game, a great many vines and fine trees and a vast number of chestnuts, the fruit of which was yet in the shell.

We left the bank of the lake, which is 80 leagues long and 25 wide. It is inhabited for the greater part by savages, along the side of streams, and we continued our journey overland some 25 to 30 leagues. In the course of four days, we traversed a number of streams and one river issuing from a lake, which empties into that of the Enctouhonorons. This lake is 25 to 30 leagues in circumference, with many beautiful islands and is the Iroquois fishing ground.

The 9th of October, our Indian scouts encountered 11 savages whom they took prisoners: four women, three boys, one girl and three men who were going fishing, four leagues distant from the enemy's fort. One of the chiefs [Iroquet] cut off the finger of one of those poor women as the commencement of their usual tortures. Whereupon I interfered and censored the Iroquet captain, telling him that a warrior, as he called himself, was not in the habit of acting cruelly towards women -- who have no defense but their tears and who, by reason of their helplessness and feebleness, ought to be treated with humanity. This act would be supposed to proceed from a vile and brutal courage and that if he committed any more of these cruelties, he would not encourage me to assist them, nor favor their war. Whereupon he replied that their enemies treated them in the same manner. But since such customs displeased me, he should not act so any more to women, but exclusively to men.

Next day, at three o'clock in the afternoon, we arrived before the enemy's fort, where the savages had some skirmishes, one against the other, though it was not our plan for them to discover ourselves until the morrow. But, the impatience of our savages would not brook this, as well the desire they felt to see us fire on their enemies, in order to liberate some of their men who had ventured too far. I advanced and presented myself, with a few men, nevertheless I shewed them what they never saw nor heard before. For as soon as they saw us, heard the reports of the arquebuses, and the balls whistling about their ears, they retired promptly within their fort, carrying off their wounded and dead. We retreated in like manner to our main body, with five or six wounded, one of whom died.

We retired within gun shot, beyond the view of the enemy, contrary to my advice and to what they had promised me. Which moved me to make use of and express to them pretty rude and angry words, in order to incite them to their duty. Foreseeing that if everything went according to their fantasy and council, nothing but misfortune would result. Nevertheless, I proposed to construct a moveable tower (cavalier) of timber to overlook their pickets. Whereupon I would post four or five of our arquebusiers, who would fire over the palisades and galleries, which were well supplied with stones. By this means the enemy, who annoyed us from their galleries, would be dislodged. In the meantime we should give orders for some boards [probably logs, where would they find sawn boards?] to form a parapet to cover and protect our men from the arrows and stones. The tower and parapets could be moved by main force. Those on the tower would do their duty with some arquebusiers posted there. And thus acting, we should so defend ourselves, that they would not be able to extinguish the fire that we would apply to their pickets. They began the next morning to construct and prepare the tower and parapets and made such progress that they were finished in less than four hours.

We were expecting 500 men that had been promised. [Consul Butterfield in his, History Of Brulé wrote, that the Carantounnais, "Had not promised anything; as there had been no communication between them and the Hurons."] Our savages were much afflicted because the promised men were not at the rendezvous. But seeing that they were numerous enough to capture the fort, and considering that delay to be always prejudicial, I urged them to attack the fort -- stating that the enemy had discovered our strength and the effect of our arms, which would pierce what was arrow proof. Their village was enclosed with strong quadruple palisades of large timbers, 30' high, interlocked one with another, with an interval of not more than half a foot between them; with galleries in the form of parapets, defended with double pieces of timber, proof against our arquebuses. On one side they had a pond with a unknown failing supply of water, from which came a number of gutters that they had laid along the intermediate space, to throw water around for the purpose of extinguishing fire.

Such was their mode of fortification and defense, which was much stronger than the villages of the Attigonuantans (Hurons).

We advanced to attack the village. Our tower was carried by 200 of our strongest men. They placed it within a pike's length in front and I posted on it four arquebusiers, well sheltered from any arrows and stones that might have been shot at them. Nevertheless, the enemy did not cease discharging and throwing a great number of arrows and stones over their pickets. The number of arquebus shots that were fired, forced them to vacate and abandon their galleries. As the tower was moved, instead of bringing the parapets, as ordered, on which the fire was to have been placed, they abandoned them. They started to yell at their enemies, shooting arrows into the fort -- which, in my opinion, did not do much

They are excusable for they are not soldiers, are averse to discipline or correction, and only do what they like. One inconsiderately applied the fire to the wrong side of the fort, or to leeward, so that it produced no results. Most of the savages began to set wood against the pickets but in such small quantities, that the fire did not do much good. The disorder was so great that it was impossible to hear. In vain I cried to them and remonstrated as well as I was able against the imminent danger to which they exposed themselves by their stupidity. They heard nothing because of the violent noise they made. By shouting, I was only splitting my skull, and that my remonstrances were in vain and that this disorder was irremediable. I resolved to do what was in my power with my men and fire on those we could discover or perceive.

The enemy profited by our disorder. They went to the water and discharged it in such abundance, that rivers, it may be said, spouted from their gutters, so that the fire was extinguished in less than no time. They continued to pour arrows on us like hail. Those on the tower killed and wounded a great many.

The engagement lasted about three hours. Two of our chiefs were wounded; one called Ochateguain, the other Orani and about 15 others. The rest seeing their folks, and some of *their chiefs wounded, began to talk of retreating without fighting any more. So they withdrew having accomplished nothing save this disorderly splutter. The chiefs have no absolute control of their companions who follow their whim and act their pleasure, which is the cause of their disorder and ruins all their affairs. In having taken a resolution, any poor devil can make them break it and change their plans. They accomplish nothing, as may be seen by this expedition.*

Having received two wounds from arrows, one in the leg and the other in the knee, which sorely incommoded me, we withdrew into our fort. Being all assembled there, I remonstrated them several times because of the disorder that had occurred. But my talk was in vain. They said many of their men had been wounded. And that it would be very inconvenient and fatiguing to carry them on the retreat. There was no way of engaging in battle, as I had proposed to them. If they would willingly wait four more days for the 500 men who were expected, upon whose arrival, they would renew their efforts and do what I had told them -- better than what they had already done. To my regret, it was necessary to stop.

Next day blew a very strong and violent wind which lasted two days, which was particularly favorable for setting the company's fort in a blaze, which I strongly urged. But fearing a failure and representing themselves as wounded, they did not do anything.

We remained encamped until the 16th of the month. Several skirmishes occurred during that time between the enemy and our people, who became engaged with them by imprudence rather than want of courage. I can assure you that every time they made a charge, we were obliged to extricate them from the difficulty not being able to extricate themselves except by the help of our arquebusiers -- which the enemy dreaded and greatly feared. As soon as they saw one of our arquebusiers, they immediately retreated, telling us not to meddle with their fights and that their families had very little courage to require our assistance.

Seeing that the 500 men were not coming, they proposed to depart and retreat at once. They began to make litters to carry their wounded ...
The Documentary History Of The State Of New York Vol 3
O'Callaghan

Champlain could not walk because of his painful wounds and was carried pinion fashion in a rude basket slung from a warrior's shoulders and in his eyes, more or less, in disgrace to a Huron village. He never considered that he was a heavy burden to the various Indians who had to carry him and who had to have suffered with his weight. Nor did he give thanks for this necessary service.

He was forced to spend the winter in their village, because strangely enough, no guide wanted to bring him to Quebec. His wounds healed but evidently his anger grew, which is apparent when reading his report on the battle.

He finally arrived back in Quebec on 11 July 1616.

conclusion

Champlain stated that the reason for this foray was that the Canadian Indians wanted it. This was 1615, and by that time, he knew that the Dutch were occupying the Hudson-Mohawk Valleys. He also knew that the Dutch were very interested in the lucrative fur trade. As was pointed out before, the man was in the tight grip of a

Champlain described how the Indians hunted deer, the winter after the battle.

hungry company who wanted a monopoly of any riches that the area possessed. Therefore, it can be assumed that this battle was to be a warning to the Indians, in the Oneida Lake region, not to wander into New France for trapping. But foremost, it was also a warning, to the Dutch in Albany, not to move in on French fur trade lines and routes.

Champlain took all the credit for the 1609 battle: never once did he give any credit to the Indians who had fought with him. This battle of 1615, did not have the same results so he whines and sniffles and shifts all the blame for the failure onto the Indians. Nowhere does he say, "I was in charge, it was my plan and things went wrong, therefore the blame rests with me."

The Onondagas were very well prepared and knew exactly what to do. Their defensive fortifications are nothing short of stunning. Was this fort a fluke, or did this defense evolve slowly? Their method of dousing a fire is unbelievable for the time and location: how did they arrive at this defense? It certainly was a touch of genius. In fact they showed more intelligence than Champlain whose moveable tower was a bit out of date. Champlain certainly did not have a clue as how to compete against this savvy tribe. He believed that a few noisy rounds from his arquebuses would stun the Onondagas so thoroughly that they would surrender immediately.

Who were the arquebusiers? Champlain did not allow the Canadian tribes to have guns. The only Frenchmen on the expedition were Champlain, his servant and Brule: but Brule had left to go to the Andastes. Since his narration says that he, "Posted four or five of our arquebusiers" and assuming that his servant might have been one, that meant that at least four Indians were operating the forbidden guns.

Champlain's chastisement of Iroquet, the chief who cut off the woman's finger was pure posturing for the officials who would read his report. He was well aware of torture, he had seen a man eaten after the 1609 battle. A native woman was no shrinking violet, she did more work than any brave: she also was involved in the torture of captives.

Because of this battle, French prestige suffered, the stone age bow and arrow proved superior to the arquebus. It has been suggested that if Champlain had won this battle, the people of the United States would be speaking French. This seems a bit far fetched because, in the future United States, there were English, Spanish, Dutch and Swedish colonies. Would he have fought all these colonies?

This culmination of Champlain's three battles, 1609, 1610 and this one, created bitter hatred of the Iroquois Confederacy against the French and their Indian allies -- and contributed to the French and Indian War.

Roasting the Dutchmen.

DANIEL van KRIECKENBEECK, 1626

A Dutch treat.

Daniel van Krieckenbeeck [Krickerbeeck/Krieckebeeck/Crieckenbeeck] was the Commis of Fort Orange in 1626 and was also the Vice Director of the Dutch West India Company According to the Tawasentha Treaty of 1618, he was expected to oversee the 25 fur traders, who were in and out of the fort and was also expected to keep the Indians peaceful.

Therefore, when some Mahicans [Mohicans] told him that a Mohawk war party was threatening their village, van Krieckenbeeck, along with six armed men, two of whom were Portuguese, left the safety of the fort accompanied by the Mahicans and headed toward the Mohawk castles.

A few miles from a castle, the Mohawks attacked so unexpectedly that the Mahicans fled in terror, while van Krieckenbeeck and three of his men were killed and burned: Tymen Bouwensen was eaten entirely; but an arm and a leg of the other two were saved and brought back to the Mohawk villages as trophies. Somehow the remaining three escaped -- even though one was shot by an arrow while swimming away from the ambush.

Pieter Barents/Barentsen, a company trader, quickly visited the Mohawks, trying to prevent further atrocities. The Mohawks claimed that they were sorry for what had happened, but only reacted the way they had, because of unwanted Dutch interference.

conclusion

The Mohawks were located to the west of Albany. Therefore van Krieckenbeeck headed west through the Pine Bush and was probably ambushed somewhere west of the Scotia area

This was the first incident of any Dutch being eaten by the Mohawks.

glossary

COMMIS ... the head of the fort, the Dutch term for commissary.

geography

CASTLE ... the larger villages of the Indians, especially in the Mohawk Valley, were called by this name.

PIERRE MAGNAN, 1627

Magnan received the same horrendous treatment that would later befall Jogues.

Pierre Magnan clubbed a man to death near Lisieux, France and fled to the New World. Little did he know the fate that awaited him in that far off land.

Some time after his arrival, a few Montagnais headed south, looking for trouble, and captured three Iroquois on Lake Champlain. One Iroquois managed to escape, but the other two were brought to Three Rivers where they were tortured. Word was sent to Champlain in Quebec who hurried to Three Rivers and immediately called together a council. He reminded his Indian audience about another miserable incident: how they had gone to the Iroquois to trade and been received with kindness, but on the way home, killed an Iroquois. Champlain chastised the Indians that now they had not only captured two Iroquois but also mistreated them.

After the various chiefs, or captains, had spoken, the council decided that one of the captive Iroquois should be sent home to his nation accompanied by an embassy of good will, consisting of: Cherououny, a Montagnais chief; two other Indians; and a Frenchman; with gifts for the captains of the Iroquois villages they would visit. The other prisoner, a young Mohawk boy, would remain with the French, as a hostage. Magnan was offered a reward if he joined the group headed for the Mohawk Valley. The group left Canada on 24 July 1627.

Unfortunately an Algonguin, from Alumette Island, who detested Cherououny, traveled south to spread hatred among the enemy. He told his Mohawk relatives that the expected embassy was a spying expedition seeking information in order to destroy them. He also related that it was Cherououny who was responsible for the unrest between the different tribes: and that 10 years ago Cherououny had slain two Frenchmen, but had been pardoned.

The Iroquois believed these falsehoods. So when the embassy arrived in the village, Cherououny, Pierre Magnan and one of the Montagnais were put to death. The second Montagnais was spared because he was a Mohawk by birth, who had been captured as a boy and brought up by the Montagnais

News of the horrible event reached the Montagnais who then killed the hostage, the Mohawk boy.

conclusion

Magnan definitely was in upper New York State. Whether the peace embassy left Lake Champlain to paddle up Lake George is not known.

JEAN NICOLET de BELLEBORNE, 1633

Consul Butterfield, the noted historian, referred to him as Sieur Nicolet and stated that Nicollet or Nicollett was incorrect. He was born c1598, probably at Cherbourg, France, the son of Thomas Nicolet, a postal courier for the king.

Jean arrived in Canada during 1618, in the service of the Compagnie des Marchands de Rouen et de Saint Malo. The population of Quebec, only 40 to 50 including the missionaries, was completely dependent on the cold hearted Compagnie des Cent Associes: Champlain was on the verge of despair. These miserable conditions must have made the young Nicolet wonder why he had come to this raw land.

Champlain sent him to live with the Algonquins at Alumette Island to learn their language, customs and to explore the regions they inhabited. Life was not too pleasant for him, at times he went without food for a week and during one desperate period of seven weeks, his only food was tree bark. But, he survived and the Indians accepted him. They accepted him so much that they made him one of their chiefs. He stayed at the island from 1620 to 1622.

It was as chief, that he led 400 Algonquins to the Mohawk Valley and made a successful peace treaty with the Iroquois. The *Jesuit Relation* of 1642 laments, "Would to God that it had never been broken, for then we would not be suffering the calamities which move us to groan." When he returned to New France, he was sent to the Nipissings and lived with them for about eight or nine years.

Father Campbell SJ, at the 1916 dedication of a memorial tablet for Nicolet on Mackinac Island, said ...

Jean Nicolet was not a great explorer, like Champlain; he was not a picturesque Governor like Frontenac; not a daring fighter like Iberville; not even a successful discoverer like Marquette; nor a martyr like his friends Brebeuf, Jogues, Daniel, Garnier and Garreau. He occupied no conspicuous position in the official world; he was not entrusted with the building or molding or modifying of a commonwealth or a colony; he was simply an employee in a trading post; and an Indian interpreter, who passed the longest and most ambitious period of his life amid surroundings that were calculated to tear out of his heart not only every noble aspiration, but every recollection of Christianity and civilization. Yet he was a man who was not influenced or harmed by them, but who made them minister to his advancement.

Father Vimont wrote in 1643, that, "His disposition and his excellent memory led one to expect worthwhile things of him." He was a man that was much admired and loved by all, even though he broke with tradition and sired an illegitimate daughter.

He drowned in a boating accident near Sillery, New France in 1642.

conclusion

Nicolet was definitely in upstate New York during 1633. The question is what route did he take to travel from the St Lawrence to the Mohawk castles? Definitely he had to follow Bressani's and Jogues' route as far as the mouth of the La Chute River where it enters Lake Champlain. Then the route would have depended on what the advance scouts told the peace party about the water level in Wood Creek to Fort Edward. The water level would have been high in spring but, later in summer or fall, it would have been low. With a party of 400, they must have taken large canoes and would they have been able to navigate Wood Creek if the water was shallow? The creek was also bordered by swampy land for some miles, definitely not favorable for a campsite.

Therefore it is more reasonable to suggest that Lake George was taken because of deeper water, excellent camp sites and more water in which to maneuver the large number of canoes.

Their exact route south from the Fort Ticonderoga point, on Lake Champlain, to the Mohawk Valley will probably never be known. Regardless it must have been an impressive sight to see so many canoes upon the northern waterways.

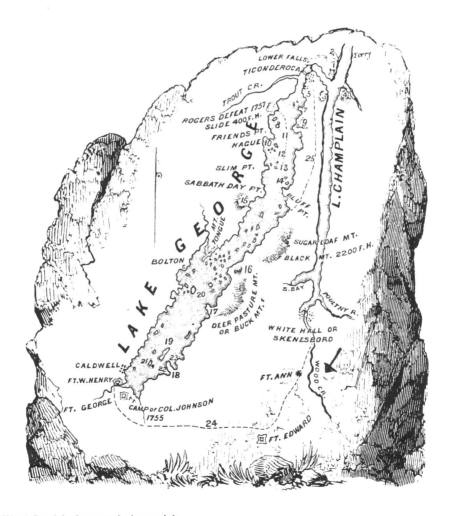

Wood Creek is shown at the lower right.

The ruins of Fort Ticonderoga.

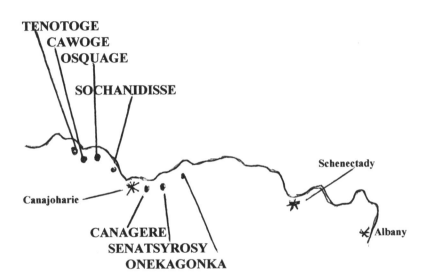

TENOTOGE
CAWOGE
OSQUAGE

SOCHANIDISSE

Canajoharie

Schenectady

Albany

CANAGERE
SENATSYROSY
ONEKAGONKA

Probable location of the Mohawk castles in 1634.

146

MEMORIAL OF THE PRINCIPAL EVENTS THAT HAPPENED DURING A JOURNEY TO THE MAQUES AND SINNIKINS INDIANS, 1634

This Journal material is by permission of the Huntington Library, San Marino, California.

On 11 December 1634, three Dutchmen and five Mohawks left Fort Orange and walked almost to Oneida Lake to investigate rumors that the French and French Indians were going there to trade for furs. These foreign traders presented a problem because the Mohawks, "Wanted to receive just as much for their skins as the French Indians did." The French had been shown the way to the area by Champlain's 1615 trip.

It is to be wondered why the trio did not wait until the Mohawk River thawed, the trip would have been a lot easier and surely would have taken less time. The fur trading season at Albany was in the summer, which would leave spring and fall as ideal times to go. The only plausible reason for setting out in the dead of winter would be that there was nothing to occupy their time in Fort Orange. The Journal backs this up with the statement that, "Trade was doing very badly just now."

The small band stopped at just about every Mohawk castle, most of which were located on the south banks of the Mohawk. Besides relating what the Iroquois were eating and the size of their villages, the journal's most important feature relates how the Dutchmen negotiated trade with the Sinnikins and the Onondagas in the last village visited ...

I saw there a good many people that I knew ... In the afternoon one of the council came to me, asking the reason of our coming into his land, and what we brought for him as a present. I told him that we did not bring any present, but that we only paid him a visit. He told us that we would not be allowed to do so, because we did not bring him a present. Then he told how the Frenchmen had come thither to trade with six men and had given him good gifts ... in the month of August of this year. We saw very good axes to cut the underwood, French shirts, and coats and razors. This member of the council said we were scoundrels, because we paid not enough for their beaver skins. They told us that the Frenchmen gave six hands of seawan [wampum] for one beaver, plus other things ... After long deliberation they made peace for four years ...

The savages came to us and told us that we had better stop another four or five days ... I told them they nearly starved us and for that reason I did not want to stay ...

The Sinnikins gave them a beaver coat and beaver skins, in turn they received some scissors, awls, knives and needles. The Indians complained that many times they had carried heavy pelts to Fort Orange only to discover that there were no trade goods and therefore had to carry the furs home. "They had done a lot of work for nothing." So, they said that if they could be assured of four handsful of wampum they would only trade with the Dutch.

147

The Sinnikins showed them, with stones and corn cakes, the location of every castle: they gave the name of each castle and the distances between them. Jeronimus de la Crois made a chart of this valuable information.

On January 9, 10 weary Onondagas arrived carrying bear skins. These people were the first, of this tribe, ever seen by the Dutch. They gave the men 14 beaver skins and said that if they received a better price, they would bring many more and invited them to visit their village during the next season. The Onondagas also told them that the French had come, in shallops, to trade for furs.

Who Wrote This Journal?

The entire trip was recorded in a journal written by the supposed leader of the group, who was accompanied by Jeronimus de la Crois and Willem Tomassen.

General James Wilson bought this copy of the earliest known New York State journal, when he was in Holland, 1895. He stated that, "It consisted of 32 pages of well-preserved foolscap, which had been buried in a Dutch garret of Amsterdam for 260 years." [The handwriting of this journal does not match van den Bogaert's handwriting, a sample of each is given in Gehring's translation. It is felt that is a copy of the original and probably was created by an employee of the Patroon.]

Wilson wasted no time in arranging for a translation to be included in the, *Independant* which was quickly followed in the, *Annual Report Of The American Historical Association* 1895.

The General declared that it had been written by, "Arent Van Curler of Corlear." But, Van Curler was not in the colony in 1634: he arrived four years later when he was 18 years old. When this fact was noticed by AJF van Laer, he then determined that the journal had been written by Dirck Cornelisz Duyster, Commis of Fort Orange. Upon further reflection of the original Dutch, van Laer decided that Duyster was in Holland at the time.

AJF van Laer searched for yet another author and thought that since the writer did a simple medical procedure and that he was asked to cure a sick man -- he was a doctor! After searching the records again, van Laer found that van den Bogaert was listed as a surgeon, for about that time. Therefore van den Bogaert became the author and he is still so considered by some historians.

Reverend Beauchamp bought the journal from the General and oddly enough never questioned that Van Curler was the author.

conclusion

It is a flimsy argument that Harmen Meyndertsz van den Bogaert is the author of this journal simply because he was a surgeon. In a frontier environment just about every adult is a potential doctor. Even today, one officer of every tanker and cargo ship automatically becomes a doctor in an emergency. Then too, some white men were considered healers by the early tribes: Alvarez Nunez Cabeza de Vaca was one. Towards the end of his aimless wanderings, where ever he went, the sick were

148

brought before him to be cured. He developed quite a reputation as a healer in the south and in Mexico, 1528-1536.

In the, *History Of New Netherland* Vol I, O'Callaghan states that, "Bogaert arrived in New Netherland, anno 1631, as surgeon of the company's ship the *Eendracht*; he continued in the company's service to 1633, after which he resided in New Amsterdam until appointed commissary to Fort Orange." There is also an entry in, *The Iconography Of Manhattan Island, 1498-1909* noting that van den Bogaert wanted to be reimbursed by the company for, "Wages and board money as he earned in the West India Company's service since 21 March 1630 ... to 1 February 1633." This plea for back wages explains his exact period of employment, 1630 to 1633 and agrees with O'Callaghan that he was not in the employment of the Company when the trip took place, 1634-1635. And, that he lived in Manhattan until he was made commis at Fort Orange: Gehring stated that this occurred in 1645.

Why would a sane man travel up the Hudson to Albany, in the winter, and then trek into the frozen unknown, if he were not in the employ of the Dutch West India Company?

At the beginning of the journal, this statement leaps out, "The Maques and the Sinnikins very often came to our commissioners (Martin Gerritsen and me)." Since this was the second sentence after the date of 11 December, it can be assumed that the "me" had to have been in Fort Orange up to that date and not 150 miles away in Manhattan, for almost two years.

Going back to the year 1626, when Daniel van Krieckenbeeck was killed, the man who ventured into the castles to soothe the ruffled Mohawks, was Pieter Barents, a company trader. Was Barents still at Fort Orange in 1634? If so, was he the author of the journal? If not, it would be plausible to think that some other company trader went on the journey and kept a record of it.

All arguments aside, the fact remains that there is no concrete proof as to who wrote this journal.

RECORDED DATES RELATING TO VAN DEN BOEGART

1630 ... 24 May, arrived [Gehring.]
1631 ... arrived [O'Callaghan, Stokes.]
1633 ... continued in Company's service until 1 February [Stokes.]
       He lived in New Amsterdam until appointed Commis to Fort Orange [O'Callaghan.]
1640 ... 22 March, tried to collect his wages from 21 March 1630 to 1 February 1633 [Stokes.]
1645 ... Commis of Fort Orange ... he had lived in Manhattan till then [Stokes.]

glossary

SINNIKINS ... the Dutch referred to the Iroquois as Senecas.

THOMAS GODEFROY, Sieur de Normanville and FRANCOIS MARGUERIE de la Haye, 1641

THOMAS GODEFROY, Sieur de Normanville was born c1610, in Lintot, Normandy. The young Godefroy arrived in New France about 1626, with his older brother Jean. He became an interpreter of the Algonquin, Iroquois and probably Huron languages for Champlain, until the English occupation of Quebec, from 1629 to 1632. He then decided to live with the Indians to learn their ways. After the French returned, he settled in the Three Rivers area and remained there until his death.

This man is best described as a go-between who was very adept at combining business and religion. He taught catechism to the Indians, led them in prayer and even baptized them -- in other words he assisted or replaced the missionaries.

He was captured by the Indians three times -- 1641, 1648 and 1652. On the first two occasions, he managed to escape, but he was not so lucky the third time, for the Indians killed him in 1652, near Three Rivers.

FRANCOIS MARGUERIE de la Haye was born in Rouen, Normandy and was baptized on 12 October 1612. He was the son of Francois Marguerie and Marthe Romaine.

One of the most daring figures of the early days of the colony, Marguerie was called, "The double man" by the Indians because he had adapted so well to their customs and to their languages. Although *The Jesuit Relations* do not mention him until 1636, it is possible that he was in Canada before 1629. He sought refuge among the Algonquins during Kirke's occupation of the colony, and became familiar with the way of life and language of this tribe. He was an interpreter.

Marguerie drowned at Three Rivers, 1648.

The Jesuit Relations of 1640-41, tells about the capture of these two young men by the Iroquois during February 1641 ...

Two young Frenchmen, one an interpreter of the Algonquin tongue for the Gentlemen Of New France, named Francois Marguerie: the other named Thomas Godefroy, who is brother to a worthy inhabitant of the country. The pair went on a hunting trip and were discovered by these barbarians [the Mohawks] who, followed the imprint of their snowshoes on the snow. The Indians approached them with stealthy steps during the night and suddenly sprung upon them -- uttering frightful shrieks and howls.

One of the two Frenchmen, had time to present his arquebus to the first Indian who endeavored to seize him. But by good luck, or rather by providence of Our Lord, it flashed in the pan. If it had taken fire, and he had killed this barbarian, both of them would have lost their lives. He came off with only the stroke of a javelin which the enemy thrust into his thigh.

The other Frenchman, promptly rose at the noise, seized his sword but a Hiroquois shot an arrow at him, which passed under his arm. Another, intending to approach him, made a false step and fell into the snow. Immediately, the Frenchman presented his naked sword at his throat, the Hiroquois saw him do this without stirring -- not one made a show of hindering

151

of killing him, for fear he might transfix his enemy whom he had at his feet. At this young man seeing that he would be massacred in a moment, if he went further, own his sword and surrendered, preferring to be burned, roasted and eaten, to dying ~~in this~~ headlong haste.

Behold, then, these two poor victims in the hands of these tigers; they bond, pinioned them and took them into their own country, with shrieks and yells, or rather with the howling of wolves. Nevertheless, having recognized that they were Frenchmen, they did not treat them as they do the savages, but used greater gentleness, for they neither tore off their finger nails, nor mutilated them in any part of their bodies.

As they did not return on the day appointed, their friends began to suspect that some misfortune had happened to them, they were waited some time longer, but as they did not appear, the French went to seek them in the place where they said they were going to hunt. They found a pole fixed in the snow, to which was attached a wretched paper, scribbled upon with a coal. They took it, read it and found these words written, "The Hiroquois have captured us: go into the woods."

They entered the woods and found a large tree from which the bark had been recently removed and on which were written these words with charcoal, "The Hiroquois have captured us tonight; they have not yet done us any harm -- they are taking us away to their own country." There were some other words which could not be read. This happened about the 20th of February. This blow somewhat bewildered our Frenchmen, who fervently commended to God these two poor captives.

All possible ways were sought to deliver them, but none seemed feasible. Our neighboring savages told us, that it was all over with them, that they had been boiled or roasted and eaten. But God, who is pleased to grant the prayers of those who have confidence in His goodness, restored them to us and, from their own lips we learned what follows.

We arrived at the village of those who captured us, after a journey of 17 or 18 days. At the report of our arrival, everyone ran to see us -- not openly from the neighboring villages, but the other Nations wished to have the satisfaction of seeing the captive Frenchmen. They made us stand up at all hours, that they might look us over from head to foot. Some derided us, others threatened to burn us, others had compassion on us. Some Hiroquois who had been prisoners at Kebec and at Three Rivers, who had been favorably treated by the French, looked kindly on us and told us that we would not die. One among them, to whom Francois Marguerie had been very kind, and whom our Fathers had aided in his necessity, said aloud that the Frenchmen were good and must not be put to death ...

A young Algonquin prisoner, whose life had been spared by the Hiroquois, recognized our Frenchmen and said to them, "Take courage, you will not die; inasmuch as you know how to pray to God, He will not fail to succor you." ...

Notwithstanding all these declarations, these young men had every reason for fear, seeing themselves in the midst of barbarism and of cruelty, without help from any creature. The question was of nothing less than fire and of the fury and teeth of these barbarians, who practice strange tortures on their prisoners.

Some savages of the upper Nations, not wishing to irritate the French, gave presents that these two poor captives might be set free. At length a council was held in the country and they concluded to negotiate peace with the French. That being done, they promised the pris-

152

oners that in the Spring, they should be taken back to Three Rivers. In the meantime, they were given to two heads of families, who treated them like their own children.

Now, these two poor Frenchmen were distressed by the severity of the cold, for, partly through force and partly out of good will, they had given the best of their clothing to these barbarians. One of them, having a knowledge of the English language, wrote to the Hollanders, who had seized a part of Acadia, which belongs to the King, and begged them to have pity upon their poverty. He used a beaver skin for paper, a little stick for a pen and some rust or soot sticking to the bottom of a kettle, for ink. The savage, to whom the beaver belonged, carried it to the Dutch who understood this writing and, touched with compassion sent to these two poor prisoners, a couple of shirts, two blankets, some provisions, an inkstand, some paper and a short letter. The savage delivered all faithfully except the letter, saying that the writing of the French was good, but that of the Hollanders was worth nothing.

Francois Marguerie, having paper, wrote the whole history of their capture and, as they feared the Hollanders might not understand the French language, inscribed his letter in French and in Latin, as he was able, and in English. He believed that it was carried, but he saw no reply. The Hiroquois doubtless were not willing to deliver one.

Neither would they ever permit them to visit the Dutch. "Those people," said they to them, "are cruel. They will put us into irons, they will plunder our countrymen, if they come into these quarters to liberate you."

The Frenchmen believed nothing of all this. Besides, they did not wish to escape from the hands of these barbarians, in order that being with them, they might better incline them to an advantageous peace.

Toward the end of the month of April, the decision to seek peace with the French was made, 500 Hiroquois, or thereabouts, set out from their country, well armed, taking with them the two Frenchmen. Some went back, others broke from the ranks in great numbers to meet the Hurons and the Algonquins, with the design of pillaging, killing and massacring all those whom they could surprise. The remainder went directly to Three Rivers.

On the 5th of June, at daybreak, 20 canoes appeared below the habitation of the French, all laden with well-armed men, others appeared in the middle of the river, equipped in like manner. Immediately, there was an alarm among the French and among the Algonquins who dwell near us -- these last cried out that all was over with their people who had gone to hunt beavers.

At that moment an Algonquin canoe, going out of the mouth of the stream, which we call Three Rivers, was taken by its enemies in the sight of the French and of the savages, without anyone being able to render it assistance. While we were in this alarm, another canoe appeared, guided by a single man, coming out from the quarter of the enemy and advancing toward the fort of the French. This canoe carried a little flag as a sign of peace. We cast our eyes upon the pilot, in dress he appeared to be a savage, but by the voice we recognized that it was Francois Marguerie, one of the two prisoners.

Having set foot on land, he was conducted to the fort, that he might pay his respects to Sieur de Chanflour, who commands there. Everyone ran, each one embraced him. He was looked upon as a man raised from the dead and as a victim escaped from the knife, that was ready to sacrifice him and from the fire, that was ready to consume him. They made him abandon his rags and reclothed him like a Frenchman.

All were full of joy and treated him affectionately and after the first caresses every one became silent, in order to listen to him. He said then, that the Hiroquois, desiring the alliance of the French, had treated them mildly. That they had set out from the country 500 in number, of whom 350 were seen prowling along the river, in sight of the fort. That they had deputed him to speak concerning peace with the French, but not with the savages -- the Algonguins and the Montagnais -- whom they hate unto death and whom they wish to exterminate entirely.

"They have," said he, "36 arquebusiers, as skillful as the French -- the remainder are very well armed in savage fashion. They are abundantly furnished with powder, with lead, with bows, arrows and javelins and with provisions. They are hoping that a present will be given them of 30 good arquebuses. They are resolute people, whom you must trust only with reserve, since an Algonguin woman -- who has lived for some time in their country and from whom these barbarians concealed little -- warned us in secret that these people wished to use our bodies as bait, in order that they might take all the savages, our confederates, ruin the whole country and make themselves absolute masters of the great river."

"I am commissioned," said he, "to return without delay. They have retained with them my companion as hostage and I have given them my word, that I will see them again as soon as possible."

Sieur de Chanflour gave us an answer, that, this matter being of great importance, it was necessary that the great Captain of the French should be notified. That they did not doubt he would approve of the pursuit of peace, that they were going to send messengers to him and that he would shortly be at Three Rivers. Our prisoner and a Frenchman, who accompanied him, re-embarked with the answer -- set off by a quantity of provisions and little presents, in order to win these barbarians. They approved our procedure, but they did not neglect to fortify themselves well, while awaiting the coming of Onontio -- it is thus they call Monsieur the Governor. They again sent back Francois Marguerie and Thomas Godefroy, his fellow captive, beseeching the Captain of Three Rivers to come and parley with them while awaiting the arrival of the Great Captain.

Father Paul Ragueneau and Sieur Nicolet -- both well versed in the Huron language, which is related to the Hiroquois language -- went to them instead of the captain, who with reason was unwilling to leave his fort. Having arrived at the rendezvous of these barbarians, they stated to them that the French had had great satisfaction in seeing their countrymen; that they all took pleasure in the news of peace; and, that they themselves had been sent to learn what was desired from the captain, whom they had asked to come. They replied that they wished to talk -- that is to say, that they wished to exchange presents -- not only restoring our prisoners, but about inviting us to make a settlement near their country, to which all the Hiroquois Nations could come for their trade.

They were answered: that they would be willingly heard, that we were awaiting the Great Captain, who had been informed of all that had occurred.

After much palaver back and forth: after the French gave gifts to the Iroquois and guided by Jean Nicolet along with Father Paul Ragneneau, it was agreed that Marguerie and Godefroy would be released. However, the Iroquois sulked that they should have been given arquebuses for the release.

The Iroquois further agreed that they would behave themselves while in New France. But the temptation was too great and they attacked one canoe, killing one woman and taking a man captive: they also attacked canoes returning from a hunt, took a woman and her child captive besides looting furs and supplies from the craft. Eventually the Iroquois returned to the Mohawk Valley.

conclusion

Godefroy and Marguerie were brought by the Iroquois up Lake Champlain and could have seen Lake George on the trip south or north. They definitely saw the land north and west of Albany.

Iroquois longhouses.

155

ISAAC
JOGUES
S·J·

1607   1646

Isaac Jogues.

156

ISAAC JOGUES, 1642

Please refer to the Buckle Press reprint of Isaac Jogues, *by TJ Campbell -- this small book contains much of the information that would only be duplicated here.*

A year after Godefroy and Marguerie had been taken captive, Father Isaac Jogues and his two companions were taken captive on the St Lawrence and dragged to the Mohawk Valley.

Godefroy and Marguerie had been treated relatively well because the Mohawks decided that they were not savages -- in other words, their enemies the Hurons or Algonquins. What had happened in only one year, that the Iroquois treated Jogues in such a despicable manner? Why did they decide that Jogues and his companions were savages?

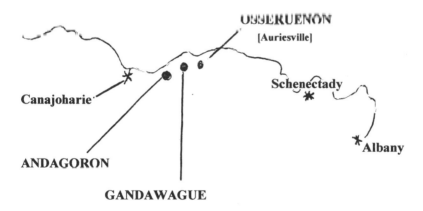

The location of the Mohawk castles 1642.

The Schuyler House at The Flatts.

ARENDT VAN CURLER, 1642

The most beautiful land that eye may wish to see.
Van Curler

Van Curler [Arent; Corler/Corlaer; sometimes a lower case "v" in Van] arrived in the Albany area during 1638, to take over the running of the manor of Rensselaerwyck. He was the grandnephew of Killian Van Rensselaer, although the question has been raised that perhaps he was a cousin because the Patroon addressed him as, "Mon Cousin" in correspondence. Whatever the relationship, Van Curler was definitely related to Van Rensselaer, the Patroon.

Different approaches had been tried by the absent landlord to run his vast holdings and none was successful. Therefore it was decided to put one man in charge of it all, a colossal job for a young person of 18 years. Even though Van Rensselaer complained now and then about how Arendt handled affairs, the colony flourished. Van Curler became loved by the Indians, so much so, they called him Corlear. They also called Lake Champlain, Lake Corlear after he drowned in it, 1667 and for years referred to New York's governors as Corlear.

Ardent was an early settler on The Flatts, having pushed Van der Donck out, and south, to Castle Island. He claimed that Van der Donck and Pieter Cornelissen were, "The dogs which bite me."

This was a man who recognized the value of The Flatts location because the road ran between the house and the river, therefore traders and Indians could be checked, or intercepted, before they reached Albany. Quickly, he built a large building for about 30 farm laborers and the farm became the foremost one in the colony.

Van Curler wrote a letter about his trip to the Mohawk Valley to try to rescue Isaac Jogues during 1642 ...

I have lately, with Labatie and Jacob Jansen van Amsterdam, been on horseback to the Maquaes [Mohawk] country, where three Frenchmen were prisoners -- one of whom was a Jesuit, a very learned scholar -- who had been very cruelly treated by the cutting off of the finger and thumb. I carried presents there and proposed that we should keep on good terms as neighbors and that they should do no injury either to the colonists or to their cattle, which all the Indians, so far as three castles, thankfully accepted. We were entertained right well, in all friendship. We were obliged to halt fully a quarter of an hour before each castle, in order that the Indians might salute us by the firing of muskets. There was also great joy among them because I had come. Indians were immediately sent out to hunt, who brought us in excellent turkeys. Then, I thoroughly inspected their castles and invited all the chiefs of the three castles to assemble together and proposed to them to release the French prisoners. But there was no appearance of this, which they refused with good reason. Said they, "We shall manifest toward you every friendship that is in our power, but on this subject we wish to be silent. Besides you well know how they treat our people who fall into their hands." Had we delayed reaching there three or four days longer, they would have been burnt. I offered them for the ransom of the Frenchmen about 600 guilders in goods, to which the entire colony would contribute, but they would in no wise accept them. However, we succeeded to this extent that they promised not to kill them, but to take them back to their country. The French captives ran screaming after us and begged us to do all that was in our power to release them out of the hands of the barbarians. But seeing that there was no chance of this, I departed: They gave me an escort of 10 or 12 men, who conducted us back home. Hardly half a day's journey from the colony, on the Maquaes Kill [Mohawk River], there lies the most beautiful land that eye may wish to see, full a day's journey long and mostly in one unbroken piece. It is impossible to reach it by boat on account of the strong current which prevails there and on the other hand on account of the shallowness of the water, but I think that it may be possible to reach it with wagons. Two of the Frenchmen, of whom the Jesuit was one, came to my house last May. They said that they hoped that now there might be a chance to procure their release. As soon as the Indians return from hunting, an effort will be made to obtain their freedom.

"Arent van Curler And His Historic Letter To The Patroon."

conclusion

Van Curler went as far as present day Auriesville, where Jogues was being kept a prisoner. He did not identify the other two villages he visited, but it can be assumed that they were east of Auriesville and on the south side of the Mohawk.

The Killian Van Rensselaer coat of arms.

glossary

PATROON ... was the title of the holder, or owner, of a vast estate granted by the Dutch West India Company. The Patroon was a feudal lord who controlled the lives of all in the colony. The Patroon of Rensselaerwyck, Killian Van Rensselaer, was granted land on both sides of the Hudson River from just above Troy down to around Coeymans. Van Rensselaer never stepped foot on the soil of the new world. The settling of the Hudson Valley was not the primary consideration of the company -- the creation of these manors was also a scheme to keep Dutch ships busy and to keep a monopoly of the fur trade.

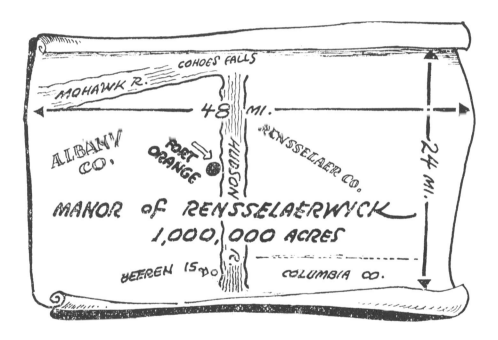

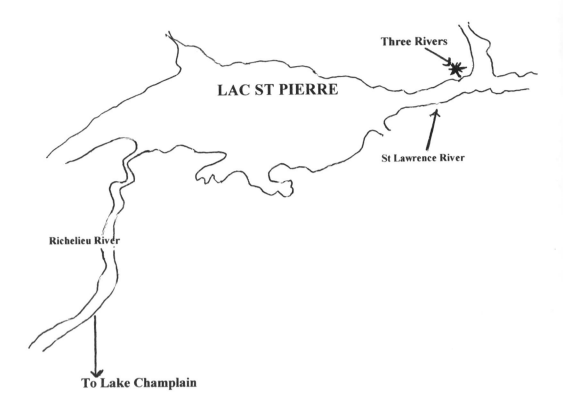

Three Rivers

LAC ST PIERRE

St Lawrence River

Richelieu River

To Lake Champlain

Lac St Pierre [Lake St Peter.]

FRANCIS BRESSANI, 1644

Some mysterious awe protected his life.
Bancroft

Francis Joseph Bressani, was another Jesuit who was cruelly tortured by the Indians in northern New York. *The Jesuit Relations*, at times, refer to him by his middle name, Joseph and spell his surname as Bressany. He was born in Rome, 6 May 1612.

As a young man, Bressani absorbed, *The Relations* which were avidly read in Europe and was so moved by them, that he joined the order to help convert the Indians of North America.

He arrived in Canada during 1642, and two years later, he was sent to minister to the Huron Nation. According to, *The Relation of 1643-44*, Bressani, along with six Christian Indians and a young French boy who accompanied him, were captured by the Iroquois. One of the six Indians was Henry Stontrats, "A man of mature age and mind" who managed to escape somewhere near the St Lawrence. Henry returned to the Jesuits and told them what had happened.

THE JESUITS WROTE HENRY'S VERSION OF THE CAPTURE ...

Our neophytes embarked in three canoes, on the 27th of April, with Father Joseph Bressany, an Italian by birth and a native of the City of Rome, whom our Reverend Father General had sent to us, two years ago, and a young French lad [Guillaume?] who was to serve our Fathers. It was believed that there would not, as yet, be much danger on the river; and our Hurons were of the opinion that, as the ice had not entirely disappeared, the Iroquois had not had time to come from their country. Moreover, they imagined that peace had already been concluded between them and the Iroquois, in consequence of overtures commenced upon this subject before they had left their own country. This induced us to risk several packages for our Fathers among the Hurons, owing to the need in which they were, after so many losses.

All these assurances did not prevent Father and the Hurons from preparing themselves as persons who might soon die. All were ready alike for life or for death, but for death rather than life, because divine providence gave them some inward presentiment of what was to happen to them.

Nor were they without some outward indications for Father Bressany's canoe was wrecked about a league from Three Rivers, at a place where there was no danger and in fine weather Owing to the proximity of the land, all in the canoe was saved, but this accident stopped them, and compelled them to sleep at this side of the entrance to the Lake (St Peter). When they started thence on the following day, the cold and the quantity of snow that fell greatly delayed them and did not allow them to proceed farther than the Marguerie River, six leagues beyond Three Rivers. Here the Hurons fired a few gunshots at some bustards. This made their presence known to 30 Iroquois who were not far away and who prepared an ambush for them beyond the river, behind a point which they had to double. Consequently, on the third day after their departure, when the canoe which carried Father Bressany, and which led the way, reached the point -- it was immediately attacked by three Iroquois canoes. On seeing them, Father commanded his people not to fight, as their side was not of equal strength, in

men or arms. *The enemies drew near, seized Father and the two Hurons who accom-
   ~~d~~ him and declared them their prisoners.*

*Meanwhile the two other Huron canoes endeavored to escape by flight, and were already
so far away that they thought they were out of danger, when, on doubling another point, they
saw two other Iroquois canoes, strongly manned, which attacked them. In this encounter, one
of our Hurons, named Betrand Sotrioskon, tried to use his gun, but was prevented from doing
so by an Iroquois who felled him in his canoe, quite dead. This so frightened the others, that
they allowed themselves to be taken without further resistance.*

*The enemies landed, with their prisoners; broke open all the packages containing the arti-
cles needed by our Fathers, who have received nothing for three years; tore up the letters that
we sent them; and equally divided the spoils. They then threw themselves upon the body of
the man whom they had killed. They tore his heart out of his breast and scalped him; they cut
off his lips; and the most fleshy parts of his thighs and legs -- which they boiled and ate in the
presence of the captives ...*

FROM BRESSANI'S NARRATIVE ...

*Then they made us cross the lake, to spend the night in a place somewhat retired, but very
damp, in which we began to sleep, bound and in the open air, as during the remainder of the
journey. It consoled me, in this matter to know that this was the will of God, as I had under-
taken this journey through obedience; and I hoped much from the intercession of the Virgin
and that of many souls who were praying for me.*

*On the following day, we embarked on a river. We had hardly made a few miles when they
commanded me to throw into the water my writings, which they had left with me till then -- as
if these had been the cause, as they superstitiously believed, of the wreck of our canoe. They
were astonished that I showed some feeling on that score, not having shown any at the loss of
everything else. We voyaged two days against the current of the river, until we were forced by
the rapids to go ashore. Then we traveled six days in the woods*

*The second day -- which was a Friday, the 6th of May -- we met with other Hiroquois, who
were going to war. They accompanied many threats with some blows which they gave us;
and, told our party about the death of one of theirs, killed by a Frenchman: the result was
that my captors began to treat me more harshly than before.*

*When they seized us, they were dying with hunger, therefore in two or three days they con-
sumed all our provisions and for the remainder of the journey there was no food, except from
either hunting or fishing, or from some wild root -- if any were found. During the extreme
hunger which we suffered, they found on the shore of the river a dead and putrid beaver,
which at evening they gave to me, that I might wash it in the river, but, having thrown it away
persuading myself that this was their intention, so stinking it was -- I paid for that with a
severe penance.*

*I will not write here what I suffered on that journey: enough to know that we marched, car-
rying burdens in the woods, where there is no road at all, but only stones, or young shoots, or
ditches, or water, or snow -- which was not melted everywhere. We traveled without shoes;
fasting sometimes till three and four o'clock in the afternoon and often whole days; exposed
to the rain and soaked in the water of the torrents and rivers which we had to cross. At evening, my office was to gather wood, carry water and do the cooking, when there was any; and*

if I was short in anything, or did not understand well, the blows were not lacking -- an[d]
less did these fail, when we happened to meet people who were going either fishing o[r]
ing. Besides, I was hardly able to rest at night, being bound to a tree and exposed to the
severity of the air -- which was still quite cold.

We finally reached their lake [Champlain], where they made other canoes, and it was necessary for me to assist them. We sailed five or six days, after which we landed, and there we
made three day's journey on foot. On the fourth day, which was the 15th of May, about the
20th hour, still fasting, we arrived at a river where about 400 barbarians were assembled for
fishing. Being already apprised of our arrival, they then came to meet us.

About 200 paces from their cabins, they stripped me naked and made me go first. On either
side, the young men of the country stood in line, every one with his stick in hand. But the first
of them had, instead of the stick, a knife. Then, as I began to proceed, one suddenly stopped
me; and took my left hand, with the knife which he held made an incision between the little
finger and the ring-finger, with so much force and violence that I believed he would split my
whole hand. The others began to load me with blows as far as the stage prepared for our
torment.

Then they made me mount upon some great pieces of bark, about nine palms above the
ground, in order that we might be seen and mocked by the people. I was now bruised all over
and covered with blood, which was flowing from all parts of my body; and exposed to a very
cold wind, which made it suddenly congeal over the skin. But, I greatly consoled myself in
see that God granted me the favor of suffering in this world some little pain in place of that
which I was under obligation, because of my sins, to pay in the other with torments incompa-
rably greater.

Meanwhile, the warriors arrived and were magnificently received by the people of the village; and, when they were refreshed with the best that they had from their fishing, they commanded us to sing. It may be wondered how we could do so, fasting, weak from the journey,
overwhelmed with blows and trembling with cold from head to foot. Some time after, a Huron
slave brought us a dish of Turkish (Indian) corn. A captain, seeing me tremble with cold, at
my urgency finally tossed to me the half of an old summer garment, all torn, which covered
rather than warmed me. They made us sing until the warriors went away; and they left us in
the hands of the young men of the place, who finally made us come down from that stage,
where we had been about two hours -- in order to make us dance in their manner -- and because I did not do so, or know how to, they beat me, pricked me, tore out my hair and beard,
etc.

They kept us in this place five or six days for their pastime, exposed to the discretion or
indiscretion of everybody. It was necessary to obey the very children, who were often contrary and unreasonable. "Get up and sing," said one. "Be quiet," said the other; and if I
obeyed one, the other ill-used me. "Here, give thy hand, which I will burn for thee," and the
other burned me because I did not extend it to him. They commanded me to take the fire in
my fingers and put it into their pipes, in which they took tobacco and then they purposely
made it fall four or five times in succession, in order to make me burn my hands by picking it
up from the ground. This was usually done at night. Toward evening, the captains shouted
through the cabins with frightful voices, "Up! assemble yourselves, O young men, come to
caress our prisoners." At this invitation they arose and gathered themselves into some large
cabin and, lifting from my back that poor rag of clothing which they had returned to me, they

left me naked. Then some pricked me with sharp sticks, others with firebrands; these burned me with red-hot stones, those with hot ashes and lighted coals. They made me walk around the fire, where they had fixed in the earth sharp sticks between the burning ashes; some tore out my hair, others my beard; and every night after having made me sing and tormented me as above.

They would burn one of my nails or fingers for the space of eight or ten minutes, often that I had, I have now only one whole one left -- and even from this one they had torn out the nail with their teeth. One evening, they burned one of my nails; on another, the first joint or section of a finger; on the next, the second. In six times, they burned nearly six of my fingers and more than 18 times they applied the fire and iron to my hands alone; and meanwhile it was necessary to sing.

Thus they treated us till one or two hours after midnight and then they left me on the bare ground, usually tied to the spot, exposed to the rain, without bed or cover other than a small skin, which covered not the half of my body -- even at times without anything, because they had already torn up that piece of garment; although, out of pity, they made of it for me enough to cover that which decency does not permit to be uncovered, even among themselves, but retained the rest.

I was treated in this way, and worse, for a whole month. But, at this first place, no longer than eight days. I would never have believed that a man could endure so hard a life. One night, while they were tormenting me as usual, a Huron who had been taken captive with me, perhaps because he had seen that one of my companions, having declared himself against us, had freed himself from the torments -- shouted in the midst of the assembly, that I was a person of rank and a captain among the French. He was heard with great attention and then they uttered a loud shout in token of joy -- resolving to treat me still worse. And on the following morning, condemned me to be burned alive and eaten. Then they began to guard me more strictly, not leaving me alone even in the necessities of nature -- wherein both the men and the boys molested me, in order to make me return as soon as possible to the cabin, fearing that I would escape.

We started thence on the 26th of May; and four days later we arrived at the first village of this nation [in the Mohawk Valley]. On this journey, made on foot, amid rains and other hardships, my sufferings were greater than before. The barbarian who conducted me was more cruel than the first, and I was wounded, weak, ill fed and half naked. Moreover, I slept in the open air bound to a stake or to a tree, trembling all night with cold and from the pain of these bonds. At difficult places in the road, I had need of some one to aid me because of my weakness, but all help was denied me; for this reason, I often fell, renewing my wounds; and to these they added new blows, in order to urge me to proceed -- thinking that I was feigning or the sake of staying behind and then taking flight. On one occasion, among others, I fell into a river and came near being drowned. However, I got out, I know not how. And all drenched with water, together with quite a heavy bundle on my shoulders, I was obliged to complete about six miles more marching until evening. They, meanwhile, jeered at me and at my stupidity in having allowed myself to fall into the river. And they did not omit, at night, to burn off one of my nails.

We finally arrived at the first village of that nation, where our entrance was similar to the former and still more cruel, because -- in addition to the blows with their fists and other blows, which they gave me on the most sensitive parts of the body -- they split for the second

166

time, my left hand between the middle finger and the forefinger. And I received beatings in so great number that they made me fall to the ground, half dead. I thought that I would lose my right eye with my sight. And, although I did not rise from the ground, for I could not, they did not cease to beat me, chiefly on the breast and on the head. Indeed, without some other hindrance they would have ended by killing me, had not a captain caused me to be dragged -- as it were, by force -- upon a stage of bark, similar to the first, where, soon afterward, they cut off the thumb of my left hand and wounded the forefinger. Meanwhile a great rain came up, with thunder and lightning and they went away, leaving us there, naked in the water, until someone, I know not who, taking pity on us, toward evening led us to his cabin. Here they tormented us with greater cruelty and impudence than ever, without a moment of rest. They forced me to eat filth, burned the rest of my nails and some fingers, wrung off my toes and bored one of them with a firebrand. And I know not what they did not do to me once, when I feigned to be in a swoon, in order to seem not to perceive something indecent that they were doing.

Surfeited with tormenting us here, they sent us to another village, nine or ten miles distant, where, besides the other torments, already mentioned, they suspended me by the feet -- sometimes with cords, again with chains, which they had taken from the Dutch. At night, they bound my hands, feet and neck to several stakes upon the bare ground. Six or seven nights they tormented me in such fashion, and in such places, that I could not describe these things, nor could they be read, without blushing. On those nights, I was awake almost all night and they appeared to me very long although they were the shortest of the year. "My God, what will purgatory be?" This thought appeased my pains not a little. In this manner of living I had become so fetid and horrible that every one drove me away like a piece of carrion. And they approached me for no other purpose than to torment me.

Scarcely did I find any one to feed me, for I could not use my hands, which were abnormally swollen and putrid. I was of course further tormented by hunger, which led me to eat raw Indian corn, not without concern for my health and made me find a relish in chewing clay, although I could not easily swallow it.

I was covered with loathsome vermin and could neither get rid of them, nor defend myself from them. In my wounds, worms were produced: out of one finger alone, more than four fell in one day. I would have regarded, by the very judgment of self-love, death as gain. I had an abscess in my right thigh, caused by blows and frequent falls, which hindered me from all repose, especially as I had only skin and bone and the earth for bed. Several times the barbarians had tried, but to no purpose, to open it with sharp stones, not without great pain to me. I was compelled to employ as surgeon, the renegade Huron who had been taken with us. The latter on the day which, as was believed the eve of my death, opened it for me with four knife thrusts and caused blood and matter to issue from it, in so great abundance and with such stench that all the barbarians of the cabin were forced to abandon it.

I desired and was awaiting death, but not without some horror of the fire: I was preparing for it, as best I could and was heartily commending myself to the Mother of Mercy ... who was, after God, the sole refuge of a poor sinner, forsaken by all creatures in a strange land ... without a language to make himself understood, without friends to console him, without Sacraments to strengthen him, and without any human remedy for alleviating his ills. The Huron and Algonquin prisoners (these are our barbarians) instead of consoling me, were the first to torment me, in order to please the Hiroquois.

I did not see the good Guillaume, except afterward, when my life was granted me. And the lad who had been taken in my company was no longer with me, especially after they perceived that I had him say his prayers -- a thing which they did not favor. But they did not leave him without torments, for, although he was no more than 12 or 13 years old, they tore out five of his nails with their teeth and, at his arrival in the country, they bound his wrists tightly with thongs, causing him the acutest pain and all in my presence, in order to afflict me more ...

The days being irksome to me and having no rest at night, I counted in the month five days more than I should, but seeing the moon one evening, I corrected my error. I knew not why they deferred my death so long. They told me that it was to fatten me before eating me, but they took no means to do so. One day, at last, they assembled in order to dispatch me. It was the 19th of June, which I reckoned as the last of my life and I entreated a captain that they would commute, if it was possible, the death by fire into some other, but another man exhorted him to remain firm in the resolution already taken. The first, nevertheless, assured me that I should die neither by fire nor by any other death. I did not believe him and knew not whether he himself spoke in good faith.

Finally they gave me, with the ceremonies of the country, to an old woman in place of her grandsire, killed some time before by the Hurons. She, instead of having me burned, as all desired and had already resolved, ransomed me from their hands for the price of some beads, which the French call "porcelain." I live here among the shadows of death, not hearing anything spoken of but murders and assassinations. They have recently slain in a cabin one of their own nation, as being useless and as one who did not deserve to live. Of course, I suffer somewhat here; my wounds are not yet healed over -- and many do not regard me with a favorable eye ... The Dutch cause me to hope for my ransom and that of the lad who was taken with me ...
Jesuit Relations Of 1653
Francis Bressani

KIEF WROTE ABOUT HOW THE DUTCH RESCUED BRESSANI ...

We, William Kieft, Director General and the Council Of New Netherland, to all those who see these presents, greeting: Francis Bressani, of the Society of Jesus, for some time a prisoner among the Iroquois savages, commonly called Maquaas, and daily persecuted by them, was, when about to be burnt, snatched out of their hands and ransomed by us for a large sum, after considerable difficulty. As he now proceeds with our permission to Holland, thence to return to France ...
20 September 1644

MEGAPOLENSIS GAVE A FEW DETAILS ...

In the year 1644, our Indians again took captive a Jesuit, [Bressani] who had been treated in the same manner as to his hands and fingers as ... [Jogues]. The Jesuit was brought to us naked, with his maimed and bloody fingers. We clothed him, placed him under the care of our surgeon and he almost daily fed at my table. This Jesuit, a native of Renen, [really of Rome] was ransomed by us from the Indians and we sent him by ship to France. He also

168

returned again from France to Canada. He wrote me a letter, as the previously mentioned one had done, thanking me for the benefits I had conferred on him.
28 September 1658

The Iroquois claimed that, "They had given Father Bressani to the Dutch because he had desired it."
He died a natural death in Florence on 9 September 1672.

conclusion

There is no doubt that Bressani was in the geographic area, but where was the fishing village, on the Hudson, where he was first tortured?

This village could have been where Fort Edward is today. Recent excavations show that there are at least four distinct levels of habitation, dating back centuries. Fort Edward was at the end of the long, or Great Carry from Lake George. Or, from Lake Champlain the group could have paddled into the now downtown area of Hudson Falls, this would have depended on the water level of Wood Creek. But considering what Bressani wrote, that it took them three days to go from Lake Champlain to the fishing village, Fort Edward does not fit the time factor.

Grassman noted that there was a fishing village on the Hudson called Ossarague, south of Glens Falls. Grassman gave Beauchamp as his source, who wrote that Ossar-a-gas or Os-sar-a-gue was a fishing place between Glens Falls and the Mohawk River in 1642 -- pronounce Os-sar-a-gue and you almost get the sound of Saratoga. This was the Iroquois favorite location for hunting and fishing and extended for quite a distance north and south of Fish Creek and on both sides of the Hudson and went west to Saratoga Lake.

Recently, a series of digs around the Fish Creek-Saratoga Lake area has proved this to be true. The remains of a fishing weir found where Fish Creek meets the Hudson at Stillwater, also argues for this location. Just about any part of this extensive area could have easily supported a group of 400.

Because of the time it took Bressani to reach the village, the Fish Creek-Saratoga Lake area is the most plausible site.

Fort Miller ford.

If the party had gone through Lake George, Bressani would have written about the portage between Lakes George and Champlain and about the portage from the south end of Lake George to the Great Carry. Since there is no mention of such a carry, the group had to have gone up Lake Champlain to Whitehall. Three days is too long a time to travel from Whitehall to Fort Edward. It is more plausible to say that it took three days to go from Whitehall to the Fish Creek-Saratoga Lake area.

glossary

CAPTAIN ... this term was used by the Jesuits in writing about Indian chiefs.

CARESS ... means tortured in every horrible conceivable way -- pricked, burned, mangled, fingers and toes cut or chewed off, nails removed, etc.

PORCELAIN ... another name for wampum, the currency of eastern Indians. Belts made of these beads were given to other tribes, to commemorate peace, or to remember special events. These beads were produced primarily by the Long Island tribes out of the shell of the quahog and exchanged by them for needed goods along the great tribal trade routes.

SINGING ... an Indian prisoner was expected to defiantly sing his death song -- to torment his captives.

geography

THEIR LAKE ... Lake Champlain was called the "Lake of the Iroquois" even though Lake Erie, according to some early maps was called the Lake of the Iroquois.

Fish Creek.

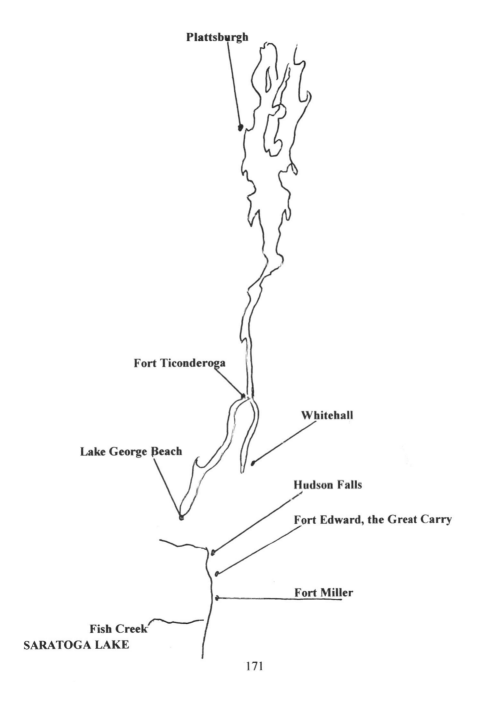

Plattsburgh

Fort Ticonderoga

Whitehall

Lake George Beach

Hudson Falls

Fort Edward, the Great Carry

Fort Miller

Fish Creek
SARATOGA LAKE

Dominie Megapolensis at the Cohoes Falls.

JOHANNES MEGAPOLENSIS, JR, c1644

The first written account of a pleasure trip to the Cohoes Falls.

Johannes Megapolensis, the minister of the congregations of Schoorl and Bergen in the Netherlands, was asked to become the first dominie for the new colony of Rensselaerwyck. He was given passage for his wife and four children; a house; a salary of 1,000 florins; a new outfit; a pension for his spouse, if he died while ministering; 30 schepels of wheat and two firkins of butter. He started preaching in Albany on 13 August 1642 and stayed there until 1649, when he went to New Amsterdam to preach there.

THE GOOD DOMINIE TOOK A PLEASURE TRIP TO VIEW THE FALLS AT COHOES AND WROTE THIS DESCRIPTION ...

Through this land runs an excellent river, about 500 or 600 paces wide. This river comes out of the Mahakas [Mohawk] country, about four leagues north of us. There it flows between two high rocky banks and falls from a height equal to that of a church, with such a noise that we can sometimes hear it here with us. In the beginning of June, 12 of us took a ride to see it. When we came there we saw not only the river falling with such a noise that we could hardly hear one another, but the water boiling and dashing with such force in still weather, that it seemed all the time as if it were raining; and the trees on the hills near by (which are as high as Schooler Duyn) had their leaves all the time wet exactly as if it rained. The water is as clear as crystal and as fresh as milk. I and another with me saw there, in clear sunshine, when there was not a cloud in the sky, especially when we stood above upon the rocks, directly opposite where the river falls, in the great abyss, the half of a rainbow, or a quarter of a circle, of the same color with the rainbow in the sky. And when we had gone about 10 or 12 rods farther downwards from the fall, along the river, we saw a complete rainbow, like a half circle, appearing clearly in the water just as if it had been in the clouds, and this is always so according to the report of all who have ever been there.

In this river is a great plenty of all kinds of fish -- pike, perch, eels, lampreys, suckers, cat fish, sunfish, shad, bass, etc. In the spring, in May, the perch are so plenty, that one man with a hook and line will catch in one hour as many as 10 or 12 can eat. My boys have caught in an hour 50, each a foot long. They have three hooks on the instrument with which they fish and draw up frequently two or three perch at once. There is also in the river a great plenty of sturgeon, which we Christians do not like, but the Indians eat them greedily

In this river, too, are very beautiful islands, containing 10, 20, 30, 50 and 70 morgens of land. The soil is very good, but the worst of it is that by the melting of the snow, or heavy rains, the river readily overflows and covers that low land. This river ebbs and flows at ordinary low water as far as this place, although it is 36 leagues inland from the sea.

"A Short Account Of The Mohawk Indians"

Sent by Megapolensis to the Netherlands on

26 August 1644

conclusion

Because Megapolensis lived on the east side of the Hudson at Greenbush, or Tuscameatick, there had to be some careful planning to bring a dozen people on such an early pleasure jaunt. A ferry ran from the east side of the Hudson River across to the Beaverkill. If the ferry could carry a horse, or a pair, could it also carry a vehicle large enough to accommodate a dozen? If not, two or more trips would have been needed.

Unfortunately he does not give a clue who accompanied him, but probably his wife was one -- that leaves 10 unknown. It is not clear if he brought his four boys: they could have fished in May, or some other time.

Quite an undertaking for the time and location.

How quiet it was then, to be able to hear the falls so many miles down river. As the Reverend had lived all his life in the flat Netherlands, seeing such a large waterfall must have been impressive. The Cohoes Falls would remain a tourist attraction for quite some time, which is rather hard to understand today, because of the series of dams that prevent much water tumbling over the rocks for most of the year.

He probably continued to go into the countryside, for in the same, "Short Account" he wrote, "I intend in process of time to preach ... to them and come ... into their own country and castles (about three days' journey from here, further inland), when I am better acquainted with their language."

It is hard to believe that sturgeon was not liked then: smoked sturgeon is quite an expensive delicacy today.

174

Megapolensis teaching the gospel to the Indians.

geography

MAHAKAS COUNTRY ... the Mohawk Valley.
MORGEN ... A Dutch land measure equal to about two acres. It was what one man could plow in a morning.
SCHOOLER DUYN .. a dune near the village of Schoorl in north Holland..

The Jesuit as a teacher.

ISAAC JOGUES, SJ, 1646

Jogues and Bressani's eulogist, Parkman, shows that the Jesuits who came in later times had not the same apostolic simplicity.

REVEREND MEGAPOLENSIS WROTE ABOUT JOGUES ...

Afterward this same Jesuit came again from France to Canada. As our Indians had made peace with the French, he again left Canada and took up his residence among the Mohawks. He indulged in the largest expectations of converting them to popery, but the Mohawks with their hatchets, put him to a violent death. They brought and presented to me his missal and breviary together with his underclothing, shirts and coat. When I said to them, that I would not have thought that they would have killed this Frenchman, they answered, that the Jesuits did not consider the fact, that their People were always planning to kill the Dutch.
28 September 1653

Megapolensis was not a Catholic priest, therefore his consideration of Jogues was extraordinary then, when hatred and intolerance by the Protestant sects against Rome was the general rule.

The Iroquois stated, "That they had always desired to bring back Father Jogues and Father Bressani, that they thought that Father Jogues had been stolen from them ..." When Father Jogues heard this discourse, he said with a smile, "The stake was all prepared, had not God preserved me they would have put me to death a hundred times. This good man says whatever pleases him."
The Jesuit Relations
1642-46

glossary

BREVIARY ... a Catholic book containing all the daily prayers read by priests every day of their lives.
THEIR PEOPLE ... the French.

CONCLUSION

I have done my best to bring together, between the covers of one book, all the people who had traveled in upstate New York before Isaac Jogues' discovery of Lake George in 1646. It is rather surprising that there are so many -- but there must more travelers, who left a "footprint" of some type.

YOU HAVE READ MY FINDINGS AND MY CONCLUSIONS -- WHAT HAVE YOU DECIDED?

bibliography

This bibliography is extensive in order that I could fully understand the time frame and/or the situation -- there are many others sources that have not been included.

For uniformity, every word of titles and publishers are capitalized because of the varied ways they had been handled.

NAVIGATION FROM 1010 to 1646

ASHE, Geoffrey, *Land To The West, St Brendan's Voyage To America*. The Viking Press, NY, 1962
"   "   *,The Quest For Arthur's Britain*. Granada Pub, St Albans, VT.
"   "   *, The Quest For America*. Praeger Publishers, Inc, NY, 1971.
"   "   *, The Ancient Wisdom*. MacMillan, London, 1977.
BABCOCK, William, *Legendary Islands Of The Atlantic*. American Geographical Society, NY, 1922.
BAIGENT, Michael, *The Temple And The Lodge*. Arcade Publishing, NY, 1989.
BAKELESS, John, *The Eyes Of Discovery*. Dover Publications, Inc, NY, 1961.
BEAZLEY, C, *The Dawn Of Modern Geography* Vol III. The Clarendon Press, Oxford, 1906.
BOLAND, Charles, *They All Discovered America*. Doubleday, NY, 1961.
BOWDITCH, Nathaniel, *The American Pratical Navigator*. US Goverment, 1995.
COHAT, Yves, *The Vikings Lords Of The Seas*. Harry N Abrams, Inc, Publishers, NY, 1992.
DUFF, Charles, *The Truth About Columbus And The Discovery Of America*. Random House, NY, 1936.
---------, *Encyclopaedia Britannica*. William Benton Publisher, USA, 1963. "John Harrison."
FELL, Barry, *Bronze Age America*. Little, Brown And Company, Boston, 1982.
"   "   *, America BC*. Quadrangle, NY, 1977.
FISKE, John, *The Discovery Of America*. Houghton, Mifflin And Company, 1892.
GODWIN, Malcom, *The Holy Grail*. Viking Studio Books, NY, 1994.
GOODRICH, Norma, *The Holy Grail*. Harper Collins Publishers, 1992.
GOODWIN, William, *The Ruins Of Great Ireland In New England*. Meador Publishing Company, 1946.
GORDON, Cyrus, *Before Columbus*. Crown Publishers, Inc, NY, 1971.
HAPGOOD, Charles, *Maps Of The Ancient Sea Kings*. Chilton Books. 1966.
HUYGHE, Patrick, *Columbus Was Last*. Hyperion NY, 1992.
JAMESON, J & BUEL, J, *Encyclopedic Dictionary Of American Reference* Vol I, II. Library Of American History, 1901.
HEALEY, Maolan, *Irish Missionaries*. Veritas Publications, Dublin, 1983.
KEHOE, Alice, *Man Across The Sea*. U Of Texas Press, London, 1971.
KRUTA, Venceslas, *The Celts Of The West*. Orbis, London, 1985.
LANDSTROM, Bjorn, *The Ship: An Illustrated History*. Doubleday, NY, 1961.
LITTLE, George, *Brendon The Navigator*. Dublin, 1946.
MARX, Robert & Jenifer, *In Quest Of The Great White Gods*. Crown Publishers, Inc, NY.
MacLEISH, William, *The Gulf Stream*. Houghton Mifflin Company, Boston, 1989.
MERTZ, Henriette, *Pale Ink*. The Swallow Press, Inc, Chicago, 1972.
"   "   *, Atlantis*. Henriette Mertz, Chicago, 1976.
MORELAND, Carl & BANNISTER, David, *Antique Maps*. Christie's, Oxford, 1986.
MORISON, Samuel, *The European Discovery Of America*. Oxford U Press, NY, 1971.
MOWAT, Farley, *Westviking*. Little, Brown And Company, Boston, 1965.
NORDENSKJOLD, A ed, *Periplus, An Essay On The Early History Of Charts And Sailing Directions*. PA Norsted & Somer Stockholm, 1847
PHRYSIVS, Gemma, "The Maner Of Fyndynge The Longitude Of Regions By Dyvers Waves After The Descrition Of Gemma Phrysius." In, *The First Three English Books On America*. Turnball & Spears, Edinburgh, 1885.
POHL, Frederick, *The Viking Explorers*. Thomas Y Crowell Company, NY, 1966.
"   "   *, Prince Henry Sinclair*. Clarkson N Potter, Inc/Publisher, NY, 1974.
SALE, Kirkpatrick, *The Conquest Of Paradise*. Knopf, NY, 1990.
SEVERIN, Tim, *Brendan Voyage*. McGraw Hill Book Co, NY, 1978.
SHARP, J, *Discovery In The North Atlantic*. Nimbus Publishing Ltd, 1991.
SINCLAIR, Andrew, *The Sword And The Grail*. Crown Publishers, Inc, NY, 1992.
SNELL, Tee, *America's Beginnings*. National Geographic Society, 1974.
SOBEL, Dava, *Longitude*. Walker & Co, NY, 1995.
SOBEL, Dava & ANDREWS, William, *The Illustrated Longitude*. Walker & Co, NY, 1998.
STRAYER, Joseph ed, *Dictionary Of The Middle Ages*. Charles Scribner's Sons, NY, 1985.
THOMPSON, Gunnar, *American Discovery*. Argonauts Misty Isles Press, Seattle, 1994.
THORDARSON, Matthias, *The Vinland Voyages*. American Geographical Society, 1930.
THWAITES, Reuben ed, *The Jesuit Relations* Vol 1-73. Pageant Book Co, 1959.
TORNOE, J, *Early American History*. Humanities Press, NY, 1965.
TORR, Cecil, *Ancient Ships*. Cambridge U Press, Chicago, 1964.
TRENTO, Salvatore, *The Search For Lost America*. Contemporary Books, Inc, Chicago, c1974.
VEBAEK, C & THIRSLUND, Soren, *The Viking Compass Guided Norsemen First To America*. Denmark, c1992.
WATERS, David, *The Art Of Navigation In England In Elizabethan And Early Stuart Times*. Yale U Press, 1958.
WILBUR, Keith, *Early Explorers Of North America*. The Globe Pequot Press,
Chester, Conn, 1989.

periodicals
HILL, John, "Amateur Archaeologist Sets Out To Prove Celtic Monks Beat Columbus By Millenium." *Post Star*, Glens Falls, NY, Sep 1995.
LANDOW, Luanne, "Charting The Course." *Good Tidings*, Jul-Aug 1997.
MOSEMAK, Jerry, "Mirages On The Artic Horizon." *USA Today*, 3 Mar 1999.
MUSHROW, Wayne, "The Mushrow Astrolabe, 1628." One page essay, [in files of Munn Library Centre For Newfoundland Studies.]
ZIMMERMANN, Jan, "Ancient Curraghs." *Wooden Boat*, Jan 1983.
[No author cited] "Tiny Object Big Find." *Science Digest* Vol 56, Nov 1964.

1010 THORFINN KARLSEFNI

ADAM OF BREMEN, *Gesta Hammaburgensis Ecclesiae Pontificum*. Hannover, 1876.
ADIRONDACK HYDRO DEVELOPMENT CORPORATION AND DOMINION ENERGY, INC, *NYS Dam Hydroelectric Facility*. 1991.
ANDERSON, Rasmus, *Viking Tales Of The North*. Scott, Foresman And Company, Chicago, 1901.
BEERS, F, *Atlas Of Hudson River Valley Country*. Waston & Co, Troy, 1891.
BEERS, S & D, *Atlas Of Albany & Schenectady Counties*. Stone & Stewart, Philadelphia, 1866.
BOLAND, Charles, *They All Discovered America*. Doubleday, NY, 1961.
"   "   *, Terra Nova*. FW Faxon Company, Boston, 1935.
BRONDSTED, Johannes, *The Vikings*. Penguin Books, Baltimore, 1965.
BROWN, Arthur ed, *Early English And Norse Studies*. Methuen & Co Ltd, London, 1963.
BRUCE, W, *The Hudson River*. Reprint - Walking News Inc, NY, 1982.
CERAM, C, *The First American, A Story Of North American Archaeology*. Harcourt Brace Jovanovich, Inc, NY, 1971.
COHAT, Yves, *The Vikings Lords Of The Seas*. Harry N Abrams, Inc, NY, 1992.
CRONE, Gerald, *The Discovery Of America*. Waybright And Talky, NY, 1969.
DASENT, George, *A Collection Of Popular Tales From The Norse And North German*. Norroena Society, London, 1907.
De COSTA, BF, *The Northmen In Maine*. J Munsell, Albany, 1870.
"   "   *, Pre-Columbian Discovery Of America, By The Northmen*. Joel Munsell's Sons Publishers, Albany, 1890.
DENYS, Nicolas, *The Description And Natural History Of The Coast Of North America*. The Champlain Society, Toronto, 1908.
DUFF, Charles, *The Truth About Columbus And The Discovery Of America*. Random House, NY, 1936.
DUNN, Shirley, *The Mohicans And Their Land*. Purple Mountain Press, 1994.
EDWARDS, John *The Vikings And L'anse aux Meadows*. National And Historic Parks, Canada, 1971.
---------, *Encyclopedia Americana*. Grolier Incorporated, Danbury, Connecticut, 1973. "Fjord"; "Grapes".
----------, *Encyclopedia Britannica*. William Benton Publisher, USA, 1963. "Salmon and Salmonidae"; "Thorfinn Karlsefni"; "Wild Rice"; "Wineberry".
FELL, Barry, *Saga America*. Times Books, NY, 1980.
FISCHER, Joseph, *The Discoveries Of The Norsemen In America*. Henry Stevens, Son & Stiles, London, 1903.
FISKE, John, *The Discovery And Colonization Of North America*. Ginn & Company, Publishers, Boston, 1905.
---------, *The Flatey Book*. Norroena Society, 1906.
FODOR, *Canada's Maritime Provinces*. Fodor's Travel Publications, Inc, NY, 1989.
FUNK, Robert, *Recent Contributions To Hudson Valley Prehistory*. NYS Museum, 1976.
GATHORNE-HARDY, G, *The Norse Discoverers Of America*. Clarendon Press, Oxford, 1970.
GOETZMANN, William & WILLIAMS, Glyndwr, *The Atlas Of North American Exploration*. Prentice Hall General Reference, NY, 1992.
GOODWIN, William, *The Truth About Leif Ericsson And The Greenland Voyages*. Meador Publishing Company, Boston, 1941.
GORDON, Kate, *The Vikings And Their Predecessors*. National Museum Of Man, Ottawa, c1981.
GREENE, Nelson ed, *History Of The Mohawk Valley*. SJ Clarke Publishing Company, Chicago, 1925.
HALE, Edward, *The History Of The United States*. Chautauqua Press, NY, 1887.
HAUGEN, Einar, *Voyages To Vineland*. Alfred A Knopf, NY, 1942.
HILL, Ralph Nading, *Lake Champlain*. The Countryman Press, Woodstock Press, VT, 1976.
HOLAND, Hjalmar, *Norse Discoveries And Explorations In America 982-1362*. Dover Publications, Inc, NY, 1968.
"   "   *, A Pre-Columbian Crusade To America*. Twayne, NY, 1962.
"   "   *, Explorations In America Before Columbus*. Twayne Publications, Inc, NY, 1956.
"   "   *, America 1355-1364*. Duell, Sloan And Pearce, NY, 1946.
"   "   *, Westward From Vinland*. Dover Publications, 1969.
HORSFORD, Eben, *The Problem Of The Northmen*. Houghton, Mifflin, 1890.
HOVGAARD, William, *The Voyages Of The Northmen To America*. The American-Scandinavian Foundation, NY, 1914.
INGSTAD, Anne, *The Discovery Of A Norse Settlement In America* Vol I. Universitetsforlaget, Olso, 1977.
"   "   "   "   "   " [etc] Vol II. Norwegian U Press, Olso, 1985.
INGSTAD, Helge, *Westward To Vinland*. St Martin's Press, NY, 1969.
JAMES, Bartlett & JAMESON, J eds *Journal Of Jasper Danckaerts*. Barnes & Noble, Inc, NY, 1941.
JAMESON, J ed, *Narratives Of New Netherland*. Charles Scribner's Sons, NY, 1909.
JONES, Gwyn, *The Norse Atlantic Saga*. Oxford U Press, London, 1964.
"   "   *, A History Of The Vikings*. Oxford U Press, London, 1973.

La FAY, Howard, *The Vikings*. National Geographic Society, DC, 1972.
LANDSVERK, O, *Runic Records Of The Norsemen In America*. Erik J Friis, Publisher, 1974.
    "   ", *Ancient Norse Messages On Ancient Stones*. Norseman Press, Glendale, 1969.
LESCARBOT, Marc, *Nova Francia*. Harper & Brothers, NY, 1928.
LONGFELLOW, Henry, "The Skeleton In Armor." In *Journeys Through Bookland* Vol 5, Bellows-Reeve Company, Chicago, 1932.
LOSSING, Benson, *The Hudson*. Reprint - Kennikat Press, Port Washington, NY, 1972.
MAGNUSSON, Magnus, *Viking Expansion Westward*. Henry Z Walck, Inc, NY, 1973.
MALLERY, Arlington, *Lost America*. Overlook Co, Washington, 1951.
MASTEN, Arthur, *The History Of Cohoes*. Reprint - Cohoes Historical Society, 1969.
McCANN, Franklin, *English Discovery Of America To 1585*. Columbia U, NY, 1952.
MORISON, Samuel, *The European Discovery Of America*. Oxford U Press, NY, 1971.
MOWAT, Farley, *Westviking*. Little, Brown And Company, Boston, 1965.
MUNSELL, Joel, *Annals Of Albany* Vol 1, 2, 9. Munsell, Albany, 1869.
MYLOD, John, *Biograph Of A River*. Hawthorne Books, Inc Publishers, NY, 1969.
OLESON, Truyggvi, *Early Voyages And Northern Approaches*. Oxford U Press, London, 1964.
OLSON, Julius & BOURNE, Edward eds, *The Northmen, Columbus and Cabot, 985-1503*. Barnes & Noble, Inc, NY, 1906.
OXENSTIERNA, Eric, *The Norsemen*. New York Graphic Society Publishers, 1965.
PHELAN, Thomas, *Hudson Mohawk Gateway*. Window Publications, US, 1985.
POHL, Frederick, *The Viking Settlements Of North America*. Clarkson N Potter, Inc/Publisher, NY, 1966.
    "   ", *Atlantic Crossings Before Columbus*. WW Norton And Company, inc NY, 1961.
    "   ", *The Viking Explorers*. Thomas Y Crowell Company, NY, 1966.
QUINN, David ed, *North American Discovery*. U Of South Carolina Press, 1971.
REEVES, Arthur, *The Finding Of Vineland The Good*. Reprint - Burt Franklin, NY, 1967.
REMAN, Edward, *The Norse Discoveries And Explorations In America*. U Of California Press, Berkeley, 1949.
RIDPATH, John, *History Of The United States*. Grosset & Dunlap, NY, 1876.
SAGARD, Theodat, *Sagard's Long Journey To The Country Of The Hurons*. Éditions du Carrefour, 1929.
SALE, Kirkpatrick, *The Conquest Of Paradise*. Knopf, NY, 1990.
SAUM, Lewis, *The Fur Trader And The Indian*. U Of Washington Press, Seattle, 1965.
SCHOOLCRAFT, Henry, *The Indian In His Wigwam*. Derby & Hewson Publishers, Buffalo, 1848.
SHARP, J, *Discovery In The North Atlantic*. Nimbus Publishing Ltd, 1991.
SKELTON, R, *The Vineland Map And The Tartar Relation*. Yale U Press, New Haven, 1965.
SLAFTER, Edmund, *Voyages Of The Northmen To America*. Printed For The Prince Society, 1877.
SNOW, Dean, *The Archaelogy Of New England*. Academy Press, Inc, NY, 1980.
SORENSON, John & RAISH, Martin, *Pre-Columbian Contact With The Americas Across the Oceans: An Annotated Bibliography* Vol 1, 2. Research Press, Provo, Utah, 1990.
STOKES, I, *The Iconography Of Manhattan Island, 1498-1909*. Arno Press, Inc, NY, 1967.
SYLVESTER, Nathaniel, *History Of Rensselaer County*. Everts & Peck, 1880.
THAWAITES, Reuben ed, *The Jesuit Relations* Vol 1-73. Pageant Book Co, 1959.
THOMPSON, Gunnar, *American Discovery*. Argonauts Misty Isles Press, Seattle, 1994.
THORDARSON, Matthias, *The Vineland Voyages*. American Geographical Society, 1930.
TORNOE, J, *Early American History*. Humanities Press, NY, 1965.
    "   ", *Columbus In The Arctic?* Boktrykkeri, Oslo, 1965.
ULMANN, Albert, *A Landmark History Of New York*. Ira J Friedman, Inc, Port Washington, NY, 1901.
VEBAER, Carl & THIRSLUND, Soren, *The Viking Compass*. Denmark, c1992.
van der DONCK, Adriaen, *A Description Of New Netherlands*. Syracuse U Press 1968.
WAGNER, W, *Romances And Epics*. Norroena Society, London, 1907.
WAHLGREN, Erik, *The Vikings And America*. Thames And Hudson, 1986.
WEISE, Arthur, *History Of The Seventeen Towns Of Rensselaer County*. JM Francis & Tucker, Troy, 1880.
    "   ", *The City Of Troy*. Edward Green, Troy, 1886.
WILBUR, C, *Early Explorers Of North America*. The Globe Pequot Press, Chester, CN, 1989.
WILCOXEN, Charlotte, *Dutch Trade And Ceramics In America In The Seventeenth Century*. Albany Institute Of History And Art, 1987.
WILLIAMS, Stephen, *Fantastic Archeology*. U Of Pennsylvania Press, 1991.
WILSTACH, Paul, *Hudson River Landings*. Tudor Publishing Co, NY, 1933.
periodicals
ASSOCIATED PRESS, "Lost Harbor Seal Takes Spring Break In Albany." *Post Star*, Glens Falls, NY, 24 May 1996.
    "   ", "Stray Seal Found Dead In Hudson." *Post Star*, Glens Falls, NY, 28 Aug 1996.
COISH, Calvin, "Shades Of The Vikings." *The Atlantic Advocate*, Jun 1984.
CRONE, Gerald, "How Authentic Is The Vineland Map?" *Encounter*, #26, 1966.

GREENBURG, "Brigitte, Researchers: Medieval Map Shows Vikings Beat Columbus." *Post Star*, Glens Falls, NY, 14 Feb 1996.
JUNGERSEN, Kenneth, "The Search For Vineland." *Oceans*, Vol 18, Sep/Oct 1985.
KELLY, Ray. "The Spuyten Duyvil Engima." *New York Folklore Quarterly*, Winter 1960.
MACPHERSON, Alan, "Norse Lessons." *The Evening Telegram*, St John's, Newfoundland, 4 Aug 1995.
MALLERY, Arlington, "The Pre-Columbian Discovery Of America: A Reply To WS Godfrey." *American Anthropologist*, Vol 60, 1958.
MARCUS, G, "The Navigation Of The Norsemen." *Mariners' Mirror*, XXIV, May 1953.
McGHEE, Robert, "The Vikings Got Here First, But Why Did They Leave?" OLESON, Trygvi, "Polar Bears In The Middle Ages." *The Canadian Historical Review*, Vol 31, 1950.
SKELTON, R, "Vinland The Good" [a grouping of articles.] *American Heritage*, Oct 1965.
SNOW, Dean, "Martians & Vikings, Madoc & Runes." *American Heritage*, Oct 1981.
STUCKER, Kenneth, "Review Of Maps Of The Ancient Sea Kings." *Geographica! Review*, Vol 57, 1967.
WALLACE, Brigitta, "The Norse In America." [No source, no date cited] Collection of Bill Maynard, Newfoundland.
not published
DEPARTMENT OF FISHERIES AND OCEANS, Communications Branch, St John's, Newfoundland, "What Is A Whale?" c1990.
HUEY, Paul, letters from etc, in the Colonie, NY, Historian's files on, "The Flatts Archeology."
THE METROPOLITAN MUSEUM OF ART Exhibition 4 Oct 1980-4 Jan 1981 [Handout] "The Vikings."
lectures
MAYNARD, Bill. His lectures on L'Anse aux Meadow during an Elderhostel Program that he conducted at Hawkes Bay, Newfoundland during June 1997.
PARKS CANADA at L'Anse aux Meadows. Tour and lecture showing where the original buildings and smithy were, data about the reconstructed buildings and the general lay of the land. June 1997.
interviews
BENNET, Jeff, on 20 Apr 1997, regarding The Flatts. Jeff is with The Pastures, the Schuyler's Albany Mansion.
BUCKELL, Ann. Ann is a graduate of SUNY Maritime; has a limited license for Master; unlimited license for Chief Mate; and is currently sailing as a deck officer for Keystone. Ann helped with information on navigational systems.
CARLSON, Sue, Sep 1997. Sue is an authority on the Sagas and discussed: L'Anse aux Meadows, especially if Thorfinn settled there, and the Ingstads.
CHRISTMAN, Beth on 28 Jun 1998. Beth, a graduate of SUNY Maritime is a Chesapeake Bay Pilot. She discussed a possibility that there could have been a sandy island at the mouth of Chesapeake Bay. She said that, "Cape Charles and Cape Henry are very sandy and low lying -- the bay has been dredged."
HUUS, Captain Bill, on 12 Jan 1997, a Sandy Hook Pilot from 1940-77. He talked about the tides around Governor's Island, Hell Gate and general information concerning the Hudson River near Albany.
tv programs
"Himalaya" showed men spinning yak hair into yarn. BBC, aired on PBS on 26 Mar 1998.
"Lief Ericson -- Voyages" on A&E shown on 10 Oct 1995.
"Nordic Sagas" on PBS shown 21 Jan 1998.
TV 6, Schenectady, NY, Local News May 1996 at 6:30. It showed the seal that swam up to Albany -- mention was also made of a seal that had appeared at Albany some 25 years prior.
"The Voyage" of *The Matthew* replica, aired on 13 Jul 1998, PBS.
correspondence
KESSLER, Selma, Philadelphia, 23 Feb 1998. Selma sent information on why there is a statue of Thorfinn in Fairmont Park, Philadelphia. It is generally believed that this Viking was not in the area.
sites visited
Aran Island Museum to view a carraugh ... L'Anse aux Meadows, Newfoundland. St Brendan's Church, Ireland ... The Gokstad Ship Museum, Oslo, Norway.

1170 PRINCE MADOC

BOLAND, Charles, *They All Discovered America*. Doubleday, NY, 1961.
BURRAGE, Henry ed, *Early English And French Voyages, Chiefly From Haktuyt, 1534-1608*. Barnes & Noble, NY, 1953.
CARVER, J, *Travels Through The Interior Parts Of North America*. Rose & Haines, Inc, Minneapolis, 1956.
CATLIN, George, *North American Indians*. Reprint - Penguin Books, NY, 1989.
DEACON, Richard, *Madoc And The Discovery Of America*. George Braziller, NY 1966.
DELAFIELD, Julia, *Biographies Of Francis Lewis And Morgan Lewis*. [No other info cited] 1887.
DEVOTO, Bernard, *The Course Of Empire*. Houghton Mifflin Company, Boston, 1952.
------------,*Encyclopaedia Britannica*. William Benton Publisher, USA, 1963. "Albinism."
------------,*Encyclopedia Americana*. Grolier Incorporated, Danbury, Connecticut, 1973. "Francis Lewis."
FOSS, Michael, *Undreamed Shores*. Charles Scribner's Sons, NY, 1974.
HOLAND, Hjalmar, *Norse Discoveries And Explorations In America, 982-1362*. Dover Publications, Inc, NY 1969.
LOSSING, Benson, *Biographical Sketches Of The Signers Of The Declaration Of American Independence*. GF Cooledge & Brother, 1848.
LOWERY, Woodbury, *The Spanish Settlements Within The Present Limits Of The United States, 1513-1661*. GP Putnam's Sons, NY, 1991.
MORISON, Samuel, *The European Discovery Of America*. Oxford U Press, NY, 1971.

MULDOON, Paul, *Madoc A Mystery*. Farrar Straus Giroux, NY, 1991.
PUGH, Ellen, *Brave His Soul*. Eyre Methuen, 1970.
SAUM, Lewis, *The Fur Trader And The Indian*. U Of Washington Press, Seattle, 1965.
SCHOOLCRAFT, Henry, *History Of The Indian Tribes Of The United States*. JP Lippincott & Co, 1857.
SCUDIERE, Paul, *New York's Signers Of The Declaration Of Independence*. NYS American Revolution Bicentennial Commission, Albany, 1975.
SNYDER, Charles, *Buckskin To Bustles*. Ira T Freidman Inc, Port Washington, NY, 1968.
THOMPSON, Gunnar, *American Discovery*. Argonauts Misty Isles Press, Seattle, 1994.
WEISE, Arthur, *The Discoveries Of America To The Year 1525*. GP Putnam's Sons, NY, 1884.
WILLIAMS, Gwyn, *Madoc: The Making Of A Myth*. Eyre Methuen, 1979.
WINSOR, Justin, *Narrative And Critical History Of America* Vol IV. Houghton, Mifflin And Company, Cambridge, 1889.

periodicals
BURDER, George, "The Welch Indians Or A Collection Of Papers Respecting A People Whose Ancestors Emigrated From Wales To America, In The Year 1170, With Prince Madoc." Reprint - William Abbott, 1922.
BUTTERFIELD, Roger, "They Signed Away Their Lives For You." *Saturday Evening Post*, 5 Jul 1947.
DAVIES, Arthur, "Prince Madoc And The Discovery Of America In 1477." *The Geographical Journal*, Vol 150, 1984.
NATIONAL GEOGRAPHIC, folded *Map* Vol 193, Feb 1998.
NEWMAN, Marshall, "The Blond Mandan." *Southwestern Journal Of Anthropology* Vol 6, 1950.
WILLIAMS, Gwyn, "Frontier Of Illusion: The Welsh And The Atlantic Revolution." *History Today*, #30,1980.

not published
SMITH, Elizabeth, "Francis Lewis Files" of the Smith Collection Supplement in the NY Historical Society, NYC. Some handwritten pages that probably were compiled by Elizabeth Smith, a descendant of Lewis, and agree with Julia Delafield's book.

1520 POMPEY STONE

BOURNE, Edward, *Spain In America*. Harper & Brothers Publishers, NY, 1906.
CLARK, Joshua, *Onondaga* Vol II. Stoddard And Babcock, Syracuse, 1849.
CLARKE, John, *Life Of James Hall*. Albany, 1923.
COFFIN, Margaret, *Death In Early America*. Elsevier/Nelson Books, NY, 1976.
------------*Encyclopedia Americana* (Grolier Incorporated, Danbury, Connecticut), 1973. "Cardiff Giant"; "Martin Luther"; "Beauchamp."
FELL, Barry, *Saga America*. Times Books, NY, 1980.
FITCH, Asa, *Historical, Topographical And Agricultural Survey Of The County Of Washington*. NY State Agricultural Society, 1849.
FRANCO, Barbara, *The Cardiff Giant*. The NYS Historical Association, Cooperstown, NY, 1990.
HOMES, Henry, *The Pompey Stone*. Ellis H Roberts & Co, Utica, 1881.
JAMESON, J & BUEL, J, *Encyclopedic Dictionary Of American Reference* Vol I, II. Library Of American History, 1901.
LEPPER, Bradley, "Just How Holy Are The Newark 'Holy Stones' ." In *Vanishing Heritage*, Hooge & Lepper eds, The Licking County Archaeology And Landmarks Society, 1992.
LOSSING, Benson, *A Pictorial History Of The United States*. Belknap, NY, 1867.
LOWERY, Woodbury, *The Spanish Settlements*. GP Putnam's Sons, NY, 1911.
MUNSELL, J, *Albany Directory For 1854*. J Munsell, Albany, 1854.
RUTTENBER, E, *The History Of Indian Tribes Of Hudson's River*. Hope Farm Press, 1992.
SCHOOLCRAFT, Henry, *Notes On The Iroquois*. Bartlett & Welford, NY, 1846.
"   "   "   "   "   "   Ernstus Pense & Co, Albany, 1847.
"   "   *, Senate Report Of New York No 24, In Senate, 1846*. [No publication info cited.]
"   "   *, History Of The Indian Tribes Of The United States*. JB Lippincott & Co, 1857.
VENERABLES, Robert, *The Six Nations Of New York*. Cornell U Press, Utica, 1995.

periodicals
ONONDAGA COUNTY LIBRARY, Syracuse; Local History, Special Collections' files, especially ...
- CANE, Richard, "Rubbing Uncovers Truth." [No newspaper cited, not dated.]
"   "   *, "How Far Can Historical Jokes Go?"* [No newspaper cited] 26 Mar 1961.
"   "   *, "Hoax May Return."* [No newspaper cited] 18[?] Mar 1976.
ONONDAGA HISTORICAL SOCIETY, Syracuse; files, especially ...
- BEAUCHAMP, Rev, "The Pompey Stone." *The Journal [Syracuse Daily Journal?]* [not dated.]
- HOLMES, Dr, "The Pompey Stone." *The Journal*, 12 & 14 Nov 1879.
- SHEPPARD, R, "Yankee Diddle Dandy." *Time*, 10 Nov 1997.
- SPICHIGER, Lynne, "The Pompey Stone." [No source cited, not dated.]
- SWEET, John, "The Pompey Stone." *The Syracuse Daily Journal*, 11 Jun 1894.
- [No author cited] "Oneida Historical Society." *Utica Morning Herald*, 19 Nov 1879.
- "   "   "   "The Onondaga Stone." [Originally in *World* - picked up by an unknown newspaper] 25 Mar 1865.

not published
BEAUCHAMP, William, "The Antiquities Of Onondaga, First Series, 1879." NYS Library; Manuscripts and Special Collections; and his diary contained on reel #29.
PARKER, Arthur, Letter To Dr John Clarke, 4 May 1909, stating that the stone is a hoax. NYS Museum Files, courtesy of Lisa Anderson.
POMPEY HISTORICAL SOCIETY, "The Pompey Stone" handout.

---

interviews
ANDERSON, Lisa, NYS Museum. Visited her office during June 1997, to check her files. She said that Schoolcraft is still considered an authority; and that the stone is on loan to a local historical society. She had never thought about its being the oldest hoax in the state, or in the country.
CHRISTOPH, Peter, Selkirk, NY, New Netherland Project. Called him on 16 Jul 1997 and he knew of the stone. Yes, it probably is the oldest hoax.
COFFIN, Margaret, author of *Death In Early America*. On 17 Oct 1997, she said that, "Type in a book would not be the same as that carved on a stone; a capital L would not necessarily have to slope forward; and that numbers could be set within an imaginary line."
GROFF, Tammis, Albany Institute Of History And Art, called her on 15 Feb 1997. She had never seen it, heard of it, nor had a file on it. The Institute has no paper memory of ever having displayed the stone for some 30 years.
HAVER, Judy, Librarian of the Onondaga Historical Association. On 6 Mar 1997, she suggested contacting the NYS Museum.
NYS HISTORICAL ASSOCIATION, Cooperstown, 1997, asking them if the stone is the oldest hoax in the state, or in the country. They had never thought about this angle.
OLCOTT, Robert, Albany Academy Historian. Called him on 11 Feb 1997, as Barry Fell had written that the stone was the property of the Boy's Academy. He had never heard of it.
SHULERIDGE, Sylvia, of the Pompey Historical Society, Oct 1997. She had not seen any transfer papers between the Albany Institute, the Pompey Historical and NYS Museum.

1568 DAVID INGRAM

ADAMS, Charles, *Guide To The Manuscript Materials For The History Of The United States To 1783*. The Carnegie Institution Of Washington, 1908.
ADAMS, Percy, *Travelers And Travel Liars*. U Of California Press, Berkley, 1962.
ANDREWS, K ed, *The Westward Enterprise*. Liverpool U Press, 1978.
ASHLEY, Roscoe, *American History*. The Macmillan Co, NY, 1907.
AXTELL, James, *Beyond 1492*. Oxford U Press, NY, 1992.
BAGROW, L, *Imago Mundi*. Mouton & Co, Gravenhage, 1960.
BAKELESS, John, *The Eyes Of Discovery*. Dover Publications, Inc, NY, 1961.
BARDEN, Renardo, *Great Mysteries, The Discovery Of America*. Greenhaven Press, Inc, San Diego, 1989.
BEAUCHAMP, William, *Onondaga* Bulletin 108, Albany, 1907.
"   "   *, The Iroquois Trail* HC Beauchamp, Fayetteville, NY, 1892.
"   "   *, Notes On David Cusick's Sketches Of Ancient History Of The Six Nations*. WM Beauchamp, Baldwinsville, NY, 1892.
"   "   *, Indian Names In New York*. HC Beauchamp, Fayetteville, NY, 1893.
BIGGAR, Henry, *The Early Trading Companies Of New France*. U Of Toronto Library, 1901.
"   "   *, The Voyages Of Jacques Cartier*. U Of Toronto Press, 1993.
BLAKE, William, *The History Of Putnam County, NY*. Baker & Scribner, 1849.
BOLTON, Charles, *Terra Nova*. FW Faxon Company, Boston, 1935.
BOLTON, Reginald, *Indian Life Of Long Ago In The City Of New York*. Harmony Books, 1972.
BRANDOW, John, *The Story Of Old Saratoga*. Fort Orange Press, Albany, 1900.
BREBNER, John, *The Explorers Of North America*. The World Publishing Company, Cleveland, 1917.
"   "   *, Canada*. U Of Michigan Press, Ann Arbor, 1970.
BROUGHTON, John, *Geology And Mineral Resources Of The Middle And Lower Hudson River Valley*. Hudson River Valley Commission, 1966.
BROWN, George ed, *Dictionary Of Canadian Biography*. U Of Toronto Press, 1966.
BROWNE, George, *The St Lawrence River*. Putnam's Sons, NY, 1905.
BULL, John & FARR, John, *The Audubon Society Field Guide To North American Birds*. Alfred Knopf, NY, 1977.
BURRAGE, Henry ed, *Early English And French Voyages, Chiefly From Hakluyt*. Reprint - Barnes & Noble, Inc, 1953.
CAMPBELL, Richard, *The People Of The Land Of The Flint*. U Press Of America, NY, 1985.
CARTIER, Jacques, *The Voyages Of Jacques Cartier*. U Of Toronto Press, 1993.
CARVER, J, *Travels Through The Interior Parts Of North America*. Reprint - Ross & Haines, Inc, Minneapolis, 1956.
CATLIN, George, *North American Indians*. Reprint - Penguin Books, NY, 1989.
CHATTERTON, E, *English Seamen And The Colonization Of America*. Arrowsmith, London, 1967.
CLINTON COUNTY HISTORICAL MUSEUM, *The Original People, Native Americans In The Champlain Valley*. Plattsburgh, 1988.
COE, Michael, SNOW, Dean, BENSON, Elizabeth, *Atlas Of Ancient America*. Facts On File Publications, NY, 1986.
COHEN, David, *Mysteries Of The World*. Doubleday & Co Inc, Garden City, NY, 1979.
COLDEN, Cadwallader, *The History Of The Five Indian Nations* Vol I. New Amsterdam Book Company Publishers, NY, 1902.
CONVERSE, Harriet, *Myths And Legends Of The New York Iroquois*. The State Education Department, Albany, 1974.
CORWIN, Edward, HASTINGS, Hugh, HOLDEN, James, *Ecclesiastical Records, State Of New York*. JB Lyon, Albany, 1901-1916.
CRICK, B & ALMON, Mirriam, *Guide To Manuscripts Relating To America In Great Britain And Ireland*. Oxford U Press, 1961.
CROWELL, Marnie, *North To The Saint Lawrence*. Raquette Press, Canton, NY, 1975.
CUMMING, W, SKELTON, R, QUINN, D, *Discovery Of North America*. American Heritage Press, NY,1972.
CYR, Donald, *King Arthur's Crystal Cave*. Stonehenge Viewpoint, Santa Barbara, CA, 1997.

181

DeBRY, Theodore, *Discovering The New World*. Harper & Row, Publishers, NY, 1976.

De COSTA, Benjamin, *The Pre Colombian Discovery Of America By The Norsemen*. Joel Munsell's Sons, Publishers, Albany, 1890.

" ", "Norumbega And Its English Explorers." In *Narrative And Critical History Of America* Vol III, Justin Winsor, Houghton, Mifflin And Company, Boston, 1884.

DeGOLYER, E, *The Journey Of Three Englishmen Across Texas In 1568*. The Peripatetic Press, El Paso, 1947.

deLAHONTAN, Baron, *New Voyages To North America* Vol I. A McClurg & Co., Chicago, 1905.

DENTON, Daniel, *A Brief Description Of New York*. Reprint - U Microfilms, Ann Arbor, 1967.

DENYS, Nichols, *The Description And Natural History Of The Coasts Of North America*. The Champlain Society, Toronto, 1908.

DOCKSTADER, Frederick, *The American Indian In Graduate Studies, A Bibliography Of Theses And Dissertations*. Museum Of The American Indian, NY, 1957.

DONOHUE, Thomas, *The Iroquois And The Jesuits*. Buffalo Catholic Publication, 1895.

DOUGLAS, David, *The Trade Of Bristol* Vol 20. JW Arrowsmith, Ltd, Bristol, 1957.

DUFF, Charles, *The Truth About Columbus And The Discovery Of America*. Random House, NY, 1936.

EDEN, Richard, *The First Three English Books On America*. Turnball & Spears, Edinburgh,1885.

EGGLESTON, Edward, *The Beginners Of A Nation*. D Appleton And Company, NY, 1897.

ELTING, Mary & FOLSON, Michael, *The Mysterious Grain - Science In Search Of The Origin Of Corn*. Evans & Co, NY, 1967.

----------, *Encyclopaedia Britannica*. William Benton Publisher, USA, 1963. "Alabama"; "Banana"; "Cotton"; " Creek [Nation]"; "Florida"; "Greensand"; "Sir John Hawkins"; "Garnet"; "Marl"; "Musk Ox"; "Roc"; "Ruby"; "Sassafras"; "Spicebush"; "Willow."

----------,*Encyclopedia Americana*. Grolier Incorporated, Danbury, Connecticut, 1973. "Alabama"; "Aspirin"; "Mammoth"; "Marl"; "Musk Ox."

FIELD, Thomas, *An Essay Towards An Indian Bibliography*. Scribner, Armstrong, And Co, NY, 1873.

FISKE, John, *The Dutch And Quaker Colonies In America* Vol I. Houghton Mifflin Company, Boston, 1899.

FLICK, Alexander, *History Of The State Of New York* Vol I. Columbia U Press, 1933.

FOSS, Michael, *Undreamed Shores*. Charles Scribner's Sons, NY, 1974.

FULOP-MILLER, Rene, *The Power And Secret Of The Jesuits*. The Viking Press, NY, 1930.

FUNK, Robert, *Report On Archeological Resource For Hudson River Valley Commission*. Hudson River Valley Commission, 1966.

" " , *Recent Contributions to Hudson Valley Prehistory*. NYS Museum, 1976.

GALVANO, Antonie, *The Discoveries Of The World*. London, 1601. Reprint - Da Capo Press, Amsterdam,1969.

GANONG, W, *Crucial Maps In The Early Cartography And Place Nomenclature Of The Atlantic Coast Of Canada*. U Of Toronto Press, 1964.

GOETZMANN, William & WILLIAMS, Glyndwr, *The Atlas Of North American Exploration*. Prentice Hall General Reference, NY, 1992.

GOODWIN, William, *The Truth About Leif Ericsson And The Greenland Voyages*. Meador Publishing Company, Boston, 1941.

GORDON, Cyrus, *Before Columbus*. Crown Publishers, Inc, NY, 1971.

GOSS, John, *The Mapping Of America*. The Wellfleet Press, Secaucus, NJ, 1990.

GOVERNMENT OF NEWFOUNDLAND AND LABRADOR, *A Self Driving Guide, Sea Birds And Major Sea Bird Colonies Of Newfoundland And Labrador*. St John's, Newfoundland, [not dated.]

GRANT, Bruce, *Concise Encyclopedia Of The American Indian*. Wings Books, NY, 1960.

GRANT, John, *Monster Mysteries*. Chartwell Books, Inc, Secaucus, NJ, 1992.

GRASSMANN, Thomas, *The Mohawk Indians And Their Valley*. Eric Hugo, Schenectady, 1969.

GREENE, Nelson ed, *History Of The Mohawk Valley*. SJ Clarke Publishing Company, Chicago, 1925.

GRIDLEY, Marion, *Indian Tribes Of America*. Rand McNally & Co, NY, 1973. *The Principal Navigations, Voyages And Discoveries Of The English Nation Made By Sea Or Over Land, To The Most Remote And Farthest Distant Quarter Of The Earth At Any Time Within The Compasse Of These 1500 Years*. Reprint - University Microfilms Inc, Ann Arbor.

HALSEY, Francis, *The Old New York Frontier*. Scribner, 1901.

HAND, Richard, *A Bookman's Guide To The Indians Of The Americas*. The Scarecrow Press, Inc, Metuchen, NJ, 1989.

HARRISSE, Henry, *The Discovery Of North America*. Reprint - N Israel, Amsterdam, 1961.

" " , *John Cabot, The Discoverer Of North America And Sebastian His Son*. Reprint - Argosy Antiquarian Ltd, 1968.

HODGE, Frederick ed, *Handbook Of American Indians North Of Mexico* Part 2. Smithsonian Institute, Washington, 1910.

HOFFMAN, Bernard, *Cabot To Cartier*. U Of Toronto Press, 1961.

HOGG, Garry, *Cannibalism And Human Sacrifice*. The Citadel Press, NY, 1966.

HORSFORD, Eben, *The Problem Of The Norsemen*. Houghton, Mifflin, 1890.

" , *Discovery Of The Ancient City Of Norumbega*. 1890.

HOWORTH, Henry, *The Mammoth And The Flood*. Sampson Low, Marston, Searle, & Rivington, London, 1887.

HUDSON, Henry, *Henry Hudson The Navigator*. Reprint - Burt Franklin, Publisher, NY, 1963.

HUDSON RIVER VALLEY COMMISSION, *The Hudson Mineral Resources*. State Of NY, 1966.

HUMBLE, Richard, *The Voyages Of Jacques Cartier*. Franklin Watts, NY, 1992.

INGRAM, David, *The Relation Of David Ingram*. Reprint - U Microfilms, 1966.

JAMES, Bartlett ed, *Journal Of Jasper Danckerts*. Barnes & Noble, Inc, 1941.

JAMESON, J ed, *Early English And French Voyages, Chiefly From Hakluyt*. Barnes & Noble, 1906.

" , *Narratives Of New Netherland*. Charles Scribner's Sons, NY, 1909.

JAMESON, J & BUEL, J, *Encyclopedic Dictionary Of American Reference* Vol I, II. Library Of American History, 1901.

JANVIER, Thomas, *The Dutch Founding Of New York*. Reprint - Ira J Friedman, Inc, Port Washington, NY, 1967.

" " , *Henry Hudson*. Harper And Brothers Publishers, NY, 1909.

JENKINS, Stephen, *The Greatest Street In The World*. GP Putnam's Sons, NY, 1911.

JOHNSON, Allen ed, *Dictionary Of American Biography*. U Of Toronto Press, 1966.

JOHNSON, Donald, *Charting The Sea Of Darkness*. International Marine, Camden, Maine, 1993.

JOHNSTON, Charles, *Famous Discoverers & Explorers Of America*. The Page Co, Boston, 1917.

KAMMEN, Michael, *Colonial New York*. Charles Scribner's Sons, NY, 1975.

KENNY, Alice, *Stubborn for Liberty*. Syracuse U Press, 1975.

LAMB, Martha, *History Of The City Of New York*. AS Barnes And Company, NY, 1877.

LAMB, Wallace, *New York State And Its Communities*. American Book Company, NY, 1942.

LEACOCK, Stephen, *The Dawn Of Canadian History*. Glasgow, Brook & Company, 1914.

LEHNER, Ernst & Johanna, *How They Saw The New World*. Tudor Publishing Company, NY, 1966.

LESCARBOT, Marc, *Nova Francia*. Harper & Brothers, NY, 1928.

LISTER, Adrian & BAHN, Paul, *Mammoths*. Macmillan, USA, 1994.

LORANT, Stefan ed, *The New World, The First Pictures Of America*. Duell, Sloan & Pearce, NY, 1946.

LOSSING, Benson, *A Pictorial History Of The United States*. Belknap, NY, 1867.

LYMAN, Kennie ed, *Gems And Precious Stones*. Simon & Schuster Inc, NY, 1986.

MacCRACKEN, Henry, *Old Dutchess Forever*. Hastings House, NY, 1956.

MACGOWAN, Kenneth & HESTER, Joseph, *Early Man In The New World*. Doubleday & Company, Inc, Garden City, 1962.

MACKENZIE, J, *The Six-Nations Indians*. The Hunter, Rose Company, Ltd, Toronto, 1896.

MALLERY, Arlington, *Lost America*. The Overlook Company, Washington DC, 1951.

MARKHAM, Clements ed, *The Hawkins' Voyage*. Reprint - Burt Franklin, Publisher, NY, 1963.

McCANN, Franklin, *English Discovery Of America*. Columbia U, NY, 1952.

McCONNIFF, John, *Illustrated Montreal*. John McConniff, Montreal, 1893.

McENANY, John, *Albany Capital City On The Hudson*. Windsor Publications, 1981.

McGANN, Franklin, *English Discovery Of America To 1585*. King's Crown Press, Columbia U, NY, 1952.

MERTZ, Henriette, *Pale Ink*. Swallow Press, Inc., Chicago, 1972.

" " , *Atlantis Dwelling Place Of The Gods*. Henriette Mertz, Chicago, 1976.

MIRSKY, Jeannette, *The Westward Crossings*. The U Of Chicago Press, 1970.

MITCHELL, Lucy & LAMBERT, Clara, *Manhattan: Now And Long Ago*. The Macmillan Company, NY, 1934.

MORELAND, Carl & BANNISTER, David, *Antique Maps*. Christie's, Oxford, 1986.

MORGAN, Lewis, *League Of The Ho-De'-No-Sau-Nee Or Iroquois* 2 Vols. Reprint - Burt Franklin, NY, 1967.

MORISON, Samuel, *Portuguese Voyages To America In The Fifteenth Century*. Octogon Books, Inc, NY, 1965.

" " , *The European Discovery Of America*. Oxford U Press, NY, 1971.

" " , *Samuel Champlain*. Little, Brown And Company, Boston, 1972.

MUIR, John, *A Thousand-Mile Walk To The Gulf*. Houghton Mifflin Company, Boston, 1981.

MUNSELL, Joel, *The Annals Of Albany* Vol 9. Joel Munsell, Albany, 1869.

NATIONAL GEOGRAPHIC SOCIETY, *The World Of The American Indian*. 1989.

NEWLAND, D, *Guide To The Geology Of The Lake George Region*. The U Of The State Of NY, 1942.

NICHOLS, Frances, *Index To Schoolcraft's "Indian Tribes Of The United States."* US Government Printing Office, Washington, 1954.

O'CALLAGHAN, E, *The Documentary History Of New York*. Weed. Parsons, & Co, Public Printers, Albany, 1850.

OLESON, Truyggvi, *Early Voyages And Northern Approaches*. Oxford U Press, London, 1964.

OVERTON, Jacqueline, *Long Island's Story*. Doubleday Doran & Company, Garden City, 1929.

PADOVER, Saul, *The Complete Jefferson*. Books For Libraries, NY, 1943.

PARKER, William, *Letters Of Thomas Jefferson*. NY, 1905.

PARKMAN, Francis, *Pioneers Of France In The New World*. Little, Brown & Company, 1905.

" " , *The Old Regime In Canada* Vol I. Little, Brown, And Company, Boston, 1902.

PELLETREAU, William, *History Of Putnam County*. WW Preston & Co, Philadelphia, 1886.

POAST, Florence, *Indian Names Facts And Games*. Thomsen-Bryan-Ellis Co, Washington, 1917.

POHL, Frederick, *Atlantic Crossings Before Columbus*. WW Norton & Company, Inc, NY, 1961.

" " , *Prince Henry Sinclair*. Clarkson N Potter, Inc/Publisher, NY, 1974.

182

"   ", *The Viking Settlements Of North America.* Clarkson N Potter, Inc/Publisher, NY, 1966.

PUTNAM COUNTY WORKSHOP, *History Workshop.* 1954.

QUINN, David ed, *North American Discovery.* U Of South Carolina Press, 1971.

"   ", *The Hakluyt Handbook* Vol I,II. The Hakluyt Society, London, 1974.

"   ", *England And The Discovery Of America.* Alfred Knopf, NY,1974.

RIDPATH, John, *History Of The United States.* Grosset & Dunlap, NY, 1876.

RINK, Oliver, *Holland On The Hudson.* Cornell U Press, Ithaca, 1986.

RISTOW, Walter & SKELTON, R, *Nautical Charts On Vellum In The Library Of Congress.* US Government Printing Office, 1971.

RITCHIE, Wm, *Aboriginal Settlement Patterns In The Northeast.* NYS Museum, 1973.

RUEDEMANN, Rudolf, *Hudson River Beds Near Albany.* U Of The State Of NY, Albany, 1901.

RUTTENBER, E, *The History Of Indian Tribes Of Hudson's River.* Hope Farm Press, 1992.

SAGAN, Eli, *Cannibalism.* Harper & Row, Publishers, NY, 1974.

SAGARD, Gabriel, *Sagard's Long Journey To The Country Of The Hurons.* Reprint - Greenwood Press, NY, 1968.

SALE, Kirkpatrick, *The Conquest Of Paradise.* Knopf, NY, 1990.

SCHOOLCRAFT, Henry, *The Indian In His Wigwam.* Derby & Hewson Publishers, Buffalo, 1848.

"   ", *Notes On The Iroquois.* Bartlett & Welford, NY, 1846.

"   ", *Memoirs Of HR Schoolcraft.* Philadelphia, c1851.

"   ", *History Of The Indian Tribes Of The United States.* JB Lippincott & Co, 1857.

SHAKESPEARE, William, *The Tempest.* In *Journeys Through Bookland* Vol VIII, Bellows-Reeve Co, Chicago, 1932.

SHARP, J, *Discovery In The North Atlantic.* Nimbus Publishing Ltd, 1991.

SIMMS, Jeptha, *History Of Schoharie County.* Munsell & Tanne Publishers, 1845.

SKINNER, Alanson, *The Indians Of Greater New York.* The Torch Press, Cedar Rapids, 1915.

"   ", *Indian Notes And Monographs.* Museum Of The American Indian, NY, 1921.

SMITH, William, *The History Of The Province Of New York.* Harvard U Press, 1972.

SNOW, Dean, *The Archaeology Of New England.* Academic Press, Inc, NY, 1980.

SPECK, Frank, *The Iroquois.* Cranbrook Institute Of Science, Bloomfield Hills, Michigan, 1960.

STONE, William, *Reminiscences Of Saratoga.* Virtue & Yorston, NY, 1875.

BUODD, Robert, *The Archaeology Of New York.* Thomas Crowell Co, NY, 1966

STUHVESAM, Joan, *History Of New York* Vol I. Lewis Historical Publishing Company, Inc, NY, 1927.

SYLVESTER, Nathaniel, *Northern New York.* Reprint - Harbor Hill Books, Harrison, NY, 1973.

THATCHER, B, *Indian Traits.* Harper & Brothers, NY, 1836.

"   ", *Indian Biography* Vol I, II. Harper & Brothers, Publishers, NY, 1869.

THOMPSON, Gunnar, *American Discovery.* Argonauts Misty Isles, Seattle, 1994.

THWAITES, Reuben ed, *The Jesuit Relations* Vol 1-73. Pageant Book Co, 1959.

TRELEASE, Allen, *Indian Affairs In Colonial New York: In The Seventeenth Century.* Kennikat Press, Port Washington, NY, 1960.

TRENTO, Salvatore, *The Search For Lost America.* Contemporary Books, Inc, Chicago, c1974.

TRUDEL, Marcel, *The Beginnings Of New France.* McClelland And Stewart, 1973.

TURCO, Peggy, *Walks And Rambles In Dutchess And Putnam Counties.* The Countryman Press, Woodstock, VT, c1996.

UNIWIN, Rayner, *The Defeat Of John Hawkins.* The Macmillan Co, NY, 1960.

VanDIVER, Bradford, *Rocks And Routes Of The North Country.* WF Humphrey Press Inc, Geneva, NY 1976.

WALDMAN, Carl, *Atlas Of The North American Indian.* Facts On File, NY, 1985.

WARD, Christopher, *The Dutch And Swedes On The Delaware.* U Of Pennsylvania Press, 1930.

WEISE, Arthur, *The Discoveries Of America To The Year 1525.* GP Putnam's Sons, NY, 1884.

WESTON, Plowden ed, *Documents Connected With The History Of South Carolina.* London, 1856.

WHITEHEAD, Ruth, *The Old Man Told Us.* Nimbus Publishing Ltd., 1991.

WILLIAMS, Sherman, *New York's Part In History.* D Appleton And Company, NY, 1915

WILLIAMSON, James, *Hawkins Of Plymouth.* Barnes & Noble, Inc, NY, 1969.

WILSON, Ian, *The Columbus Myth.* Simon & Schuster, London, 1991.

WILSON, James ed, *The Memorial History Of The City Of New York* Vol I. NY History Company, NY,1892.

WILSTACH, Paul, *Hudson River Landings.* Tudor Publishing Co, NY, 1933.

WINSOR, Justin, *Geographical Discovery In The Interior Of North America.* Houghton, Mifflin And Company, Boston, 1894.

"   ", *Narrative And Critical History Of America* Vol I. Houghton, Mifflin And Company, Cambridge, 1889.

WISSLER, Clark, *Indians Of The United States.* Doubleday & Company, Inc, Garden City, NY, 1948.

WOLFE, Art, *Penguins, Puffins, And Auks: Their Lives And Behavior.* Crown Publishing Group, NY, 1993.

WRIGHT, Louis & FOWLER, Elaine eds, *West And By North.* Delacorte Press, NY, 1971.

periodicals

ATHINEOS, Doris & ALSOP, Eliza, " Crystal Rocks." *Traditional Home,* May 1999.

AXTELL, James, "Who Invented Scalping?" *American Heritage,* Apr 1977.

CARACI, Roma, "The Reputed Inclusion Of Florida In The Oldest Maps Of The New World." *Image Mundi,* Vol 15.

CARSON, Sue, "Letter To The Editor - Etymology Of Norumbega." *NEARA Journal,* Vol XXXI #1, Summer 1997.

DOLD, Catherine, "The Corn War." *Discover,* Dec 1997.

EISELEY, Loren, "The Mastodon And Early Man In America." *Science,* Vol 102, 1945.

ELIOT, John, "Polar Bears Stalkers Of The High Arctic." *National Geographic,* Jan 1998.

GUTHRIE, James & McGLONE, William, "Fantastic Scholarship, A Comment On Stephen Williams And Fantastic Archaeology." *NEARA Journal,* Vol 3 & 4, Winter/Spring, 1992.

HALL, Robert, "The Etymology Of Norumbega." *NEARA Journal,* Vol XXX, 3 & 4, Winter/Spring, 1996/7.

HOOPER, F, "Rocks And Minerals Of The Adirondacks." *Top Of The World News,* Lake George, NY, Nov 1938.

JAMIESON, Paul, "First White Man." *The Quarterly,* Vol 13-15, 1968-1970.

MENON, Shanti, "This Not So Dumb Englishman." *Discover,* Jan 1997.

MURPHY, Reg, "The Easy Way Of The Altamaha." *National Geographic,* Jan 1998.

OGBURN, Charlton, "The Longest Walk; David Ingram's Amazing Journey." *American Heritage,* April/May 1979.

OLESON, Truyggvi, "Polar Bears In The Middle Ages." *The Canadian Historical Review,* Vol 31, 1950.

PATTON, Joan, "Former Garnet Mine Started By Colorful Characters." *Post Star,* Glens Falls, NY, 12 May, 1991.

PLEASANT, Jane, "The Iroquois Sustainers." *Northeast Indian Quarterly,* Spring/Summer 1989.

SCHUMACHER, Muriel, "Manufacturing And Industry In Rensselaerswyck." *The Dutch Settlers Society Of Albany,* Vol 37, 1962-3.

TIPPETTS, W, "Northern New York State Mines." *Lake George Mirror,* Lake George, NY, 1 Oct 1898.

"   ", "Graphite, Garnet And Mica All found In Paying Quantities In Warren County." *The NewYork Sun,* 3 Jan 1890.

[no author cited]"The Spanish Plymouth Rock." *Discover,* Jan 1994.

"   " "The Product Of Genius." *Warrensburgh News,* 12 Jan 1893.

"   " "Towers Of Tufa." *Discover,* Mar 1998.

"   " "Armillary Spheres." *Antiques Journal,* Mar 1996.

"   " "Founders Of New England." *National Geographic,* Jun 1953.

"   " "Commanded By An Expert." *Warrensburgh News,* 26 Jan 1893.

"   " "Ruby Crystals." *House Of Onyx,* Vol 239.

"   " "Portuguese Dispute Cabot Discovery." *Evening Telegram,* St John's, Newfoundland, Vol 116, 17 Feb 1995.

not published

SABAL'S CASSAVA FOOD PRODUCTS, "Cassava" script Dumpligan Town, Belize.

interviews

BAKER, Rebecca, The House of Onyx, Inc, Greenville, KY. On 13 Jan 1994, Rebecca said that rubies are still found in North Carolina. A 2"x 4" stone, found today, would not be of a good gem quality, but would be a cabochon stone. *Star Of India* garnets can weigh up to a pound.

BECKLER, Ed, Natural Stone Bridge And Caves, Pottersville, NY, on 1 Jul 1997. He felt that at that size the stone would be a garnet. Stones have been picked up by people just walking.

HAMIL, George, NYS Museum, 7 Jul 1997. He thought that the white substance that was burned probably was marl. When vegetation builds up in a peat bog -- lime secreting organisms build up a lens under the peat to form a precipitate of calcium carbinate. Tufa, on the other hand, would be found in a clear spring, or a stream, with a high lime content. He had never heard of a white earth substance that was used by the Indians.

HAWKIN, Michael, NYS Museum, 1 Jul 1997. Very unlikely that the stone would be a ruby. There are no workable ruby deposits *today* and the North Carolina mine is very inaccessible. He felt that a garnet would be the best bet.

La ROSE, Gail, Feulier Museum of Natural History, Granville, NY during Feb 1999. Discussed that Carolina parakeets would flash green when flying and that the color of passenger pigeons would be gray, like a mourning dove; and that they were both numerous. Gail could not think of any bird that would fit "russet parrots."

WOLFERS, Harvey, geologist, Hudson Falls, Apr 1994. Discussed iron carbide, calcium, acetelyne and crushed limestone as possibilities of "sweet turf to burn." He suggested calling the NYS Museum.

tv programs

"Mammoths Of The Ice Age" *Nova,* aired on PBS, 28 Dec 1997.

"Richard Wheeler Traces The Migration Of The Now Extinct Great Auk" *Nova* aired on PBS, 25 Oct 1994.

The Frugal Gourmet, cooked and discussed plantain, on PBS, 17 Feb 1997.

correspondence

NATIONAL GEOGRAPHIC SOCIETY, 8 Feb 1995, had no information regarding Ingram in their book, *The World Of The American Indian.*

FISH AND FUR

The bibliography for FISH AND FUR, before 1609, and DUTCH FUR, have been combined because much of the source material is intertwined.

ANDREWS, K ed, *The Westward Enterprise.* Liverpool U Press, 1978.

ANSON, Peter, *Mariners Of Brittany.* JM Dent And Sons Ltd, NY, 1931.

BACON, Edgar, *The Hudson River From Ocean To Source.* GP Putnam's Sons, 1902.

BAKELESS, John, *The Eyes Of Discovery.* Dover Publications, Inc, NY, 1961.

BALCOM, B, *The Cod Fishery Of Isle Royale, 1713-58.* National Historic Parks And Sites Branch, Canada, 1984.

BARKHAM, Michael, "French Basque 'New Found Land' Entrepreneurs ..." In *Newfoundland Studies,* 1994.

BARKHAM, Selma, *The Basque Coast Of Newfoundland.* Great Northern Peninsula Development Corporation, 1989.

BARRETT, William, *The History And Antiquities Of The City Of Bristol.* Reprint - 1982.

BAYER, Henry, *The Belgians, First Settlers*. The Devin-Adair Co, NY, 1925.

BENNETT, C, *Many Mohawk Moons*. Gazetee Press, 1935.

BEST, George, *The Three Voyages Of Martin Frobisher, 1578*. Reprint - B Franklin, 1963.

BESTON, Henry, *The St Lawrence*. Rinehart & Company, 1942.

BIGGAR, H, *A Collection Of Documents Relating To Jacques Cartier And The Sieur DeRoberval*. Public Archives Of Canada, 1930.

"   ", *The Early Trading Companies Of New France*. U Of Toronto Library, 1901.

BIRCH, John, *The Markers Speak*. The Schenectady County Historical Society, 1962.

BISHOP, Mark, *Champlain: The Life Of Fortitude*. Alfred A Knopf, NY, 1948.

BISSON, Douglas, *The Merchant Adventurers Of England*. U Of Delaware Press, Newark, 1993.

BOLTON, Charles, *Terra Nova*. FW Faxon Company, Boston, 1935.

BOLTON, Reginald, *Indian Life Of Long Ago In The City Of New York*. Harmony Books, 1972.

BOLTON, Theodore & CORTELYOU, Irwin, *Ezra Ames*. The NY Historical Society, NY, 1953.

BOWMAN, Wm, *Bristol And America*. R Sydney Glover, London, 1929.

BOYD, C, *Shad Fishing*. Crown Publishers, NY, 1975.

BOYER, Henry, *The Belgians, First Settlers*. The Devin-Adair Co, NY, 1925.

BREBNER, John, *The Explorers Of North America 1492-1806*. The World Publishing Company, Cleveland, 1907.

"   ", *Canada*. U Of Michigan Press, Ann Arbor, 1970.

BRIERE, Jean, *La Peche Francaise En Amerique Du Nord Au XVII Siecle*. Collection Fleure de Lys, 1990.

BRISTOL DEVELOPMENT BOARD, *Bristol -- Birthplace Of America*. Partridge Love & Ltd, Bristol.

BRITTEN, Evelyn, *Chronicles Of Saratoga*. Published by the author, Saratoga Springs, c1959.

BRODHEAD, John, *Documents Related To The Colonial History Of The State Of New York* Vol I. Weed, Parsons And Company, Albany, 1856.

BROWN, George ed, *Dictionary Of Canadian Biography*. U Of Toronto Press, 1966.

BROWN, H & HARRIS, P, *Bristol England*. The Burleigh Press, Bristol, 1946.

BRUCE, Wallace, *The Hudson River*. Reprint - Walking News, Inc, NY, 1982.

BURKE, Thomas, *Mohawk Frontier*. Cornell U Press, Ithaca, 1991.

CARUS-WILSON, E, *The Overseas Trade Of Bristol*. Barnes & Noble, NY, 1967.

"   ", *Medieval Merchant Venturers*. Methuen & Co Ltd, England, 1967.

CHATTERTON, E, *English Seamen And The Colonization Of America*. Arrowsmith, London, 1967.

COE, Michael, SNOW, Dean, BENSON, Elizabeth, *Atlas Of Ancient America*. Facts On File Publications, NY, 1986.

COMMITTEE ON THE CELEBRATION OF THE 250th ANNIVERSARY OF THE GRANTING OF THE DONGAN CHARTER, Albany, *A Cradle Of America*. Albany, 1936.

CONDON, Thomas, *New York Beginnings*. NY U Press, 1968.

CORWIN, Edward, HASTINGS, Hugh, HOLDEN, James, *Ecclesiastical Records, State Of NY*. JB Lyon, Albany, 1901-1916.

CRISTY, Miller, *The Voyages Of Captain Luke Foxe* Vol I, II, Hakluyt Society. Reprint - Burt Franklin Publisher, NY, 1966.

DENYS, Nichols, *The Description & Natural History Of The Coasts Of North America*. The Champlain Society, Toronto, 1908.

DOUGLAS, David ed, *The Trade Of Bristol In The Eighteenth Century* Vol XX. JW Arrowsmith Ltd, Bristol, 1957.

DUNN, Shirley, *The Mohicans And Their Land*. Purple Mountain Press, 1994.

ECCLES, W, *The Canadian Frontier*. U Of Toronto, 1969.

EDEN, Richard, *The First Three English Books On America*. Turnball & Spears, Edinburgh, 1885.

-----------, *Encyclopaedia Britannica*. William Benton Publisher, USA, 1963. "Fishing"; "Labadists."

-----------, *Encyclopedia Americana*. Grolier Incorporated, Danbury, Connecticut, 1973. "Canada: Growth Of The Fisheries"; "Dutch West India Company"; "Fur Trade"; "Lent."

FARR, Grahame, *Somerset Harbours*. Christopher Johnson, London. 1954.

FISKE, John, *The Dutch And Quaker Colonies In America* Vol I. Houghton Mifflin Co, Boston, 1899.

"   ", *The Discovery & Colonization Of North America*. Ginn & Company, Publishers, Boston, 1905.

"   ", *The Discovery Of America*. Houghton, Mifflin And Company, 1892.

FLICK, Alexander ed, *History Of The State Of New York*. Columbia U Press, 1933.

FOSS, Michael, *Undreamed Shores*. Charles Scribner's Sons, NY, 1974.

GEHRING, Charles & STARNA, William, translators, *A Journey Into Mohawk And Oneida Country, 1634-1635*. Syracuse U Press, 1988.

GOETZMANN, William & WILLIAMS, Glyndwr, *The Atlas Of North American Exploration*. Prentice Hall General Reference, NY, 1992.

GRAS, Norman, *The Early English Customs System*. Harvard U Press, Cambridge, 1918.

GRASSMANN, Thomas, *The Mohawk Indians & Their Valley*. Eric Hugo, Schenectady, 1969.

GREENE, Nelson ed, *History Of The Mohawk Valley*. SJ Clarke Publishing Company, Chicago, 1925.

"   ", *History Of The Valley Of The Hudson*. SJ Clarke Publishing Co, Chicago, 1931.

GRIFFIS, William, *The Story Of The Walloons*. Houghton Mifflin Company, Boston, 1923.

HARRISSE, Henry, *The Discovery Of North America*. Reprint - N Israel, Amsterdam, 1961.

HART, Larry, *Tales Of Old Schenectady*. Old Dorp Books, Scotia, NY, c1996.

HILL, William, *Old Fort Edward*. Bullard Press, Glens Falls, 1929.

HISLOP, Codman, *Albany, Dutch, English, And American*. The Argus Press Publishers, Albany, 1936.

HODGE, Frederick ed, *Handbook Of American Indians North Of Mexico*. Goverment Printing Office, Washington, 1910.

HOLDEN, Austin, *History Of The Town Of Queensbury*. J Munsell, Albany, 1874.

HORWOOD, Joan, *Viking Discovery*. Jeperson Press & Newfoundland Historic Parks Association, St John's, Newfoundland, 1985.

HORWOOD, Harold & BUTTS, Edward, *Pirates & Outlaws Of Canada 1610-1932*. Doubleday Canada Limited, Toronto, 1984.

HUDSON, Henry, *Henry Hudson The Navigator*. Reprint - Burt Franklin, Publisher, NY, 1963.

HUDSON RIVER VALLEY COMMISSION, *The Hudson Fish & Wildlife*. State Of NY, 1966.

HUMBLE, Richard, *The Voyage Of Jacques Cartier*. Franklin Watts, NY, 1992.

HUYGHE, Patrick, *Columbus Was Last*. Hyperion, NY, 1992.

INNIS, Harold, *The Fur Trade In Canada*. Yale U Press, New Haven, 1930.

"   ", *The Cod Fisheries*. Yale U Press, New Haven, 1940.

"   ", *Select Documents In Canadian Economic History 1497-1783*. The U Of Toronto Press, 1929.

JAMES, Bartlett & JAMESON, J eds, *Journal Of Jasper Danckaerts*. Barnes & Noble, Inc, NY, 1941.

JAMES, Thomas, *The Strange & Dangerous Voyages Of Captaine Thomas James, In His Intended Discovery Of The Northwest Passage Into The South Sea*. London, 1633.

JAMESON J & BUEL, J eds, *Encyclopedic Dictionary Of American Reference* Vol I, II. Library Of American History, 1901.

JAMESON, James ed, *Narratives Of New Netherland*. Charles Scribner's Sons, NY, 1909.

JONES, Gwyn, *The Norse Atlantic Saga*. Oxford U Press, London, 1964.

KERLING, Nelly, *Commercial Relations Of Holland And Zeeland With England From The Late 13th Century To The Close Of The Middle Ages*. EJ Brill, Leiden, 1954.

KIMBALL, Francis, *The Capital Region Of New York State*. Lewis Historical Publishing Company, Inc, NY, 1942.

KINGSFORD, C, *Prejudice And Promise*. Barnes & Noble, Inc, NY, 1962.

LAHONTAN, Louis, *New Voyages To North America*. Reprint - Burt Franklin, NY, 1970.

LAMB, Harold, *New Found World*. Doubleday & Company, Inc, Garden City, 1955.

LAMB, Wallace, *New York State & Its Communities*. American Book Company, NY, 1942.

LEACOCK, Stephen, *The Mariner Of St Malo*. Glasgow, Brook & Company, 1915.

LESCARBOT, Marc, *Nova Francia*. Harper & Brothers, NY, 1928.

LINGELBACH, W, *The Internal Organisation Of The Merchant Adventurers Of England*. Philadelphia, 1903.

LLOYD, T, *Alien Merchants In England In The Middle Ages*. St Martin's Press, NY, 1982.

LOUGHEED, Sharon, *Port Of Albany*. Ft Orange Press, Albany, 1982.

MacCRACKEN, Henry, *Old Dutchess Forever!* Hastings House, NY, 1956.

MACINNES, C, *A Gateway, Of Empire*. JW Arrowsmith, Bristol, 1968.

McGRATH, Patrick, *Records Relating To The Society Of Merchant Venturers Of The City Of Bristol In The Seventeenth Century*. JW Arrowsmith Ltd, Bristol, 1952.

MEDEIROS, William, *The Hudson River Shad Fishery: Background, Management Problems And Recommendations*. State U Of NY At Stony Brook, 1974.

MILLER, Ernest, "The West India Company And The Walloons." In *Transactions Of The Albany Institute* Vol XII. Weed Parsons & Co, Printers, 1893.

MIRSKY, Jeannette, *The Westward Crossings*. The U Of Chicago Press, Chicago, 1970.

MORISON, Samuel, *Portuguese Voyages To America In The Fifteenth Century*. Octagon Books, Inc, NY, 1965.

"   ", *Samuel de Champlain*. Little, Brown & Co, Boston, 1972.

MORSE, Eric, *Fur Trade Canoe Routes Of Canada/Then And Now*. Queen's Printer, Ottawa, 1969.

MOWAT, R ed, *The Deposition Books Of Bristol* Vol VI, XIII. Bristol Record Society's Publications.

MUNRO, William, *Crusaders Of New France*. Yale U Press, New Haven, 1921.

MUNSELL, Joel, *The Annals Of Albany* Vol 1, 2, 5, 9. Joel Munsell, Albany, 1869.

"   ", *Collections Of The City Of Albany*. J Munsell, Albany, 1865.

NEALE, W, *At The Port Of Bristol* Vol I. The Port Of Bristol Authority, 1968.

NETTLE, Richard, *The Salmon Fisheries Of The St Lawrence*. J Lovell, 1857.

NEW YORK STATE, *State Of New York Conservation Departmen Thirty-Second Annual Report*. Williams Press, Albany, 1942.

NEW YORK STATE JOINT LEGISLATIVE COMMITTEE ON LAKE GEORGE WATER CONDITIONS, *Lake George*. Revised March, 1945.

NISSENSEN, Samuel, *The Patroon's Domain*. Columbia U Press, NY, 1937.

NORTON, Thomas, *The Fur Trade In Colonial NY*. The U Of Wisconsin Press, Madison WI, 1974.

NUTE, Grace, *Ceasars Of The Wilderness*. Minnesota Historical Society Press, St Paul, 1978.

O'CALLAGHAN, E, *Documents Relative To The Colonial History Of The State Of New York* Vol I. Weed, Parsons And Company, Printers, Albany, 1856.

O'DEA, Agnes, *Bibliography Of Newfoundland* Vol I, II. U Of Toronto Press, 1986.

OLESON, Truyggvi, *Early Voyages And Northern Approaches*. Oxford U Press, London, 1964.

PARKMAN, Francis, *Pioneers Of France In The New World*. Little, Brown, And Company, Boston, 1905.

PFEIFFER, C, *Shad Fishing*. Crown Publishers, Inc, NY, 1975.

PHILLIPS, Paul, *The Fur Trade* Vol I. U Of Oklahoma Press, 1961.

PROULX, Jean-Pierre, *Basque Whaling In The 16th Century*. Parks Service Environment Canada, 1986.

QUINN, David ed, *North American Discovery c1000-1612*. U Of South Carolina Press, 1971.

184

REEVES, Arthur, *The Finding Of Wineland The Good*. Reprint - Burt Franklin 1967.
REYNOLDS, Cuyler, *Albany Chronicles*. JB Lyon Co, Printers, Albany, 1906.
RIDPATH, John, *History Of The United States*. Grosset & Dunlap, NY, 1876.
ROSS, Stewart, *Fact Or Fiction: Pirates*. Copper Beech Books, Brookfield, Connecticut, 1995.
SACKS, David, *The Widening Gate*. U Of California Press, 1991.
SAGARD, Gabriel, *Sagard's Long Journey To The Country Of The Hurons*. Reprint - Greenwood Press, NY, 1968.
SALE, Kirpatrick, *The Conquest Of Paradise*. Knopf, NY,1990.
SALSMAN, L, *English Trade In The Middle Ages*. The Clarendon Press, Oxford, 1931.
SAMMURTOK, M & SURETTE, R, "Newfoundland And Labrador." In *Fodor's 89 Canada's Maritime Provences*, 1989.
SAUM, Lewis, *The FurTrader And The Indian*. U Of Washington Press, Seattle, 1965.
SCHUYLER, George, *Colonial New York* Vol 1. Charles Scribner's Sons, NY, 1885.
SHACKLETON, Michael, *The Politics Of Fishing In Britain And France*. Gower, 1986.
SHARP, J, *Discovery In The North Atlantic*. Nimbus Publishing Ltd, 1991.
SHILTON, Dorothy & HOLWORTHY, Richard, *High Court Of Admiralty Examinations 1637-1638*. Publications Of The Anglo-American Records Foundation, 1932.
SHIPSIDES, Frank & WALL, Robert, *Bristol: Maritime City*. The Redcliffe Press, Bristol, 1981.
SHORTT Adam & DOUGHTY, Arthur eds. *Canada And Its Provinces* Vol 1, 2, 15, 23. Glasgow, Brook And Company, 1914.
SLOANE, William, *The French War And The Revolution*. Charles Scribner's Sons, 1910.
SMALLWOOD, Joseph ed, *The Book Of Newfoundland* Vol II. Newfoundland Book Publishers, Ltd, St John's, 1967.
    "   ", *Encyclopedia Of Newfoundland And Labrador*. Newfoundland Book Publishers Limited, 1967.
SMITH, George, *Religion And Trade In New Netherland*. Cornell U Press, Ithaca, NY, 1973.
SNELL, Tee, *The Wild Shores*. National Geographic Society, 1974.
STOKES, I, *The Iconography Of Manhattan Island*. Arno Press, Inc, NY, 1967.
STRAYER, Joseph ed, *Dictionary Of The Middle Ages*. Charles Scribner's Sons, NY, 1985. "Fasting."
SULLIVAN, James, *History Of New York State* Vol 1. Lewis Historical Publishing Company, Inc, NY, 1927.
SYLVESTER, Nathaniel. *Northern New York*. Reprint - Harbor Hill Books, Harrison, NY, 1973.
THWAITES, Reuben ed, *Jesuit Relations* Vol 1-73. Pageant Book Co, 1959.
TORNOE, J, *Columbus In The Artic?*. Boktrykkeri, Oslo, 1965.
TRUDEL, Marcel, *The Beginnings Of New France*. McClelland And Stewart Limited, 1973.
TUCK, James & GRENIER, Robert, *Red Bay, Labrador, World Whaling Capital AD 1550-1600*. Atlantic Archaeology, Ltd, St John's Newfoundland, 1989.
VAN LAER, A, *Correspondence Of Maria van Rensselaer*. The U Of The State Of NY, Albany, 1935.
VIERECK, Philip, *The New Land*. The John Day Company, NY, 1967.
WARD, Christopher, *The Dutch And The Swedes*. U Of Pennsylvania Press, 1930.
WATERFORD STUDY CLUB, *Waterford, 1794-1912*. 1912.
WEISE, Arthur, *History Of The Seventeen Towns Of Rensselaer County*. JM Francis & Tucker, Troy, 1880.
    "   , *The City Of Troy*. Edward Green, Troy, 1886.
WELLS, Charles, *A Short History Of The Port Of Bristol*. JW Arrowsmith, London, 1909.
WESTOVER, Myron ed, *Schenectady Past And Present*. Shenandoah Publishing House, Inc, Straburg, VA, 1931.
WILCOXEN, Charlotte, *Seventeenth Century Albany*. Albany Institute Of History And Art, 1981.
WILLIAMS, Sherman, *New York's Part In History*. D Appleton And Company, NY, 1915.
WILLIAMSON, James, *Maritime Enterprise 1485-1558*. The Clarendon Press, Oxford, 1913.
WILSON, Ian, *The Columbus Myth*. Simon & Schuster, London, 1991.
WILSON, James ed, *The Memorial History Of The City Of New York* Vol I. NY History Company, NY, 1892.
WILSTACH, Paul, *Hudson River Landings*. Tudor Publishing Co, NY, 1933.
WINSOR, Justin, *Geographical Discovery In The Interior Of North America*. Houghton, Mifflin And Company, Cambridge, 1894.
    "   , *Narrative And Critical History Of America* Vol III. Houghton, Mifflin And Company, Cambridge, 1889.
WORTH, Gorham, *Random Recollections Of Albany From 1800-1808*. J Munsell, Albany, 1866.

periodicals

BARKHAM, Selma, "The Basques: Filling A Gap In Our History Between Jacques Cartier And The Champlain." *Canadian Geographical Journal*, Feb/Mar 1978.
BARRETT, John, "Does Island Hide Gains Of Pirates?" *Western Star*, 14 Apr 1950.
BASILO, Tony, "Hearsay & History." *The Greenwich Journal*, Greeenwich, NY, 27 Apr 1949.
COISH, Calvin, "The Jolly Roger And Pieces Of Eight." *The Atlantic Advocate*, Oct 1982.
CURTSINGER & SCHLECHT, "Discovery In Labrador: A 16th-Century Basque Whaling Port And Its Sunken Fleet." *National Geographic*, Jul 1985.
DAVIES, Arthur, "Prince Madoc And The Di,scovery Of America In 1477." *The Geographical Journal*, Nov 1984.
ENGLISH, I, "The Basques." *The Newfoundland Quarterly*, [no date, etc, cited.]
FLANAGAN, Chris, "Buried Treasure, Port Aux Basques, Milkman's Driving Discovery." *Sunday Telegram*, St John's, Newfoundland, 5 Mar 1995.

HALL, Alice & SPIEGEL, Ted, "The Hudson: That River's Alive." *National Geographic*, Jan 1978.
HARDING, Leslie, "The Smell Of A Newfoundland Pirate Ship." *The Newfoundland Quarterly*, Christmas, 1979.
HARRINGTON, Michael, "The White Fleet Of Portugal." *The Atlantic Advocate*, Vol 48, Jul 1958.
HILL, Michael, "Shad-ow Of Doubt." Associated Press in the *Post Star*, Glens Falls, NY, 16 May 1996.
HORWOOD, Harold, "French Beginnings In Newfoundland" Part I. The Newfoundland Collection files in St John's Library, St John's, Newfoundland, [no newspaper cited, not dated.]
JACKSON, Donald, "Who The Heck *Did* Discover The New World?" *Smithsonian*, Sep 1991.
LANKEN, Dane, "Selma Barken Traces Our Basque Heritage." *Route*, May 1984.
MARTIN, Dudley, "Shad In The Shadow Of Skyscrapers." *National Geographic*, Mar 1947.
McGHEE, Robert, "Early Whalers Of Labrador." *Canadian Heritage*, Feb/Mar 1983.
McKINNEY, Wayne, "Newfoundland Pirate Ports." *The Atlantic Advocate*, Sep 1973.
MURRAY, Neil, "Father Of The Lake." *Post Star*, Glens Falls, NY, 31 May 1996.
RAYBURN, Alan, "The Basque Legacy On Canada's East Coast." *Canadian Geographic*, Vol 114, Jul/Aug 1994.
ROBBINS, Doug, "Labrador's Spanish-Basque Heritage." *Impact*, Vol 4 & 5, Sep 1992.
RUDDOCK, Alwyn, "John Day Of Bristol & The English Voyages Across The Atlantic." *The Geographical Journal*, Vol 132, 1966.
STEGEMANN, Eileen and STANG, Douglas, "The Herring Of New York." *The Conservationist*, April 1993.
WHEELER, D, "The Portuguese In Newfoundland Waters." *Historic Newfoundland*, The Newfoundland Department Of Tourism, Newfoundland, 1979.
[No author cited] "Historic Connections To The Basques." *Where It's At*, 1996.
    " " " "Red Bay, First Industrial Complex In North America." *The Newfoundland Herald*, 23 Jul 1983.
    " " " "Portuguese Dispute Cabot Discovery Claim." *Evening Telegram*, St John's, Newfoundland, 17 Feb 1995.

not published

"Collections For Bristol." Handwritten notes, and some old newspaper clippings regarding the history of Bristol in The Avon County Library, Bristol, England.
GATH, E, "Bristol Voyages To The New World Between 1576 And 1612." Thesis offered for the Bristol MA Examination, U of Bristol, 1914
RINK, Oliver, "Merchants And Magnates." A dissertation presented to the Graduate School, U of Southern California for the degree Doctor of Philosophy, Jan 1976.
STENTON, CF, "An Investigation Of The Antiquities And Importance Of English Pirates 1603-40." A Thesis Presented For Doctor Of Philosophy At The U Of Bristol, 1972.
[No author cited] "Saga Of A River Town, Watertown, NY." A typed paper in Waterford Public Library files, [not dated.]

1598 THE GREENLAND COMPANY

BAKELESS, John, *The Eyes Of Discovery*. Dover Publicaations, Inc, NY, 1961.
De COSTA, BF, *Sailing Directions Of Henry Hudson*. J Munsell, Albany, 1869.
MIRSKY, Jeannette, *The Westward Crossings*. The U of Chicago Press, 1970.
O'CALLAGHAN, E, *History Of New Netherland* Vol I, II, III. D Appleton & Company, NY, 1845.
SULLIVAN, James, *History Of New York State* Vol I. Lewis Historical Publishing Company, Inc, NY, 1927.
THWAITES, Reuben ed, *Jesuit Relations* Vol 1-73. Pageant Book Co, 1959.
VAN LINSCHOTEN, Jan, *Discours Of Voyages Into Y[e] East & West Indies*. Reprint - Walter Johnsson, Inc, Amsterdam, 1974.
WILSON, James ed, *The Memorial History Of The City Of New York* Vol I. NY History Company, NY, 1892.

1609 CASTLE ISLAND

BACON, Edgar, *The Hudson River From Ocean To Source*. GP Putnam's Sons. 1902.
BARNES, William, *The Settlers & Early History Of Albany*. J Munsell, Albany, 1864.
BISBEE, Ernest, *The Empire State Scrap Book*. The Bisbee Press, 1947.
BURKE, Thomas *Mohawk Frontier*. Cornell U Press, Ithaca, 1991.
BUTTERFIELD, Consul, *History Of Brule's Discoveries And Explorations*. The Hellman-Taylor Company, 1898.
COMMITTEE ON THE CELEBRATION OF 250th ANNIVERSARY OF THE GRANTING OF THE DONGAN CHARTER, *Albany, A Cradle Of America*. Albany, 1936.
CONDON, Thomas, *New York Beginnings*. NY U Press, 1968.
De COSTA, BF, *Sailing Directions Of Henry Hudson*. J Munsell, Albany, 1869.
DUNN, Shirley, *The Mohicans And Their Land*. Purple Mountain Press, 1994.
----------, *Encyclopaedia Britannica*. William Benton Publisher, USA, 1963. "Jean La Badie."
FLICK, Alexander ed, *History Of The State Of New York*. Columbia U Press, 1933.
GREENE, Nelson, *History Of The Valley Of The Hudson*. SJ Clarke Publishing Company, Chicago, 1931.
HALSEY, Francis, *The Old New York Frontier*. Scribner, 1901.
HOWELL, George, "Evidence Of The French Discoveries In New York Previous To The Colonization By The Dutch." In *Transactions Of The Albany Institute* Vol XI, Weed, Parsons & Co, Printers, Albany, 1887.
JAMES, Bartlett & JAMESON, J eds, *Journal Of Jasper Danckaerts*. Barnes & Noble, Inc, NY, 1941.
JAMESON, J ed, *Narratives Of New Netherland*. Charles Scribner's Sons, NY, 1909.
LOSSING, Benson, *The Hudson*. Reprint - Kennikat Press, Port Washington, NY, 1972.

O'CALLAGHAN, E *Documents Relative To The Colonial History Of The State Of New York* Vol I. Weed, Parsons And Company, Printers, Albany, 1856.
McENANY, John, *Albany Through Time*. Windsor Publications, Inc, Woodland hills, CA, 1981.
MUNSELL, Joel, *Annals Of Albany* Vol 2, 10. Joel Munsell, Albany, 1869.
NISSENSAN, Samuel, *The Patroon's Domain*. Columbia U Press, NY, 1937.
REYNOLDS, Cuyler, *Albany Chronicles*. JB Lyon Printers, Albany, 1906.
SCHOOLCRAFT, Henry, *State Of New York No 24, In Senate, 1846.* [No publication info cited.]
  "   "   , *Notes On The Iroquois*. Erastus H Pease & Co, Albany, 1847.
SULLIVAN, James, *History Of New York State* Vol I. Lewis Historical Publishing Company, Inc, NY, 1927.
SYLVESTER, Nathaniel, *Northern New York*. Reprint - Harbor Hill Books, Harrison, NY, 1973.
TRELEASE, Allen, *Indian Affairs In Colonial New York, The Seventeenth Century*. Kennikat Press, Port Washington, NY, 1960.
VIERECK, Philip, *The New Land*. The John Day Company, NY, 1967.
WEISE, Arthur, *The History Of The City Of Albany*. EH Bender, Albany, 1884.
  "   "   , *History Of The Seventeen Towns Of Rensselaer County*. JM Francis & Tucker, 1880.
WILCOXEN, Charlotte, *Seventeenth Century Albany*. Albany Institute Of History And Art, 1981.
WILSON, James ed, *The Memorial History Of The City Of New York* Vol I. NY History Company, NY, 1892.
WILSTACH, Paul, *Hudson River Landings*. Tudor Publishing Co, NY, 1933.

interviews
CHRISTOPH, Florence, on 16 Jul 1997 suggested getting in touch with Paul Huey.

... ALLEFONSCE ...
ANDERSON, George, *Landmarks Of Rensselaer County*. D Mason & Company, 1897.
BAKELESS, John, *The Eyes Of Discovery*. Dover Publications, Inc, NY, 1961.
BIGGAR, H, *A Collection Of Documents Relating To Jacques Cartier And The Sieur De Roberval*. Public Archives of Canada, Ottawa, 1930.
  "   "   , *The Early Trading Companies Of New France*. U of Toronto Library, 1901.
BOLTON, Charles, *Terra Nova*. FW Faxon Company, Boston, 1935.
BREBNER, John, *The Explorers Of North America*. The World Publishing Company, Cleveland, 1917.
BRISTOL DEVELOPMENT BOARD, *Bristol, Birthplace Of America*. Partridge Love, Ltd, Bristol.
BRODERICK, Frances, *Lansingburgh*. Lansingburgh Historical Society, 1971.
BRODERICK, Warren, *Brunswick, A Pictorial History*. The Brunswick Historical Society, 1978.
BROWN, Arthur, *Early English And Norse Studies*. Methuen & Co, London, 1963.
BROWN, Jennifer, *Strangers In Blood*. U Of British Columbia Press, Vancouver, 1980.
CARTIER, Jacques, *The Voyages Of Jacques Cartier*. U Of Toronto Press, 1993.
CARUS-WILSON, E, *Medieval Merchant Venturers*. Methuen & Co Ltd, England, 1967.
DAVIDSON, Charles, *Hoosick Falls Historic Guide*. Hoosick Valley Publishing Co, Mineola, NY, 1990.
DUNN, Shirley, *The Mohicans And Their Land*. Purple Mountain Press, 1994.
FITCH, Asa, *A Historical, Topographical And Agricultural Survey Of The County Of Washington*. NY State Agricultural Society, 1849.
FLICK, Alexander ed, *History Of The State Of New York* Vol I. Columbia U Press, 1933.
GANONG, W, *Critical Maps In The Early Cartography And Place Names Of The Atlantic Coast Of Canada*. U Of Toronto Press, 1964.
GRASSMANN, Thomas, *The Mohawk Indians And Their Valley*. Eric Hugo, Schenectady, 1969.
GEHRING, Charles ed, *A Guide To Dutch Manuscripts Relating To New Netherland In United States Repositories*. U Of The State Of NY, 1978.
GOODWIN, William, *The Truth About Leif Ericsson And The Greenland Voyages*. Meador Publishing Company, Boston, 1941.
HOFFMAN, Bernard, *Cabot To Cartier*. U Of Toronto Press, 1961.
HUDSON, Henry, *Henry Hudson The Navigator*. Reprint - Burt Franklin, Publisher, NY, 1963.
JAMES, Bartlett & JAMESON, J eds, *Journal Of Jasper Danckaerts*. Barnes & Noble, Inc, NY, 1941.
JENKINS, Stephen, *The Greatest Street In The World*. GP Putnam's Sons, NY, 1911.
JOHNSON, Allen ed, *Dictionary Of American Biography*. U Of Toronto Press, 1966.
KELLER, Jane, *Adirondack Wilderness*. Syracuse U Press, 1980.
LAMB, Harold, *New Found World*. Doubleday & Company, Inc, Garden City, NY, 1955.
LAMB, Wallace, *New York State And Its Communities*. American Book Co, NY, 1942.
LEACOCK, Stephen, *The Mariner Of St Malo*. Glasgow, Brook & Company, Toronto, 1915.
  "   "   , *The Dawn Of Canadian History*. Glasgow, Brook & Company, 1914.
LESCARBOT, Marc, *Nova Francia*. Harper & Brothers, NY, 1928.
McENEANEY, John, *Albany, Capital City On The Hudson*. Windsor Publications, 1981.
MIRSKY, Jeannette, *The Westward Crossing*. The U of Chicago Press, 1970.
MORISON, Samuel, *Samuel de Champlain*. Little, Brown & Co, Boston. 1972.
NILES, Grace, *The Hoosac Valley*. GP Putnam's Sons, NY, 1912.
NISSENSAN, Samuel, *The Patroon's Domain*. Columbia U Press, NY, 1937.
O'CALLAGHAN, E, *The Documentary History Of New York* Vol II. Weed, Parsons & Co, Public Printers, Albany, 1850.
PARKMAN, Francis, *Pioneers Of France In The New World*. Little, Brown, And Co, Boston, 1905.

PUBLIC ARCHIVES OF CANADA, *Preliminary Inventory - Fur Trade And Indians*. 1954.
REEVES, Arthur, *The Finding Of Wineland The Good*. Reprint - Burt Franklin, NY, 1967.
REYNOLDS, Cuyler, *Albany Chronicles*. JB Lyon Co, Printers, Albany, 1906.
RUTTENBER, E, *Indian Tribes Of Hudson's River* Vol II. Hope Farm Press, 1992.
SALE, Kirpatrick, *The Conquest Of America*. Knopf, NY, 1990.
SCHOOLCRAFT, Henry, *The Indian In His Wigwam*. Derby & Hewson Publishers, Buffalo, 1848.
SULLIVAN, James, *History of New York State* Vol I. Lewis Historical Publishing Company, Inc, NY, 1927.
THOMPSON, Gunnar, *American Discovery*. Argonauts Misty Isles Press, Seattle, 1994.
THWAITES, Reuben ed, *Jesuit Relations* Vol 1-73. Pageant Book Co, 1959.
TRUDEL, Marcel, *The Beginnings Of New France 1524-1663*. McCelland And Stewart Limited, 1973.
WEISE, Arthur, *History Of The Seventeen Towns Of Rensselaer County*. JM Francis & Tucker, Troy, 1880.
WILSON, James ed, *Memorial History Of The City Of New York* Vol I. NY History Co, NY, 1892.
WILSTACK, James, *Hudson River Landings*. Tudor Publishing Co, NY, 1933.
WINSOR, Justin, *Narrative And Critical History Of America* Vol IV. Houghton, Mifflin And Company, Boston, 1889.
  "   "   , *Geographical Discovery By The Interior Of North America*. Houghton, Mifflin And Company, Cambridge, 1894.

periodicals
BALL, Levi, "Annals Of Hoosick." *Rensselaer County Standard*, 1873-1874.
MUSSET, George, " Jean Fonteneau dit Alfonse de Saintonge." *Bulletin de la Section de Geographie*, 1895.
[No author cited] "Interesting Indian Lore Told Of White Creek Early Years", *Falls Standard Press*, 10 Sep 1953.

not published
HOOSICK TOWNSHIP HISTORIC SOCIETY files, especially these letters ...
- BANNON, W, to NYS Historical Association, 11 May 1959.
-   "   "   , to James McGuire Historian, Town of Hoosick, 18 May 1960.
- ROBINSON, W, to Wm Bannon, 20 Feb 1959.

1609 SAMUEL de CHAMPLAIN
BAILEY, Horace, *Historical Booklet Of Lake Champlain*. Lake Champlain Tercentenary Commission Of Vermont, 1909.
BAKELESS, John, *The Eyes Of Discovery*. Dover Publications, Inc, NY, 1961.
BIGGAR, H ed, *The Works Of Samuel de Champlain*. The Champlain Society, Toronto, 1922-23.
BISHOP, Morris, *Champlain The Life Of Fortitude*. Alfred A Knopf, NY, 1948.
BUCKELL, Betty, *Stuff*. Buckle Press, Queensbury, NY, 1992.
CHAMPLAIN, Samuel, *Voyages Of Champlain*. Allerton Book Co, NY 1904.
CLARKE, T, *The Bloody Mohawk*. IJ Freidman, Port Washington, NY, 1968.
CLAYTON, W, *History Of Onondaga County*. D Mason & Co, 1878.
COLDEN, Caldwallader, *History Of The Five Indian Nations* Part I. New Amsterdam Book Co, 1902.
COOLIDGE, Guy, *The French Occupation Of The Champlain Valley*. Reprint - Harbor Hill Books, Mamaroneck, NY, 1979.
de LAHONTAN, Baron, *New Voyages To North America* Vol I. McClurg & Co., 1905.
DIONNE, N, *Champlain*. Morang & Co, Limited, Toronto, 1910.
DONOHUE, Thomas, *The Iroquois And The Jesuits*. Buffalo Catholic Publication Co, 1895.
---------, *Encyclopaedia Britannica*. William Benton, Publisher, Chicago, 1963. "Arquebus"; "Champlain."
EVERTS and ENSIGN, *History of Washington County, New York*. JB Lippincott & Co, Philadelphia, 1878.
FITCH, Asa, *A Historical, Topographical And Agricultural Survey Of The County Of Washington*. NY State Agricultural Society, 1849.
FLICK, Alexander ed, *History Of The State Of New York*. Columbia U Press, 1931.
GOETZMANN, William & WILLIAMS, Glyndwr, *The Atlas Of North American Exploration*. Prentice Hall General Reference, NY, 1992.
GOODRICH, Chauncey, *Lake Champlain*. G Goodrich & Co, Burlington, 1857.
GRANT, John, *Monster Mysteries*. Chartwell Books, Inc, Secaucus, NJ, 1992.
GRANT,W, *Voyages Of Samuel de Champlain, 1604-1618*. Charles Scribner's Sons, NY, 1907.
GRASSMANN, Thomas, *The Mohawk Indians & Their Valley*. Eric Hugo, Schenectady, 1969.
GRESHAM PUBLISHING COMPANY ed, *History And Biography Washington County*. Gresham Publishing Company, Chicago, 1894.
HAMILTON, Edward, *Fort Ticonderoga Key To A Continent*. Little, Brown And Company, Boston, 1964.
HERTZBERG, Hazel, *The Great Tree And The Longhouse*. The Macmillan Company, NY, 1966.
LESCARBOT, Marc, *Nova Francia*. Harper & Brothers, 1928.
LOUNSBURY, Floyd, *Iroquois Place Names In The Champlain Valley*. The State Education Department, Albany, 1960.
McARTHUR, Thomas, *History Of Putnam*. Reprint by the Town of Putnam Historical Society [no date cited.]
McCONNIFF, John, *Illustrated Montreal*. John McConniff, Montreal, 1893.
MORGAN, Lewis, *League Of The Ho-De'-No-Sau-Nee or Iroquois* 2 Vols. Reprint Burt Franklin, NY, 1967.
MORISON, Samuel, *Samuel de Champlain*. Little, Brown And Company, Boston, 1972.
O'CALLAGHAN, E, *Documentary History Of New York* Vol 3. Weed, Parsons & Co, Public Printers, Albany, 1850.
PALMER, Peter, *History Of Lake Champlain*. J Munsell, Albany, 1866.
PARKMAN, Francis, *Champlain And The Indians*.
  "   "   , *Pioneers Of France In The New World*. Little, Brown,

And Company, Boston, 1907.
"   "   , The Great Republic. .
QUINN, David ed, North American Discovery. U Of South Carolina Press, 1971.
SAGARD, Theodat, Sagard's Long Journey To The Country Of The Hurons. Editions du Carrefour, 1929.
SAMSON, Paul, Mohican Point On Lake George. Bixby, 1913.
SCHOOLCRAFT, Henry, Notes On The Iroquois. Erastus H Pease & Co, Albany, 1847.
SLAFTER, E, Voyages Of Samuel Of Champlain. The Prince Society, 1880.
SMITH, H, History Of Warren County. D Mason & Co, Publishers, Syracuse, 1885.
"   ", History Of Essex County.   "   "   "   "   .
SULLIVAN, James, History Of New York State Vol I. Lewis Historical Publishing Company, Inc, NY, 1927.
SYLVESTER, Nathaniel, Saratoga And Kay-Ad-Ros-Se-Ra. William B Young, Troy, 1876.
TEHANETORENS, Wampum Belts. Irografts, 1983.
THOMPSON, Z, Lake George & Lake Champlain. Burlington, 1845.
THWAITES, Reuben ed, Jesuit Relations Vol 1-73. Pageant Book Co, 1959.
TRUDEL, Marcel, The Beginnings Of New France. McClelland And Stewart Limited, 1973.
TYRRELL, William, Champlain And The French In New York. NYS Education Department, Albany, 1959.
WINSOR, Justin, Geographical Discovery In The Interior Of North America. Houghton, Mifflin And Company, Cambridge, 1894.
WRIGHT, Louis & FOWLER, Elaine eds, West And By North. Delacorte Press, NY, 1977.

periodicals
BLOW, David, "Modern Dinosaur, Or Big Sturgeon?" Post Star, Glens Falls, NY, 20 Feb 1994.
CAMPBELL, Thomas, "Nicolet Day On Mackinac Island." Michigan Historical Collections, Bulletin 6, 1916.
CONE, Gertrude, "Travel In The Champlain Valley In Pioneer Times." North Country Life, Summer 1959.
COOPER, Susan Fenimore, "The Hudson River And Its Early Names." Magazine Of American History, June 1880.
HOLDEN, A, " The Early History Of Queensbury." Glens Falls Messenger, 24 May 1867. In Holden's Scrapbook #9, Local History Collection, Crandall Library, Glens Falls, NY.
O'NEAL, Glenn, "Study Links Early Settler's Difficulties To Droughts." USA Today, 24 Apr 1998.
WAGNER, John, "Au Plaisir." Adirondack Life, Jan 1988.
[No author cited] "Grimness Of Mythic Proportions." Discover, Jan 1999.
not published
HILL B B B files. Feinberg Library, SUNY Plattsburgh, NY, has a vast collection of Dr David Kellogg's notes, articles and lectures regarding Indian settlements of the area. He noted that there were 45 prehistoric dwelling places on or near Lake Champlain. Kellogg found over 20,000 stone artifacts, pottery, stone implements, pipes and copper weapons -- he sold 15,000 of these to Amherst College.
interviews
FEISTER, Lois, NYS Historic Preservation Office, Peebles Island, on 19 Jan 1999, to determine the correct latitude of Crown Point.
FISHER, Captain Marty, on 2 Jun 1998. Marty never thought to look for snow when he operated the now retired Ticonderoga on Lake Champlain.
OULETTE, Sue, 19 Nov 1995. She suggested that I check the Kellogg Collection at the Feinberg Library, SUNY, Plattsburgh.
RANSON, Stan, Plattsburgh, NY, 20 Jun 1997. Stan agreed that mountains, to the south, are first seen in the Chazy area.
SHIELDS, Addie, Clinton County Historian, Mar 1998. Mrs Shields agreed that the mountains to the south can be seen from the Plattsburgh area; and that she has seen snow on the Vermont Mountains from her house in the summer.
TYKES' BAIT SHOP, Whitehall NY, 5 Jul 1997 -- agreed that the fish that Champlain saw is the gar pike, which is still found in the lake.
YOUNG, Walter, Lake George Planning Board, 19 Jan 1999, to determine the correct latitude of the Beach Road, southern end of Lake George.
WESTBROOK, Nick, Town of Ticonderoga Assessor, 19 Jan 1999, to determine the correct latitude of Fort Ticonderoga.

1609 HENRY HUDSON

ADAMS, Arthur, The Hudson Through The Years. LP Lind Publications, Westwood, NJ, 1983.
ALBANY PORT DISTRICT COMMISSION, The Port Of Albany. Albany, c1932.
ASHER, G, Henry Hudson, The Navigator. Reprint - Burt Franklin, Publisher, NY, 1963.
BACON, Edgar, The Hudson River From Ocean To Source. GP Putnam's Sons, 1902.
BANKS, A, Albany Bi-Centennial. Banks & Brothers, Albany, 1888.
BAKELESS, John, The Eyes Of Discovery. Dover Publications, Inc, NY, 1961.
BARNES, William, The Settlement And Early History Of Albany. J Munsell, Albany, 1864.
BAYER, Henry, The Belgians, First Settlers In New York And In The Middle States. The Devin-Adair Company, NY, 1923.
BISBEE, Ernest, The Empire State Scrap Book. The Bisbee Press, 1947.
BOLTON, Reginald, Indian Life Of Long Ago In The City Of New York. Harmony Books, 1972.
BOYLE, Robert, The Hudson River: A Natural And Unnatural History. Norton, 1969.
BRITTEN, Evelyn, Chronicles Of Saratoga. Published by the author, Saratoga Springs, c1959.
BRUCE, Wallace, The Hudson Three Centuries Of History, Romance And Invention. Walking News, Inc, NY, 1982.
BUTTERFIELD, Consul, History Of Brule's Discoveries And Explorations. The Helman-Taylor Company, 1898.
CARMER, Carl, The Hudson. Grosset & Dunlop Publishers, NY, 1939.

CHRISTOPH, Peter & Florence, eds, New York Historical Manuscripts. Genealogical Publishing Co, 1980.
COMMITTEE ON THE CELEBRATION OF THE 250th ANNIVERSARY OF THE GRANTING. OF THE DONGAN CHARTER, Albany A Cradle Of America. Albany, 1936.
CONDON, Thomas, New York Beginnings. NY U Press, 1968.
De COSTA, BF, Sailing Directions Of Henry Hudson. J Munsell, Albany, 1869.
DUNN, Shirley, The Mohicans And Their Land. Purple Mountain Press, 1994.
---------, The Dutch Settlers Society Of Albany Yearbook. Albany, 1927-1987.
---------, Encyclopaedia Britannica. William Benton Publisher, USA, 1963. "Henry Hudson."
FISKE, John, The Dutch And Quaker Colonies In America Vol 1. Houghton Mifflin Company, Boston, 1899.
"   "   , The Discovery And Colonization Of North America. Ginn & Company, Boston, 1905.
GREENE, Nelson ed, History Of The Mohawk Valley. SJ Clarke Publishing Company, Chicago, 1925.
GRIFFIS, William, The Story Of The Walloons. Houghton Mifflin Company, Cambridge, 1923.
HALE, Edward, History Of The United States. Chautauqua Press, NY, 1887.
HALFMOON BICENTENNIAL COMMITTEE, Halfmoon -- A Peaceful Passageway. 1976.
HALSEY, Francis, The Old New York Frontier. Scribner, 1901.
HAMILTON, Milton, Henry Hudson & The Dutch In New York. U Of The State Of NY, Albany, 1964.
HAMMERSLEY, Sydney, The History Of Waterford, NY. Waterford, NY, 1957.
HILL, William, Old Fort Edward. Bullard Press, Glens Falls, 1929.
HISLOP, Codman, Albany: Dutch, English, And American. The Argus Press, Publishers, Albany, 1936.
HOFFMAN, Bernard, Cabot To Cartier. U Of Toronto Press, 1961.
HOWELL, George, History Of The County Of Albany, NY From 1609 To 1886. J Munsell, Albany, 1886.
HUDSON, Henry, Henry Hudson The Navigator. Reprint - Burt Franklin, Publisher, NY, 1963.
INNES, J, New Amsterdam And Its People. Charles Scribner's Sons, NY, 1902.
IRVING, Washington, A History Of New York. JB Lippincott & Co, Philadelphia, 1871.
JAMES, Bartlett & JAMESON, J eds, Journal Of Jasper Danckaerts. Barnes & Noble, Inc, NY, 1941.
JAMESON, J ed, Narratives Of New Netherland. Charles Scribner's Sons, NY, 1909.
JANVIER, Thomas, The Dutch Founding Of New York. Reprint - Ira J Friedman, Inc, Port Washington, NY, 1967.
"   "   , In Old New York. Harper & Brothers Publishers, NY, 1894.
JARA I, Cornell ed, Historic Chronicles Of New Amsterdam, Colonial New York And Early Long Island. Ira J Friedman, Inc Port Washington, NY.
JOHNSON, Donald, Charting The Sea Of Darkness. International Marine, Camden, Maine, 1993.
JUET, Robert, Juet's Journal. The New Jersey Historical Society, Newark, 1959.
KENNEY, Alice, Stubborn For Liberty. Syracuse U Press, 1975.
LOSSING, B, The Hudson. Reprint - Kennikat Press, Port Washington, NY, 1972.
LOUGHEED, Sharon ed, Port Of Albany. Ft Orange Press, Albany, 1982.
MASTEN, Arthur, The History Of Cohoes. Reprint - Cohoes Historical Society, 1969.
MUNSELL, Joel, The Annals Of Albany Vol 1, 2, 5, 6, 7. Joel Munsell, Albany, 1869.
"   "   , Collections Of The History Of Albany Vol I, II, III. J Munsell, Albany, 1865.
MURPHY, Henry, Henry Hudson In Holland. The Brothers Giunta D'Albani, The Hague, 1859.
MYLOD, John, Biography Of A River. Hawthorn Books, Inc Publishers, NY, 1969.
THE NATIONAL SAVINGS BANK OF THE CITY OF ALBANY, Albany's Historic Street. Albany, 1918.
THE NATIONAL SAVINGS BANK OF THE CITY OF ALBANY, Birthplace Of The Union. Albany, 1940.
O'CALLAGHAN, E, History Of New Netherland Vol I, II, III. D Appleton & Company, NY, 1845.
"   "   ", Remonstrance Of New Netherland. Weed, Parsons And Company, Albany, 1856.
OLTON, Jean compiler, The Town Of Colonie. Town Of Colonie, NY, 1990.
OVERTON, Jacqueline, Long Island's Story. Doubleday Doran & Company, Garden City, 1929.
PECKHAM, Mary, Waterford, 1794-1912. Waterford, c1912.
POUND, Arthur, Murals In The State Bank Of Albany. Albany, 1943
QUINN, David ed, North American Discovery. U Of South Carolina Press, 1971.
REYNOLDS, Cuyler, Albany Chronicles. JB Lyon, Printers, Albany, 1906.
SCHUYLER, George, Colonial New York Vol 1, 2. Charles Scribner's Sons, NY, 1885.
SMITH, William, The History Of The Provence Of New York. Harvard U Press, 1972.
STOKES, I, The Iconography Of Manhattan Island, 1498-1909. Arno Press, Inc, NY, 1967.
SULLIVAN, James, History Of New York State Vol I. Lewis Historical Publishing Company, Inc, NY, 1927.
SYLVESTER, Nathaniel, Northern New York. Reprint - Harbor Hill Books, Harrison, NY, 1973.
"   "   , Saratoga & Kay-Ros-Se-Ra. William B Young, Troy, 1876.
TRUDEL, Marcel, The Beginnings Of New France. McCelland And Stewart Limited, 1973.
VAIL, Philip, The Magnificent Adventures Of Henry Hudson. Dodd, Mead, 1965.
VAN DER ZEE, Henri & Barbara, A Sweet And Alien Land. The Viking Press, NY, 1978.
VAN LAER, A, Minutes Of The Court Of Rensselaerswyck 1648-1652 Vol I, II.

The U Of The State Of NY, Albany, 1922.
"   ", *Correspondence Of Maria van Rensselaer*. The U Of The State
        Of NY, Albany, 1935.
VIERECK, Phillip, *The New Land*. The John Day Company, NY, 1967.
WARD, Christopher, *The Dutch And Swedes On The Delaware*. U Of
Pennsylavania Press, 1930
WEISE, Arthur, *The History Of The City Of Albany*. EH Bender, Albany NY,
        1884.
"   ", *The City Of Troy*. Edward Green, Troy, 1886.
"   ", *The Discoveries Of America To The Year 1525*. GP Putnam's
        Sons, NY, 1884.
WESLAGER, C, *Dutch Explorers, Traders And Settlers In The Delaware Valley*.
U Of Pennsylvania Press, 1961.
WILCOXEN, Charlotte, *Seventeenth Century Albany*. Albany Institute Of
        History And Art, 1981.
"   "   , *Dutch Trade & Ceramics In America In The
        Seventeenth Century*. Albany Institute Of History
        And Art, 1987.
WILSTACH, Paul, *Hudson River Landings*. Tudor Publishing Co, NY, 1933.
WING, Judith, *Bibliography On The Albany, New York Area*. Hudson Mohawk
Library Association, 1995.
WRIGHT, Louis & FOWLER, Elaine eds, *West And By North*. Delacorte Press,
NY, 1971.

periodicals
ATWOOD, Albert, "The Mighty Hudson." *National Geographic*, Jul 1948.
CONLON, Kevin, "Historian Tells Of Waterford's Long-Gone Fort Halfmoon."
The Sunday Gazette, 10 Sep 1995.
PRICE, Willard, "Henry Hudson's River." *National Geographic*, May 1980.
VOSBURGH, Frederick, "Henry Hudson Magnificent Failure." *National
Geographic*, May 1980.

not published
BUREAU OF HISTORIC SITES MASTER PLAN COMMITTEE, "A Structure
Report On The Former Cluett, Peabody And Co, Inc Bleachery Complex At Pebles
Island State Park, Waterford, NY." NYS Office of Parks & Recreation, 1980.
DOUGLAS, G, Historian of the Village of Waterford - typed notes contained in the
Waterford Public Library's files.
SARATOGA COUNTY HISTORICAL SURVEY, "Brief Narrative History Of
Founding And Erection Of The Town [Of Waterford.] 1935.

interviews
BIELINSKI, Stefen, former Director of Colonial Albany Project, on 27 Apr 1995.
He felt that Hudson landed near Bethlehem, "On the Overslaugh, a sand bar just
below the city" of Albany.
RIVAGE, Dennis, Historian for the Town of Waterford, on 28 Apr 1998.

1614 KLEYNTIES
BISHOP, Mark, *The Life Of Fortitude*. Alfred A Knopf, NY, 1948.
BREBNER, John, *The Explorers Of North America*. The World Publishing
Company, Cleveland, 1917.
DUNN, Shirley, *The Mohicans And Their Land*. Purple Mountain Press, 1994.
GRASSMANN, Thomas, *The Mohawk Indians And Their Valley*. Eric Hugo,
Schenectady, 1969.
SULLIVAN, James, *History Of New York State* Vol I. Lewis Historical Publishing
Company, Inc, Ny, 1927.
THWAITES, Reuben ed, *The Jesuit Relations* Vol 1-73. Pageant Book, Co, 1957.

1615 ETIENNE BRULE
BAKELESS, John, *The Eyes Of Discovery*. Dover Publications, NY, 1961.
BISHOP, Mark, *Champlain: The Life Of Fortitude*. Alfred A Knopf, NY, 1948.
BREBNER, John, *The Explorers Of North America, 1492-1805*. The World
        Publishing Company, Cleveland, 1917.
"   ", *Canada*. The U Of Michigan Press, Ann Arbor, 1970.
BROWN, George ed, *Dictionary Of Canadian Biography*. U Of Toronto Press,
1966.
BUTTERFIELD, Consul, *History Of Brule's Discoveries And Explorations*.
        The Helman-Taylor Company,1898.
"   "   , *History Of Seneca County*. D Cambell, Sandusky, 1884.
CRANSTON, J, *Etienne Brule Immortal Scoundrel*. The Ryerson Press, Toronto,
1949.
DIONNE, N, *Champlain*. Morang & Co, Limited, Toronto, 1910.
GIFFORD, Stanley, *Fort Wm Henry -- A History*. Bullard-Glencraft Printing, Inc,
1966.
HORWOOD, Harold & BUTTS, Edward, *Pirates & Outlaws, 1610-1932*.
Doubleday Canada Limited, Toronto, 1984.
MORISON, Samuel, *Samuel de Champlain*. Little, Brown And Company, Boston,
1972.
NISSENSON, Samuel, *The Patroon's Domain*. Columbia U Press, NY, 1937.
PARKMAN, Francis, *Pioneers Of France In The New World*. Little, Brown, And
Company, Boston, 1905.
PRITCHETT, John, *Black Robe And Buckskin*. College And U Press Services,
1960.
THWAITES, Reuben ed, *The Jesuit Relations* Vol 1-73. Pageant Book Co, 1959.
TRUDEL, Marcel, *The Beginnings Of New France*. McClelland And Stewart, 1973.
WALDMAN, Carl, *Atlas Of The North American Indian*. Facts On File, NY, 1985.
WILLIAMS, Sherman, *New York's Part In History*. D Appleton And Company, NY,
1915.
WINSOR, Justin, *Geographical Discovery In The Interior Of North America*.
Houghton, Mifflin And Company, Boston, 1894.

periodicals
CAMPBELL, Thomas, "Nicolet Day On Mackinac Island." *Michigan Historical
Collections*, Bulletin 6, 1916.
SELDON, George, "Etienne Brule The First White Man In The Genesee Country."
Rochester History Society, Vol I, 1925.

VANDERLIP, William, "Etienne Brule, First Exchange Student." *New York State
Tradition*, Winter 1964.

1615 SAMUEL de CHAMPLAIN
BUTTERFIELD, Consul, *History Of Brule's Discoveries And Explorations*. The
Helman-Taylor Company, 1898.
CLARKE, T, *The Bloody Mohawk*. IJ Friedman, Inc, Port Washington, NY,1968.
DONOHUE, Thomas, *The Iroquois And The Jesuits*. Buffalo Catholic Publication
Co, 1895.
FITCH, Asa, *A Historical, Topographical And Agricultural Survey Of The County
Of Washington*. NY S Agricultural Society, 1849.
GOETZMAN, William & WILLIAMS, Glyndwr, *The Atlas Of North American
Exploration*. Prentice Hall General Reference, NY 1992.
MORISON, Samuel, *Samuel de Champlain*. Little, Brown and Company, Boston,
1972.
O'CALLAGHAN, E, *The Documentary History Of The State Of New York* Vol 3.
Weed, Parsons & Co, Albany, 1850.
SCHUYLER, George, *Colonial New York* Vol 1. Charles Scribner's Sons, NY,
1885.
SLAFTER, Edmund, "Champlain." In *Narrative And Critical History Of America*
Vol IV. 1884-c1889.
SNYDER, Charles, *Oswego From Buckskin To Bustles*. Ira J Friedman, Inc, Port
Washington, NY, 1968.
SYLVESTER, Nathaniel, *Northern New York*. Reprint - Harbor Hill Books,
Harrison, NY, 1973.
THWAITES, Reuben ed, *Jesuit Relations* Vol 1-73. Pageant Book Co, 1959.
TRUDEL, Marcel, *The Beginnings Of New France*. McCelland And Stewart
Limited, 1973.
WINSOR, Justin, *Geographical Discovery In The Interior Of North America*.
Houghton, Mifflin And Company, Cambridge, 1894.

periodicals
THE ONONDAGA HISTORICAL ASSOCIATION files, especially ...
- GALLIPEAU, William, "They've Overlooked Important Facts" Letter to the
        Editor. *Post-Standard*, 29 Jan 1949.
-    "   , [untitled typed copy of a] "Letter To The Editor"
        regarding Champlain's battle.   29 Jul 1937., [no
        newspaper cited.]
- WALTER, George, "Roy Cary & Nichols Pond." *Mid-York Week*, 25 Nov 1965.
[No author cited] "Bates Proves Site Of First Battlefield." [No newspaper cited]
        2 Apr 1929.
"   "   "Canadians Want 1603 [sic] Device Back."   "   "   "
        [not dated.]
"   "   "Champlain At Onondaga.   "   "   "
        14 Jan 1965.

1626 van KRICKERBEECK
CLARKE, T, *The Bloody Mohawk*. IJ Friedman, Inc, Port Washington, NY, 1968.
GREENE, Nelson, *History Of The Valley Of The Hudson*. SJ Clarke, Publishing
Co, Chicago, 1931.
NISSENSON, Samuel, *The Patroon's Domain*. Columbia U Press, NY, 1937.
TRELEASE, Allen, *Indian Affairs In Colonial New York: The Seventeenth Century*.
Kennikat Press, Port Washington, NY, 1960.
VAN DER ZEE, Henri & Barbara, *A Sweet And Alien Land*. The Viking Press, NY,
1978.

1627 PIERRE MAGAN
DIONNE, N, *Champlain*. Morang & Co, Limited, Toronto, 1910.
GRASSMANN, Thomas, *The Mohawk Indians And Their Valley*. Eric Hugo,
Schenectady, 1969.
THWAITES, Reuben ed, *Jesuit Relations*. Pageant Book Co, 1939.

1633 JEAN NICOLET
BISHOP, Mark, *Champlain: The Life Of Fortitude*. Alfred A Knopf, NY, 1948.
BREBNER, John, *The Explorers Of North America, 1492-1806*. The World
Publishing Company, Cleveland, 1917.
BROWN, George ed, *Dictionary Of Canadian Biography*. U Of Toronto Press,
1966.
BUTTERFIELD, Consul, *History Of The Discovery Of The Northwest*. Robert
Clarke & Co, Cincinnati, 1881.
----------, *Encyclopedia Americana*. Grolier Incorporated, Danbury, Connecticut,
1973. "Nicolet."
GARNEAU, F & FERLAND, J, "Jean Nicolet." In *Collections Of The State
Historical Society Of Wisconsin* Vol X, Democrat Printing Co, Madison, 1888.
PRITCHETT, John, *Black Robe And Buckskin*. College And U Press Services,
1960.
SCHOOLCRAFT, Henry, *The Indian In His Wigwam*. Derby & Hewson Publishers,
Buffalo, 1848.
THWAITES, Reuben ed, *The Jesuit Relations* Vol 1-73. Pageant Book Co, 1959.
RUBLEE, Horace, "Jean Nicolet." In *Collections Of The State Historical Society
Of Wisconsin*, Vol X, Democrat Printing Co, Madison, 1888.
WALDMAN, Carl, *Atlas Of The North American Indian*. Facts On File, NY, 1985.
WINSOR, Justin, *Geographical Discovery In The Interior Of North America*.
Houghton, Mifflin And Company, 1884.

periodicals
BROSHAR, Helen, "The First Push Westward Of The Albany Traders." *Mississippi
Valley Historical Review*, Vol 17, 1920.
CAMPBELL, Thomas, "Nicolet Day On Mackinac Island." *Michigan Historical
Collection*, Bulletin #6,1916.
RODESCH, Jerold, "Jean Nicolet." *Voyageur, The Historical Review Of Brown
County & Northeast Wisconsin*, Spring 1984.

1634 JOURNAL

FLICK, Alexander ed, *History Of The State Of New York* Vol 1. Columbia U Press, 1933.

GEHRING, Charles & STARNA, William translators, *A Journal Into Mohawk & Oneida Country 1634-35 The Journal Of Harmen Meyndertsz van den Bogaert.* Syracuse U Press, 1988.

GOODWIN, Maud, *Dutch And English On The Hudson.* Yale U Press, USA, 1919.

GRASSMANN, Thomas, *The Mohawk Indians & Their Valley.* Eric Hugo, Schenectady, 1969.

GREENE, Nelson ed, *History Of The Mohawk Valley.* SJ Clarke Publishing Company, Chicago, 1925.

JAMES, Bartlett & JAMESON, J eds, *Journal Of Jasper Danckaerts.* Barnes & Noble, Inc, NY, 1941.

JAMESON, J ed, *Narratives Of New Netherland.* Charles Scribner's Sons, 1909.

KIMBALL, Francis, *The Capital Region Of New York State.* Lewis Historical Publishing Company, Inc, NY, 1942.

MUNSELL, Joel, *The Annals Of Albany* Vol 1. J Munsell, Albany, 1869.

O'CALLAGHAN, E, *History Of New Netherland* Vol 1. D Appleton & Company, NY, 1845.

STOKES, I, *The Iconography Of Manhattan Island, 1498-1909.* Arno Press Inc, NY, 1967.

TRELEASE, Allen, *Indian Affairs In Colonial New York: The Seventeenth Century.* Kennikat Press, Port Washington, NY, 1960.

[No author cited] *Memorial Of The Principal Events That Happened During A Journey To The Maques And Sinnikins.* Written in Dutch; 32 pages. [This journal is the property of The Huntington Library, San Marino, CA.]

periodicals

WILSON, General James, "Arent Van Curler And His Journal Of 1634-35." *Annual Report Of The American Historical Association,* 1895.

correspondence

THE HUNTINGTON LIBRARY, San Marino, CA. From ...
- LEWIS, Dan, Curator of American Historical Manuscripts, 29 Oct 1997.
- ZEIDBERG, David, Director of the Library, 13 Nov 1997.

1641 GODEFROY and MARGUERIE

BISHOP, Mark, *Champlain: The Life Of Fortitude.* Alfred A Knopf, NY, 1948.

BROWN, George ed, *Dictionary Of Canadian Biography.* U Of Toronto Press, 1966.

BROWNE, George, *The St Lawrence River.* Putnam's Sons, NY,1905.

GRASSMANN, Thomas, *The Mohawk Indians And Their Valley.* Eric Hugo, Schenectady, 1969.

THWAITES, Reuben ed, *The Jesuit Relations* Vol 1-73. Pageant Book Co, 1959.

periodicals

CAMPBELL, Thomas, "Nicolet Day On Mackinac Island." *Michigan Historical Collections,* Bulletin #6,1916.

1642 & 1646 ISAAC JOGUES

See Buckel Press' reprint of *Isaac Jogues* by TJ Campbell for bibliography that I added.

1642 ARENDT VAN CURLER

BARTH, Laura, *The Mohawk River And Its Valley.* FA Davis Company, Publishers, Philadelphia, 1941.

BEAUCHAMP, William, *The Iroquois Trail.* HC Beauchamp, Fayetteville, NY, 1892.

BENNETT, C, *Many Mohawk Moons.* Gazettee Press, 1938.

BIRCH, John, *The Markers Speak.* Schenectady County Historical Society, 1962.

BURKE, Thomas, *Mohawk Frontier.* Cornell U Press, Ithaca, 1991.

CORWIN, Edward, HASTINGS, Hugh, HOLDEN, James, *Ecclesiastical Records, State Of NY.* JB Lyon, Albany, 1901-1916.

GRIFFIS, Wm, "Ardent Van Curler ..." In *Transactions Of The Albany Institute* Vol XI. Weed, Parsons & Co, Printers, Albany, 1887.

GREENE, Nelson ed, *History Of The Mohawk Valley.* SJ Clarke Publishing Company, Chicago, 1925.

HALSEY, Francis, *The Old New York Frontier.* Scribner, 1901.

HART, Larry, *Tales Of Old Schenectady.* Old Dorp Books, Scotia, NY, c1996.

JAMESON, J & BUEL, J, *Encyclopedic Dictionary Of American Reference* Vol I, II. Library Of American History, 1901.

MUNSELL, Joel, *Annals of Albany* Vol 1. Joel Munsell, Albany, 1869.

NISSENSON, Samuel, *The Patroon's Domain.* Columbia U Press, NY, 1937.

O'CALLAGHAN, F, *History Of New Netherland.* D Appleton & Company, NY, 1845.

REYNOLDS, Cuyler, *Albany Chronicles.* JB Lyon, Printers, Albany, 1906.

SHEA, John, *History Of The Catholic Missions.* PJ Kenedy, NY, 1899.

STOKES, I, *The Iconography Of Manhattan Island, 1498-1909.* Arno Press Inc, NY, 1967.

THWAITES, Reuben ed, *The Jesuit Relations* Vol 1-73. Pageant Book Company, 1959.

TRELEASE, Allen, *Indian Affairs In Colonial New York: The Seventeenth Century.* Kennikat Press, Port Washington, NY, 1960.

van der DONCK, Adriaen, *A Description Of New Netherland.* Syracuse U Press, 1968.

WESTOVER, Myron ed, *Schenectady Past And Present.* Shenandoah Publishing House, Inc, Strasburg, VA, 1931.

periodicals

SCHENECTADY COUNTY HISTORICAL SOCIETY files, especially ...
- BURNHAM, Koert, "Arent Van Corlaer Alias Corlaer." [No magazine cited] Summer, 1973.
- REYNOLDS, Neil, "Raw Materials Of History." *Schenectady Gazette,* [not dated.]
- STAFFA, Susan, "As It Was." *The Stockade Spy.*

VAN LAER, A, "Arent van Curler And His Historic Letter To The Patroon." In *Dutch Settlers Society Of Albany Yearbook,* Vol III.

not published

HUEY, Paul, misc correspondence in the Colonie Historian's "Van Curler Files" especially about the archeological digs at the Flatts.

1644 FRANCIS BRESSANI

BARTH, Laura, *The Mohawk River And Its Valley.* FA Davis Company, Philadelphia, 1941.

BEAUCHAMP, W, *Indian Names In New York.* HC Beauchamp, Fayetteville, NY, 1893.

BISHOP, Mark, *Champlain: The Life Of Fortitude.* Alfred A Knopf, NY, 1948.

BRANDOW, John, *The Story Of Old Saratoga.* Fort Orange Press, Albany, 1900.

BRIADDY, Katherine, *Ye Olde Days.* Journal Press, Ballston Spa, 1974.

BRITTEN, Evelyn, *Chronicles Of Saratoga.* Published by the author, Saratoga Springs, c1959.

CAMPBELL, T, *Pioneer Priests Of North America* Vol III. The American Press, 1911.

     ", *The Martyrs Of The Mohawk.* Apostleship Of Prayer, NY, 1926.

PALMERS, Harvey, *Mohawk Valley Tales.* Mac Printing Co, 1971.

CLARKE, T, *The Bloody Mohawk.* IJ Friedman, Inc, Port Washington, NY, 1968.

COMMITTEE ON THE CELEBRATION OF 250th ANNIVERSARY OF THE GRANTING OF THE DONEGAN CHARTER, *Albany - A Cradle Of America.* Albany, 1936.

CORWIN, Edward, HASTINGS, Hugh, HOLDEN, James, *Ecclesiastical Records, State Of NY.* JB Lyon, Albany, 1901-1916.

DIEFENDORF, Mary, *The Historic Mohawk.* Putnam, 1910.

DONOHUE, Thomas, *The Iroquois And The Jesuits.* Buffalo Catholic Publication Co, Buffalo, 1895.

FULOP-MILLER, Rene, *The Power And Secrets Of The Jesuits.* The Viking Press, NY, 1930.

FUNK, Robert, *Recent Contributions To Hudson Valley Prehistory.* NYS Museum, 1976.

GRASSMANN, Thomas, *The Mohawk Indians And Their Valley.* Eric Hugo, Schenectady, 1969.

GREENE, Nelson ed, *History Of The Mohawk Valley.* SJ Clarke Publishing Company, Chicago, 1925.

HILL, William, *Old Fort Edward.* B ullard Press, Glens Falls, 1929.

JAMESON, J ed, *Narratives Of New Netherland.* Charles Scribner's Sons, 1909.

MARQUIS, Thomas, *The Jesuit Missions.* Glasgow, Brook & Company, Toronto, 1916.

MORGAN, Lewis, *League Of The Ho-De-Sau-Nee Or Iroquois* 2 Vols. Reprint - Burt Franklin, NY, 1967.

MUNSELL, Joel, *The Annals Of Albany* Vol 9. Joel Munsell, Albany, 1869.

NATIONAL GEOGRAPHICAL SOCIETY, *The World Of The American Indian.* 1989.

PRITCHETT, John, *Black Robe & Buckskin.* College And U Press Service, 1960.

RITCHIE, William, *The Chance Horizon An Early Stage Of Mohawk Iroquois.* NYS Museum, Albany, 1952.

SHEA, John, *History Of The Catholic Missions.* PJ Kenedy, NY, 1899.

SHEEHAN, Harold, "A Look At Our Early History." In the *Mechanicville Centennial,* Centennial Committee 1959.

SMITH, HP, *Historical & Statistical Gazetteer Of New York State, 1860.* HP Smith Publishers, Syracuse, c1860.

STARBUCK, David ed, *Archaeology Of The French & Indian War Military Sites Of The Hudson River, Lake George And Lake Champlain Corridor.* Adirondack Community College, Queensbury, NY, 1994.

THWAITES, Reuben ed, *The Jesuit Relations* Vol 1-73. Pageant Book Co, 1959.

VEEDER, Millicent, *Door To The Mohawk Valley.* Cromwell Printery Inc, Albany, 1947.

WILLIAMS, Sherman, *New York's Part In History.* D Appleton And Company, NY, 1915.

periodicals

POST, Paul, "Fishkill Site In Jeopardy?" *The Moreau Sun,* Moreau, NY, 10 Jul 1994.

[No author cited] "Peter Kalm's Travels In The Adirondacks." *Lake George Mirror,* Lake George, NY, 31 Jul 1970.

     "   "Thanks To Fr Bressani." *Pilgrim From The Martyrs Shrine,* Auriesville, NY, Winter,1968.

interviews

~ Called the following people, but none knew of anyone who had done, or is doing, research on Bressani to try to determine where the fishing village was located, near the Hudson River, the site of his first torture ~

CARRON, Ferne, Auriesville, NY; 22 Jun 1997.

FULLER, Jo Ann, Fort Edward, NY on 3 Jan 1997. She said that Ft Edward had been an early Native American fishing village.

KANE, Patrice, Fordham U Library, the Bronx, NY during Jun 1997.

LIGHT, Sally, Albany, NY on 14 Jan 1997. Sally has done historical research for the Albany Diocese.

PADENI, Scott, Ballston Spa, NY on 3 Jan 1997. Scott mentioned that in the fall, Indians, from the Schenectady area, went to Saratoga Lake to fish.

PARET, John SJ, Auriesville, NY on 22 Jun 1997.

1644 JOHANNES MEGAPOLENSIS

HALSEY, Francis, *The Old New York Frontier.* Scribner, 1901.

JAMESON, J ed, *Narratives Of New Netherland.* Charles Scribner's Sons, NY, 1909.

MASTEN, Arthur, *The History Of Cohoes.* Reprint - Cohoes Historical Society, 1969.

MUNSELL, J, *Annals Of Albany* Vol 1. Joel Munsell, Albany, 1869.

THWAITES, Reuben ed, *Jesuit Relations.* Pageant Book Co, 1959.

ACKNOWLEDGMENTS
A very special thanks to ...

- SHIRLEY McFERSON
Director
Caldwell-Lake George Library
Lake George, NY

- Southern Adirondack Library System
Saratoga Springs, NY, for filling my
myriad requests for books -- within the
SALS and Mohawk Valley Systems
- The Neil Hellman Library, College of St
Rose, Albany, for the loan of their 73
volumn set of *The Jesuit Relations*

archives
New York State Archives, Albany

libraries and historical societies
~ in the united states ~
Alexander Library, Rutgers U, New
Brunswick, NJ.
The Huntington Library, San Marino
California; John Rhodehamel, Norris F
Foundation Curator Of American History

~ in new york state ~
Adirondack Community College Library
Queensbury
Cohoes Library -- Walt Lipka, Historian
Crandall Library, Glens Falls -- Albert Fowler
Greenwich Free Library
Hillview Library, Diamond Point
Hoosick Township Historical Society
John Jay College Library, New York City
Keating Library, Fordham U, The Bronx
Lake George Historical Association
McKinney Library, Albany Institute Of
History And Art -- Scott McCloud
Mechanicville District Public Library
Neil Hellman Library, College Of Saint Rose,
Albany
New York City Public Library:
Fifth Ave -- Rare Books And Manuscripts;
Fordham Branch, The Bronx
New York Historical Assoc, Cooperstown
New York Historical Society, New York City
New York State Library, Albany

Queensbury High School Library
Peru Free Library
Saratoga Springs Public Library
Schenectady County Historical Society
Stillwater Free Library
SUNY:
  Benjamin Feinberg Library, Plattsburgh
  Joe Swinyer, Former Director Of Special
  Collections;
  Stephen B Luce Library, SUNY Maritime
  Bronx -- John Lee
Town Of Colonie Historian -- Jean Olton
Warren County Historian -- Marge Swan
Waterford Public Library
William K Sanford Library, Loundonville

~ in england ~
National Maritime Museum, Greenwich
  Clive Powell
Avon County Library, Bristol -- Elizabeth
  Jeffery, Assistant, Reference Library
U Of Bristol Library, Bristol
Bristol Record Office, Bristol
U Of The West Of England, Bristol
  Cathryn Gallacher, User Services Librarian
Royal Greenwich Observatory, Greenwich
  Dr Peter Andrews, Head Of Information
  Services

~ in st john's, newfoundland ~
Munn Library Centre For Newfoundland
  Studies
St John's Library, Provincial Resource
  Library -- Joan Grandy, Library Technician

people
Virginia Bowers, City of Albany Historian
Bill Maynard, Hawkes Bay, Newfoundland
Charline Phelps, Samerset, KY -- researching
  fur traders of the east coast
Marilyn Van Dyke, Queensbury, NY
Don & Barbara Wilford, Altamont, NY.

190

INDEX

194